THE
HAND-ME-DOWN
PC

The Hand-Me-Down PC

Upgrading and Repairing Personal Computers

Morris Rosenthal

McGraw-Hill, Inc.
New York · San Francisco · Washington, D.C.
Auckland · Bogotá · Caracas · Lisbon · London
Madrid · Mexico City · Milan · Montreal · New Delhi
San Juan · Singapore · Sydney · Tokyo · Toronto

Library of Congress Cataloging-in-Publication Data

Rosenthal, Morris.
    The hand-me-down PC : upgrading and repairing personal computers /
Morris Rosenthal.
        p.   cm.
    Includes index.
    ISBN 0-07-053523-X
    1. Microcomputers—Upgrading. 2. Midrocomputers—Repairing.
I. Title.
TK7887.R67   1997
621.39'16—dc21   97-31095
                                                            CIP

McGraw-Hill

A Division of The McGraw·Hill Companies

    3 4 5 6 7 8 9 0   DOC/DOC   9 0 2 1 0 9 8

ISBN 0-07-053523-X

*The sponsoring editor for this book was Scott Grillo, the editing supervisor was Sally
Glover, and the production supervisor was Sherri Souffrance. It was set in Vendome ICG
per the Trade Comp. specs by McGraw-Hill's Professional Book Group composition unit,
Hightstown, N.J.*

Printed and bound by R. R. Donnelley & Sons Company.

McGraw-Hill books are available at special quantity discounts to use as premi-
ums and sales promotions, or for use in corporate training programs. For more
information, please write to the Director of Special Sales, McGraw-Hill, 11 West
19th Street, New York, NY 10011. Or contact your local bookstore.

This book is printed on recycled, acid-free paper containing
a minimum of 50% recycled, de-inked fiber.

Disclaimer

Personal risk and limits of liability.

Neither the author, the publisher, nor anyone directly or indirectly connected with the publication of this book shall make any warranty either expressed or implied, with regard to this material, including, but not limited to, the implied warranties of quality, merchantability, and fitness for any particular purpose. Further, neither the author, publisher, nor anyone directly or indirectly connected with the publication of this book and computer software shall be liable for errors or omissions contained herein, or for any incidental or consequential damages, injuries, or financial or material loses resulting from the use, or inability to use, the material contained herein. The material is presented as-is, and the reader bears all responsibilities and risks connected with its use.

Notices

The following trademarked names may appear in this book. Every effort has been made to cover each appropriate reference. All other trademarked names remain the property of their respective owners.

IBM, PC-XT, PC-AT, OS/2, VoiceType and Microchannel are a trademarks of International Business Machines. MS-DOS, Word, Excel, Windows, Windows for Workgroups, Windows NT, Windows 95, Plus, Active X, InPort Mouse and Internet Explorer are trademarks of Microsoft Corporation. Sound Blaster is a trademark of Creative Labs. Disk Manager is a trademark of ONTRACK Inc. Netscape Navigator is a trademark of Netscape Corporation. Indeo, Pentium, Pentium PRO, and OverDrive are trademarks of Intel Corporation. Bernoulli, Zip and Jaz are trademarks of Iomega. SyQuest is a trademark of SyQuest Inc. PostScript and Pagemaker are a trademark of Adobe Inc. Bubble Jet is a trademark of Canon Inc. 123 and Notes are a trademark of Lotus Corporation. Ventura Publisher is a trademark of Xerox. WordPerfect is a trademark of WordPerfect Corporation. AutoCad is a trademark of Autodesk Inc. Cyrix is a trademark of Cyrix Inc. AMD is a trademark of American Micro Devices. AMI is a trademark of American Megetrends Inc. Phoenix is a trademark of Phoenix Inc. Award is a trademark of Award Inc. Trident 9000 is a trademark of Trident Inc. Novel NE2000 is a trademark of Novel Inc. Computer Shopper is a trademark of Ziff Davis Publishing, Inc. Java is a trademark of Sun Microsystems Inc.. Alpha and DEC are a tradmark of Digital Equipment Corporation. HP is a trademark of Hewelett Packard Inc. Sportster is a trademark of U.S Robotics Inc.

CONTENTS

Contents

Contents

Contents

Acknowledgments

My thanks to the following:

- Franklyn Dailey, Jr. for his proofreading and suggestions.
- Ken Fetterhoff for allowing me to photograph and thoroughly disorder his large collection of computer parts on multiple occasions.
- Mary Rosenthal and Reva Rubenstein for their illustrations and balanced meals.

INTRODUCTION

In fifteen short years, PCs have gone from being workplace curiosities to outselling color television sets. Ironically, one of the factors that has helped make PCs so wildly popular also makes them a little hard to explain. A PC isn't just a word processor, a game machine, or an accounting system; a PC is all of these things and more. PCs are general-purpose computers that can run a vast array of software which instantaneously transforms them into an electronic checkbook, an F-16 cockpit, or a window onto the World Wide Web. Through the addition of internal components called "adapters" and external components called "peripherals," PCs can be enhanced to do almost any job in the factory or the office.

PCs are currently entering their seventh major generation of hardware, yet some people continue to work away on PCs from the first three generations: the original IBM PC, the IBM PC-XT, and the IBM PC-AT. Starting with the PC-XT, other computer manufacturers began producing copies of these machines, called compatibles. At some point, the copies got so good that they became known as "clones." After the PC-AT, IBM decided to recapture market share by selling PCs that couldn't be legally cloned, called PS/2s. The copy makers kept right on making improvements to the PC-AT, sticking to the basic design, known as Industry Standard Architecture (ISA). Eventually, IBM gave up on the proprietary PS/2 and began building clones to the standard they had originally set. Today's Pentium PCs are direct descendants of the IBM PC-AT.

With the introduction of each new generation of PC, the prices of older models fall through the floor. In addition, many purchasers of new PCs are replacing an older model. These "hand-me-down" PCs are sold to employees, donated to schools and charities, or given to friends and family. Unfortunately, even when free, these PCs are not always the bargain they first appear to be. Some require hardware upgrades to run the software that the new owner wants to use; others require "minor" repairs. There are sad stories about individuals who have paid good money to upgrade an older PC into something less than a new PC, for more than a new PC's price. A thread of discussion runs throughout this book with the point of empowering owners and potential buyers of hand-me-down PCs so they can determine whether it makes financial sense for them to invest in upgrading or repairing their hand-me-down PCs.

The book is divided into five basic parts. The first part gives an overview of all of the parts that make up a PC. Readers new to the world of computers may have a little trouble at first with some of the new vocabulary, which is always explained in the text. Just remember that while we all know that a light year is a lot farther than a league, few of us know exactly how long either is in feet. Likewise, the computer terms will be important to most users only in their relative measure, i.e., 100 megahertz is better than 25 megahertz. Pricing information is introduced in this part to provide context and is repeated in later parts. Some areas, like the discussion of monitors (TV displays), are a little heavy on technical jargon for the same reason that descriptions of high-fidelity stereo systems are loaded with esoteric terms. The high prices that manufacturers charge for upscale models have to be justified somehow!

The second part of the book looks at the various tasks a PC can be called upon to fulfill. Software is treated first because there are some software components every computer must have, like an operating system. Applications software is also introduced, since users in a wide spectrum of situations will need some of the same programs, such as a word processor. The role the PC can play is entirely dependent on the hardware required by different programs. Students, moonlighting accountants, secretaries, and artists all need different software and peripherals to get the most out of their PC. A hand-me-down PC might become the core office equipment for a home office or startup new business. Twenty identical PCs might be donated in one clump to create a computer lab in a classroom, or one might be left in a basket on the steps of a church. This part also covers multimedia computers, which are standard PCs with a couple of extra parts thrown in. In addition, peripherals like laser printers and scanners, and networks for office and classroom environments, will be discussed.

The third part addresses upgrading hand-me-down PCs. We'll consider the options from two viewpoints: people who will do their own work, and people who will pay someone else for their labor. The stress here is on money for both parts and labor. Cost of components is discussed in detail, with an emphasis on mail-order pricing. The value of knowing good mail-order pricing, even for readers with no intention of doing their own work, is that competitive mail-order prices come within a few percentage points of true wholesale. A couple of minutes spent leafing through Ziff Davis' *Computer Shopper* will arm readers with the knowledge of what their repair person or computer store is paying for parts. The pricing used in this book is based on the best information available to the author during the preparation of the manuscript. Pricing of basic commodity items, such as memory, are subject to price fixing by overseas cartels, and prices may vary by as much as 100 percent in the course of a couple of months. Good mail-order pricing is found only in magazines that take advertising from hundreds of different suppliers. Catalogs which offer one-stop shopping, no matter how highly recommended they come, are generally overpriced and loaded with already obsolete close-out items.

The fourth part of the book is a hardware troubleshooting guide. There is no attempt to give the reader a cram course in electronics or to explain in great detail the underlying principles of PC operation. The goal of the troubleshooting guide is to enable the reader to determine which component is causing a problem. Failed computer components in PCs are always replaced rather than repaired. There simply isn't enough value in any individual component to justify the expense of the equipment and training that would be needed to repair these mass-produced parts. The only tools ever required are a screwdriver and a willingness to dive in.

The final part of the book in intended to give the reader a feel for the direction that computing is headed, and the probable future of the hand-me-down PC. An entire chapter is dedicated to a discussion of the World Wide Web and how to get the most out of an Internet connection and make your presence felt. Other topics include CD recording, digital video disc (DVD), speech recognition, and using the PC as a video phone. Finally, we discuss the PC life cycle to illustrate why buying the latest, greatest product is often the wrong financial decision.

Three generations of PCs are the main focus of this book: Pentiums and those known generically as 486s and 386s. These PCs represent about 80 percent of all clones currently in use. Older PCs are occasionally mentioned and are treated in the troubleshooting guide but are generally excluded from discussion due to their limitations with the Windows operating system. Newer PCs, based on the Pentium PRO and Intel's MMX (multimedia extension) technology, are often referenced in order to make comparisons on price/performance. The upgrading part and troubleshooting guide are applicable to PCs of all generations, thanks to the standard parts and procedures used across generational boundaries.

PART 1

PCs and Their Parts in Plain English

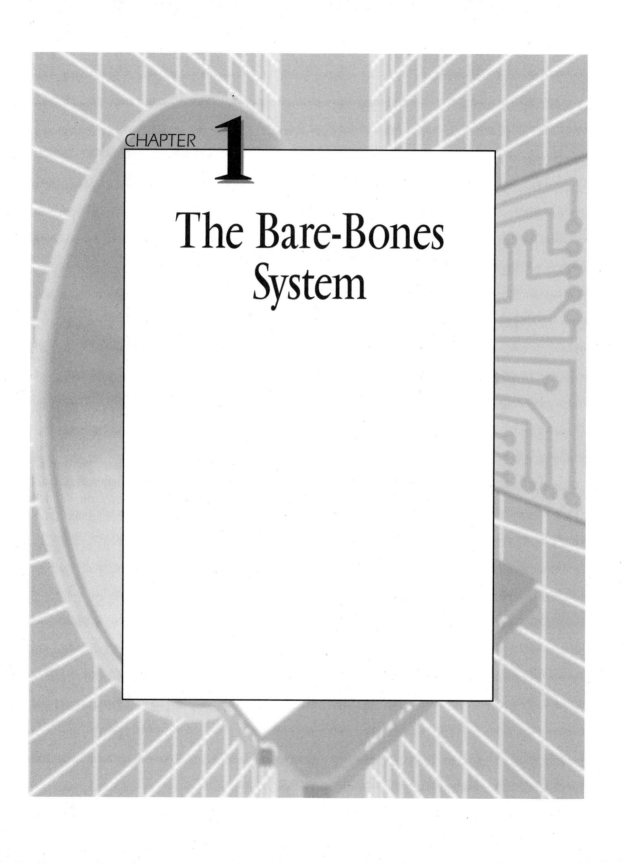

CHAPTER 1

The Bare-Bones System

Most people who buy a car are not automotive engineers, yet the vast majority of us make comparisons between cars as a part of the buying process. If you have a lot of kids, you want a lot of seats. If you have a lot of tools, a pickup or van may be a good choice. Big motors usually pull more weight; turbo-chargers make it go faster. Cruise control and air-conditioning are luxuries for some and necessities for others. You don't need to be a musician to decide on a stereo, and you don't need to know how a transmission works to choose between a manual and an automatic. When the car gets old and the transmission shop wants $1000 to put in a rebuilt with a 90-day warranty, the decision to invest the money or buy a new car often has as much to do with the condition of your bank account as with the overall condition of the car.

The purpose of Part 1 is to give you a feel for how all the parts in a PC add up to make a working computer. Like automobiles, many models are built on the same chassis, with the most expensive "loaded" models costing more than twice as much as the stripped-down economy version. There are many "after-market" enhancements you can make, some are add-ons, and some replace the original components. The expensive models have the potential to get you where you're going faster and in more comfort. However, there are a few fundamental differences between PCs and cars that make buying and owning a PC a whole lot easier. One difference is that PCs are all built to standards such that their component parts, even across brands, are largely interchangeable. Another difference is that most of these parts are either commodities or available from a single source only, i.e., you can buy memory or a floppy drive from any manufacturer, but Intel chips come from Intel Corporation and Windows—in a variety of flavors—comes from Microsoft.

The System Box or Case

There are two kinds of computer parts. There are things that go inside the system box and things that attach to it. The system box itself is either a flat metal box with a couple of buttons and lights on the front with at least one place to insert a floppy disk, or the same flat metal box stood on end. The flat box laying down is called a "desktop case" and the flat box standing up is called a "minitower." Big minitowers that sit on the floor are called "towers." The system box has one power cord that gets plugged into the wall, and all sorts of connection points called "ports" are provided for parts outside the system box to get attached. Two things that every computer will have plugged into ports are a keyboard and a monitor (TV display). Other things that are commonly plugged into ports on the system box include: a mouse, a printer, a telephone wire, a joystick, and speakers. The parts that get plugged into ports on the system box are called "peripherals."

Before we start to examine things that go in the system box, let's look at the box itself. The front of the system box is covered by a plastic faceplate, with several rectangular cutouts, a couple of buttons and LEDs

Figure 1-1
Minitower to desktop.

(lights), a keyhole, and a power switch. The power switch is often on the side of the older desktop cases. The rectangular cutouts cover the drive bays, where floppy drives, CD-ROM drives, and hard drives are mounted. The larger bays house 5$\frac{1}{4}$" floppy drives, CD ROM drives, and older hard drives. The small bays house 3$\frac{1}{2}$" floppy drives and newer hard drives. The two push buttons, besides the power switch, are labeled "reset" and "turbo." The reset button is for restarting the computer if it stops responding to keyboard and mouse input. The turbo button switches the machine between its top speed and a slow speed, which is only useful for playing games or troubleshooting. On the high speed, the turbo LED should be lit. Turbo switches and LEDs are no longer used on the newest PCs. The power LED should be lit all the time when the computer is on, and the HDD LED will blink when the hard drive is being accessed. The LEDs are for the benefit of the user, and the computer will work fine even if they are hooked up wrong or broken.

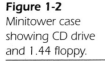

Figure 1-2
Minitower case showing CD drive and 1.44 floppy.

Inside the box is normally where the confusion begins. Here we have RAM, ROM, megabytes, motherboards, drives, and adapters. All of these things are necessary for even the most stripped-down computer, but they need no assembly beyond plugging connectors together and turning in the occasional screw. The cost of each part can be as high as $200 or as low as $10 or $20. The first part we'll consider, the power supply, is usually purchased with the system box itself, and in some brand name machines it will have a unique shape (form factor). A unique and painful replacement cost goes hand-in-hand. Power supplies and system boxes are normally sold together for a price between $30 and $40 dollars for a cheap minitower to $70 for a desktop and over $100 for a tower. The cheapest cases often have metal burrs inside that scratch unwary hands and lack fit and finish.

Figure 1-3
The innards of the author's hand-me-down PC.

A bare bones system consists of a case, power supply, motherboard, CPU (brain), and memory. New computers are often sold to computer stores and other resellers as "bare bones" for a couple of reasons. One is the FCC (Federal Communications Commission) approval sticker that should appear on the back of every computer, certifying that it won't interfere with your neighbor's TV or radio. Manufacturers will sell "bare-bones" systems as FCC approved, although there is no guarantee they would pass the test with other parts added. Another reason is that screwing in the motherboard and connecting all the little lights and switches is a dreary job that most resellers are willing to pay a few dollars to avoid. We have taken advantage of the "bare-bones" approach and divided up the parts inside the system box into three categories; "bare bones," "drives," and "adapter cards."

The Power Supply

The power supply, which is attached to the case with four to six screws, takes the 115 volts of AC power from your wall plug and turns it into the small DC voltages that all computer components operate on. The only continuous sound that should come from an operating computer is the small fan cooling the power supply. If the fan fails, the power supply will soon overheat and fail. The cost of a standard power supply, for both minitower and desktop cases, is around $35. Note that you can often buy a new case and power supply for less

Figure 1-4
Standard power supply for mintower or desktop.

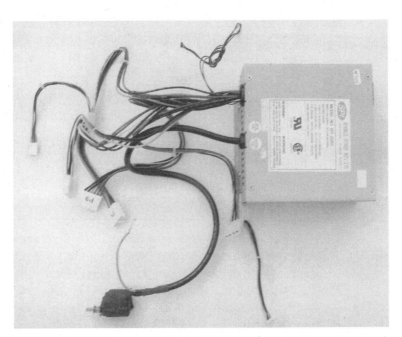

than the cost of a replacement power supply by itself. Old-fashioned "AT"-type power supplies, with a large paddle switch on the side, run over $50. The main figure of merit for power supply connoisseurs to boast about is their power output, in watts. The standard power supply delivers 200 watts, which is more than you'll ever need. The power supply performs two jobs inside the box. One is to supply power to the motherboard in a wide variety of voltages, and the other is to provide power to the drives.

The Motherboard

Figure 1-5
A 486 clone
motherboard.

All of the parts that go into the system box have a direct connection to the motherboard. The motherboard, besides serving as the traffic cop for routing information to all the parts, also serves as the home of the brain (CPU) and the memory (RAM), which fit into special sockets. A lot of terminology is used to describe different versions of motherboards and their capabilities, but most variations have little real impact on the user. The main point to get is that the motherboard is where the software you will run on your computer actually executes, as the brain works with the information stored in the memory. Motherboards are often sold with the CPU (brain), and a new generation of motherboard must be designed for each new CPU (386, 486, Pentium) that's released. A 386 motherboard, with CPU, has no value on the market, while a new 486 motherboard with a 133-MHz CPU might sell for up to $100. Pentium motherboards, with CPU, range from $200 to $700, depending on the exact model and clock speed.

CPU (The Brain)

The vast majority of all CPUs mounted on PC motherboards since the beginning of time (the early 1980s in this case) are manufactured by Intel. Other companies that have tried competing include NEC, AMD, Texas Instruments, Cyrix, IBM (under Intel licensing), and Motorola, which makes the CPUs for Apple Computers. However, the only CPUs besides Intel that you're likely to find inside a hand-me-down PC are manufactured by AMD (American Micro Devices) or Cyrix. Fortunately, they follow the same nomenclature, so we can usually omit the manufacturer and refer to older CPUs generically as 386s or 486s. With the advent of the trademarked Pentium processor, AMD and Cyrix continued using the "86" nomenclature, adding the numeral "5" or "6" in the CPU name to express next-generation technology. The primary figure of merit for CPUs of a similar generation is the clock speed, measured in MHz (megahertz). To understand the speed at which CPUs operate, let's compare them to alarm clocks.

Alarm clocks come in two basic types: digital and analog. An analog alarm clock motor runs directly off the 115-volt, 60-Hz AC power from the wall outlet. Through a series of gears, like an automobile transmission, the alarm clock motor moves the second hand around the face once a minute, the minute hand once an hour, and the hour hand twice

Figure 1-6
Intel 486 CPUs with passive and fan-cooled heatsinks.

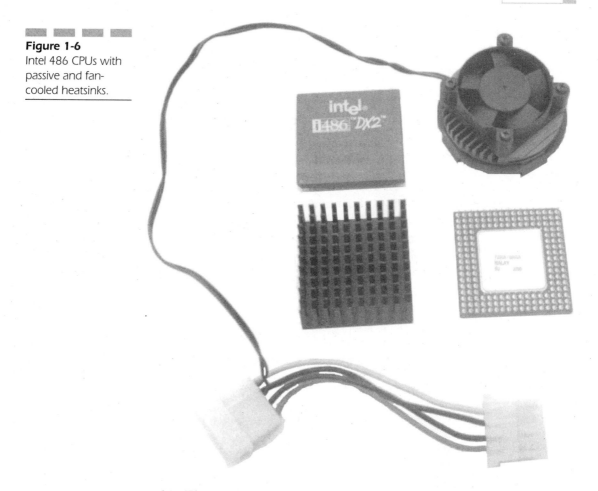

a day. Those of us with cheap analog alarm clocks and good ears can hear the alarm faintly building up before it goes off. That's because time, in the analog world, is continuous, so things never happen "all at once." A digital alarm clock displays the time in Arabic numerals and changes the time displayed once a minute. If the alarm is set for 6:30 AM, when the clock changes from 6:29 AM to 6:30 AM, the alarm starts to beep. In effect, there has been a step change, an "all at once," and there are no faint warning beeps before the alarm sounds.

CPUs are digital. The CPU clock speed tells us how many step changes, or operations, the CPU will make in one second. For example, a 386SX-25 CPU does 25 million operations per second. A 486DX-25 CPU also does 25 million operations per second, although each operation of the 486 CPU may do twice as much work as the 386SX CPU operating at the same clock speed. A 486DX/4-100 CPU does 100 million operations per second, and a 200-MHz Pentium takes 200 million steps per second. CPUs all do millions of operations per second, expressed as "MHz," so we only need to comprehend the smaller number, 25, 66, 150. The speed of the CPU isn't the only thing that determines how fast the computer runs your software (imagine putting a race car engine in a truck), but the higher the number, the faster the machine. AMD recently introduced a "PR" performance rating on their CPUs, which expresses the Pentium clock speed that their K5 CPU is comparable to.

There are three other parts to the nomenclature, which you may have noticed above. First is whether we have a 386, a 486, or a Pentium. CPU manufacturers improve their chips with each generation, and the 486 is the minimum required by many software packages. The 486 replaced the 386, just as the 386 replaced the 286, which was the CPU in the IBM PC-AT. Never spend money to obtain a 386-based PC. Another part to the nomenclature relevant to older CPUs is the "DX" or "SX" part, and the last bit is the "4" that appears in the 486DX/4-100. In both 386 and 486 CPUs, the DX does complicated math (engineering calculations) better than the SX. Some software may require that you have a DX type CPU, or that you buy another CPU-like chip known as a math coprocessor to compensate. Just remember DX is better than SX, and don't buy a machine with an SX CPU at any price, unless it comes with a real nice monitor you can use on your next machine. The "4" that appears in 486DX/4-100 or the "2" in 486DX/2-66 tells us that the CPU is a clock multiplier. The CPU runs at the stated speed, 100 or 66, but it talks with the motherboard it's plugged into at a lower speed. That means it can work very quickly with information held in the CPU, but if it has to go out and get something from memory, things slow down.

Overdrive processors with Pentium or Pentium PRO "cores" are available from Intel to replace some 486 CPUs. The "core" includes the next-generation technology, along with a large amount of super fast memory known as *internal cache* that allows the CPU to crunch data without having to wait for the slower motherboard to fetch it from other locations. The overall situation in this case is similar to running a clock-multiplied 486 CPU (DX2/66 or DX4/100) on an older 486 motherboard. The newest MMX- enhanced Pentium CPUs boost the performance of compliant software whether they are added on the oldest motherboard that supports the CPU or the newest motherboard designed for MMX processors. Of course, performance will always be best when a CPU is used on a motherboard that was designed to support it.

RAM (The Memory)

Memory is what the CPU shuffles through in order for the software to accomplish anything. The CPU never looks directly at the information on your floppy disk, your hard drive, or your CD-ROM. This information must first be copied into memory by one of the traffic cops on the motherboard. The CPU then reads this information from the memory and acts on it. Random Access Memory (RAM) is called by this name because the CPU can get information from any location in the memory in much less than a millionth of a second. Even picking locations at random, the retrieval speed will remain unchanged. This is very different from the case with a floppy drive or other disc media. Bits of

Figure 1-7
Collection of 72-pin SIMMs in carrier.

information stored next to each other on the floppy can be read relatively quickly, while bits which are recorded a couple of inches away on the disk take much longer to retrieve, actual fractions of a second! Sometimes a "D" is added to the front of "RAM," which makes the word "DRAM." The "D" stands for dynamic, because the RAM will actually forget what it's holding if the motherboard doesn't continually refresh (read and rewrite) the information. Everything in DRAM disappears when the computer is turned off.

Computers work with very small bits of information, intelligently known as "bits," which have to be combined into larger clumps to be of much use. The basic clump used by computers consists of 8 bits and is known as a *byte*. Memory size is measured in bytes, and more is always better. Since computers need huge numbers of bytes to do anything useful, the measure of a "megabyte," one million bytes, is used. Early 386 machines running DOS could limp by on 1 or 2 megabytes (MB) of RAM, but 4 MB is the minimum required to run Windows in a reasonable fashion. 4 MB works fine with most older software, but 8 MB is being required by many new programs. Programs requiring 16 MB, the next logical increment due to the way memory is installed in most machines, are becoming increasingly common. Today RAM costs under $5/MB, down from about $35/MB one or two years ago, meaning that the 16 MBs of RAM that cost $500 in 1995 costs around $50 today.

CHAPTER **2**

Drives

Drives provide the permanent storage for your computer. When the computer is turned off, all of the parts except for the drives are effectively wiped clean. Drives all use electric motors to spin disks or tapes, and drives require a power lead directly from the power supply. Most drives—like floppies, CDs, and tapes—use a removable medium that is slid into the drive where it protrudes through the front of the system box. Some special-purpose drives called external drives sit entirely outside the system box and are connected to the system box by a cable. Hard drives are sealed against the atmosphere and dust contamination and have no removable media. These drives can rarely be seen from the outside of the system box, which is why manufacturers include a "HDD" LED (light) on the front panel to show when they are being accessed.

The Floppy Drive

Floppy drives and floppy disks come in two sizes: the older, flexible, 5¼" disks and the newer, rigid, 3½" disks. Floppy disks, which are read by a floppy drive, provide permanent, removable storage for your computer. The storage is permanent because it is recorded in the magnetic material of the disk the same way that audio or video cassettes are recorded. As long as you keep the disks away from big magnets and don't spill hot coffee on them, they'll hold the information for a couple of years. Several different formats for floppy disks exist which describe how much information can be recorded on them. Old floppy drives only read and write the low-capacity, or low-density formats. These old double-density (DD) formats are measured in KB (thousands of bytes): 360 KB for the double-density 5-¼" disk, and 720 KB for the double-density 3-½" disk. New drives, with high-density (HD) floppies, record 1.2 MB on a 5-¼" disk and 1.44 MB on a 3-½" disk. The drives are cheap. A brand new 1.44-MB drive costs about $20; a 1.2-MB drive about $25. There is no reason for buying or using a 1.2-MB (5-¼") drive unless you are stuck with a bunch of old disks filled with information. Even then, your best bet would be to copy them onto newer disks. Most PCs will support 2.88-MB, 3-½" drives, but they never came into common use, and there's little reason to invest in one.

A tip about buying floppy disks, which can get pretty confusing. 1.44-MB disk, hopefully the only kind you would be out buying, is labeled 3-½" HD. The 720-KB disks are labeled 3-½" DD. Both types are

Figure 2-1
1.2-MB floppy drive.

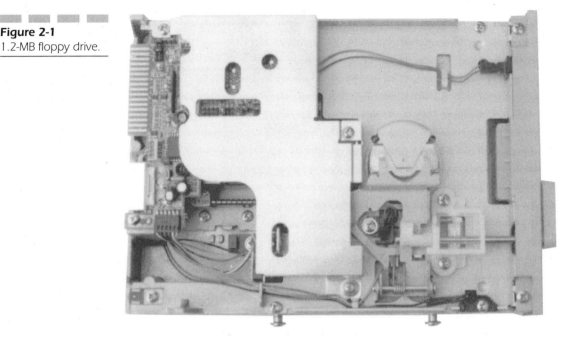

double sided (DS); the information is written on both sides. The 1.2-MB disks are labeled 5-$\frac{1}{4}$" HD, and 360-KB disks, if they are still sold, are labeled 5-$\frac{1}{4}$" DD. Again, both are double sided, and the description is sometimes run together as DSDD, in the case of the 360 KB. Single-sided, single-density disks exist only in super-old word-processing systems and museums.

Hard Drives

Now we're getting to the real storage. The hard drive is essentially several nonremovable, rigid floppy disks stacked together with a drive built around them. Because the disks are rigid, the read/write heads can be positioned much more accurately, allowing more information to be written (higher density). Another advantage is the disks can spin much faster, thousands of rpms (revolutions per minute). As a result of higher recording density and faster spinning, hard drives can write and retrieve information much faster than floppy drives. The most important measure associated with a hard drive is the capacity, how many megabytes it can

Figure 2-2
The inside of an IDE
hard drive.

store. The smallest hard drives being sold today can hold about 700 flop-py disks worth of information, though older drives in hand-me-down PCs will likely have a more modest capacity.

About the smallest drive you'll find in an old 386 is a 40-MB drive, which could just about hold DOS and Windows with a couple of small programs. Drives up to about 500 MB are commonly found in older PCs, and many machines will have a second drive installed. Pricing for old drives is irrelevant, since they quickly disappear from the market when new drive prices fall. About the smallest hard drive commonly available today is the 1.2-GB drive (1 GB = 1000 MB) for $175. Hard drives are very reliable (much more so than floppies), and the newer drives have a pro-jected average operating life approaching 20 years, much longer than they will be practically useful. However, if you have important informa-tion on your hard drive, say your checkbook or your unfinished novel, it's always a good idea to make a fall-back copy onto a floppy disk, tape, or removable cartridge. This procedure is known as *backing up.* Store the backup disk(s) away from the computer, so in case of fire or theft, you still have your copy.

Hard drives come in different price/performance ranges, with the main figures of merit being access time and transfer rate. The access time is an average figure for how long it takes the drive electronics to mechanically position the read head at the beginning of a block of information that a program has requested. Access times are measured in milliseconds (ms) and range between about 7 ms for the newest high-performance drives to 15 ms for older models. Very old hard drives, those with capacities in the 5- to 40-MB range, had access times as slow as 65 ms. The transfer rate expresses a measure of how fast information can be taken from the drive, once the beginning of a block of data is located. Transfer rates vary from a few hundred kilobytes per second to several megabytes per second, and you'll need the proper adapter card to take full advantage of high-performance drives.

CD-ROM Drives

CD drives are relative newcomers to PCs, coming into common use about five years ago. CD drives made possible the delivery of huge software programs and games to the user that would otherwise require hundreds of floppy disks. CDs are very cheap to mass manufacture at about 60 cents each, and they have a tremendous projected shelf life of over 50 years. All CD drives are capable of playing regular music CDs and come equipped with a headphone jack on the front of the player. If the system box contains a sound card, the music can be amplified and played

Figure 2-3
An external CD drive.

out of speakers. CDs come in one physical size, with a maximum capacity of about 680 MB. The main competitive comparison between CD drives is the transfer speed, how fast they can hand information to the motherboard to be placed in memory. This is expressed as a multiple (2X, 3X, 4X, 12X, and so on) of the original CD drive transfer speed, which was the same as that of a stereo CD player. While any speed CD drive is better than nothing, 2X (double speed) is the minimum needed for crude video playback, and with the cost of 4X drives already under $50, the slower ones are no longer sold. A 12X drive still costs over $100, and the 16X drives aren't worth the price differential.

Portable Cartridge Drives

Two companies, SyQuest and Iomega, dominate the removable media market. These drives are especially popular with artists who work with many large files, sometimes over 100 megabytes for a single image. Thanks to the higher performance and capacity of the newest cartridge drives, many people are turning to them as their primary storage system, sometimes purchasing cartridge arrays with many gigabytes of storage.

SyQuest makes both 3.5" and 5.25" cartridge drives, with capacities ranging from 44 MB all the way up to 1.5 GB. The SyQuest drives are based on Winchester technology and are essentially hard drives with removable platter cartridges. Iomega manufactures Bernoulli, Zip, and Jaz drives. Bernoulli and Zip drives are a cross between hard-drive and floppy-drive technology and offer capacities between; the 100-MB Zip disks are the same size as a 3.5" floppy. Bernoulli cartridges hold up to 230 MB. The new Jaz drive is similar to the leading SyQuest drives, both in performance and in capacity, with a 1.0-GB cartridge model. Prices for both brands range from $150 to $500 for the drives and $15 to $99 for the cartridges, depending on model and capacity.

Tape Drives

Many older PCs are equipped with tape drives for backing up the information on the hard drive. The most common drives had a capacity of 120 or 250 megabytes, stored on a removable tape about half the size and

Figure 2-4
A 3-½" tape drive
mounted in a 5-¼"
frame kit.

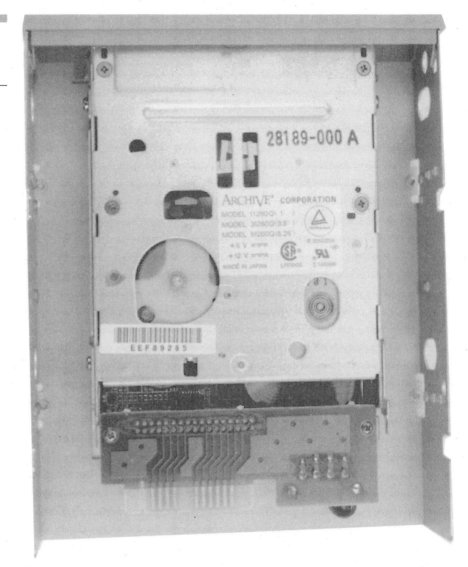

twice the thickness of an audio cassette. These one-sided tapes are easily
recognized by the thick metal bottom of the cartridge that helps con-
duct away heat. Some more expensive or obsolete drives use tapes as
small as a telephone answering machine cassette or as large as a VHS
tape cartridge. Tape drives in individual computers have gone out of
vogue for two reasons. First, they proved less reliable than the hard drives
they back up. Second, as hard-drive capacity skyrocketed, the cheap tape

drives required several tapes (and hours) to back up the data. Another reason is that most companies have installed networks, which allow the administrator to back up individual computers onto a shared hard drive or a single fast tape drive at a central location. Second-hand tape drives have no market value unless they were niche products, and they are often "orphans," i.e., the tapes or controllers are no longer available.

Newer tape drives using DAT (Digital Audio Tape) technology are much quicker and more reliable than older drives but can cost over $500 and are rarely found outside of business settings. Travan tape drives, discussed in the upgrading section, are a stable technology, and the more expensive models are capable of backing up a large hard drive on a single tape. The home user will normally want an internal tape drive that works off the floppy drive controller, or an external drive that connects to the printer port. Business users should purchase drives that require or come with a special adapter card, as these will create backups much faster than their less-expensive counterparts. Removable cartridge drives from SyQuest or Iomega are a better choice than tape drives for most small businesses and home users.

CHAPTER 3

Adapters

Adapter cards, which are plugged into the motherboard, give PCs the tremendous flexibility to do all of the jobs we can think up for them. As computer technology has evolved, the "bus slots" on the motherboard into which the adapter cards are placed have evolved as well. The latest adapter cards used in Pentium computers can move four times as much information in a single cycle as the older cards used in 386 computers. These cycles, known as *bus cycles*, occur with another digital clock called the *bus clock*, which runs at different speeds for different bus technologies. See Chapter 14 for a more detailed description of bus architecture.

The classification of these adapters is important if you are buying replacements, and they go as follows: 8- and 16-bit ISA adapters (286 motherboards and higher), VESA adapter (486 systems), EISA adapter (some 386 systems and higher, very expensive) and PCI adapter (Pentium and very new 486 systems). All motherboards, including the newest Pentiums, leave a couple of old-fashioned 16-bit slots (sometimes even 8-bit slots!) for compatibility with old technology. The standard motherboard can support (has space for) six or seven adapters to plug into the bus. Don't automatically assume that a more recent adapter type means higher performance. The fastest modems are still built on 8-bit ISA cards because the performance limit is in the phone lines, not in the PC.

Video Adapters

The video adapter performs the job of the cable box or the antenna and tuner on your TV. It takes the information the motherboard tells it to display and generates the signals that the monitor understands. In the case of old video adapters—Hercules, CGA (Color Graphics Adapter), EGA (Extended Graphics Adapter)—this was a digital code. Do not pay for a computer with this type of adapter or monitor, characterized by a nine-pin connector on the end of the monitor cable. The new generation of adapters, VGA (Video Graphics Adapter), operates more like a traditional television, providing the monitor with color (red, green, blue—RGB) information and some timing signals.

There are several distinct levels of performance associated with VGA adapters, namely how many colors they can display at one time, how much information they can squeeze onto a screen, and how often they update the information. How fast the different video adapters can refresh the monitor is dependent on both the adapter and the monitor and is set

Figure 3-1
VESA local bus
adapter.

aside for the monitor discussion. VGA adapters come equipped with their own RAM for temporarily storing what will be drawn on the monitor, and the amount of RAM usually corresponds somewhat with the overall performance of the adapter. The brand of VGA adapter, and the amount of RAM it carries in kilobytes (KB) or megabytes (MB), is usually the first thing displayed on the monitor when the computer is turned on.

VGA Adapters with 256 KB RAM

VGA adapters with 256 KB RAM are no longer sold. These adapters limit even the most expensive monitors to displaying a maximum of 256 colors at VGA screen resolution. By VGA screen resolution, we are talking about the number of pixels (separate points) the monitor uses to fill the screen. VGA resolution uses 640 pixels horizontally across the monitor and 400 pixels vertically, up and down. This compares well with broadcast television, which uses 512 pixels horizontally by 384 pixels vertically to fill up your TV screen, which is usually much larger than your monitor. For the math lovers, you can multiply 640 and 400 together, coming up with 256,000, or 256 K. These 256-K pixels require one byte of memory each, which is where we get the 256 KB of memory. One important note is that the video adapter requires special software called a "driver" to be installed on your computer for it to work to its highest potential. Without the driver installed, Windows and other software will only display 16 simultaneous colors, instead of 256. Also, while 256 K is sufficient memory to handle 256 colors at VGA resolution, the adapter may be limited to 16 colors by a 4-bit DAC (Digital-to-Analog Converter), which is the chip that turns the digital information into the analog signals that the monitor requires.

SVGA Adapters with 512 KB RAM

SVGA adapters (you caught the "S" sneaking in front of the VGA) are capable of displaying "super" VGA resolutions, beyond the 640-by-400 resolution of plain VGA. As you can guess, more resolution means more pixels, and more pixels at one byte of memory per pixel means more memory. SVGA adapters can display 800 pixels horizontally by 600 pixels vertically on the screen. Or, at two bytes of memory per pixel, they can still display regular VGA resolution. The extra byte per pixel at regular VGA resolution lets the adapter display 256 multiplied by 256 equals 64,356 colors at one time. Over 64,000 colors is enough to make most images appear as clear as photographs on a good monitor. For this reason (the ability to display "high color"), SVGA adapters are a minimum requirement for multimedia software. Some people will use the SVGA adapter to display the 800-by-600 pixel resolution instead, which fits almost twice as much information on the screen in one shot. The penalty for doing this is that everything appears proportionally smaller (remember, the size of the monitor hasn't changed), and only 16 colors can be displayed at one time.

These adapters are sold in the $20 to $30 range, but if replacing a failed part, you should buy a 1-MB adapter. Again, software from the manufacturer controls how the SVGA adapter operates. Also, while 512 K is sufficient memory to handle 64-K colors at VGA resolution, the adapter may be limited to 256 or 32-K colors by a low-resolution DAC (Digital-to-Analog Converter), the chip that turns the digital information into the analog signals that the monitor requires.

Video Adapters with 1 MB RAM and Beyond

The standard video adapter sold today comes with 1 MB (1024 KB) of video memory, and many 486 PCs were equipped with these cards. With double the memory of the 512-KB adapters, they can send the monitor over 16 million colors to be displayed simultaneously at VGA resolution. This creates a picture-perfect image known as *true color*. Likewise, there is now enough memory per pixel at SVGA (800-x-600) resolution to display over 64,000 colors simultaneously. Most of these adapters can operate at even higher resolutions, displaying 256 colors at 1,024-by-768 resolution, or 16 colors at 1,280-by-1024 resolution. These higher resolutions are normally only used by artists or computer draftspeople who have large monitors (over 17") and buy video adapters with 2 MB of memory or more to allow them to display more colors at these super-high resolutions.

Input/Output (I/O) Adapter

Before we even begin the discussion of the I/O adapter, we must note that in almost all 386 and 486 computers, the functions of this card have been combined with the disk controller functions into a single adapter, the SIDE (Super IDE) adapter, which will be discussed in the next section. On Pentium and Pentium PRO systems, plus most newer 486s, these functions have been integrated into the motherboard, and the separate adapter card no longer exists. The I/O functions we discuss here operate exactly the same way whether combined into the SIDE adapter or integrated with the motherboard.

The I/O adapter provides several ports, through which the computer communicates with the outside world. There are three types of ports provided: serial communications, parallel communications, and the game port. Two serial ports are provided, normally called *Com1* and *Com2*, one parallel port called the *printer port*, and the *game port*, normally used to connect a joystick for arcade-type games. Nearly all computers will have a mouse (pointing device) connected to the Com1 port, and the vast majority of printers sold today will work when hooked up to the printer port. The second serial port normally goes unused, unless an external modem (which connects your computer to the outside world through a telephone line) or some other special equipment is purchased. An I/O adapter costs less than $10.

SIDE Adapter

In the early 1990s, a type of hard drive using Intelligent Drive Electronics (IDE) began to take over the PC market. An intelligent hard drive allows for a simple controller, which really just ties the drive

Figure 3-2
ISA SIDE adapter.

Figure 3-3
VESA SIDE adapter.

directly to the motherboard bus. At first, these hard drives shipped with an adapter known as an IDE Paddle card, which doubled as the controller for the floppy drives. Ribbon cables, many wires molded into a flat plastic cable, connect the adapter to the hard drive(s) and the floppy drive(s). Manufacturers soon figured out that there was enough room on the adapter to add all the functions of the I/O adapter, and they created the Super IDE (SIDE) adapter. All of the functions of the SIDE adapter, including a second IDE connector to support additional drives, are integrated on Pentium, Pentium PRO, and newer 486 motherboards.

These adapter cards sell for less than $15, which makes them the least expensive component in the box. Unfortunately, since these adapters are so "low-tech" and inexpensive, the quality tends to be poor and they are the weakest link in most computers. I once sent a new technician out for her first afternoon of field service with three new SIDE adapters, with which she was able to effect different repairs on three computers. SIDE cards are also liberally sprinkled with jumpers, a type of switch that can select between two options. These jumpers can enable and disable the different functions, and in some cases, change the locations of the ports (i.e., Com1 becomes Com3 or Com2 becomes Com4).

Other Adapters

A video adapter and a SIDE adapter are the minimum number of adapters required for a PC to operate. Millions of computers complete their life cycle with no additions to these two basic adapters. There are literally hundreds of other adapters available for PCs, many of them designed to let the computer talk to a specific piece of equipment in a laboratory or on a shop floor. While your hand-me-down PC might contain a leftover adapter from some obsolete system, guidelines for guessing at what it might be are beyond the scope of this book. In the next few topics we will cover the more common adapters you might find in a hand-me-down or used PC, but a final word about unknown adapters. Leave them where they are, and don't start plugging things in unused ports at random to see if they do anything. In other words, "If it's not broke, don't fix it."

Internal Modem

About the most common and most useful extra adapter you can have in your PC is an internal modem. A *modem* is a device that gets plugged into a telephone jack and enables communications between your computer and other computers. These other computers could be at work, at your bank, or the gatekeepers (servers) on the Internet and the World Wide Web. Like most computer parts, modems have evolved to communicate faster and faster over the last 10 years. Because of the premium prices commanded by faster modems, most older computers

will come with slow modems. Modems are categorized by their line data rate in bits per second (bps). The slowest modem you'll find in an old 386 will run at 1,200 bps, compared to the newest modems in Pentiums which run at 33,600 bps (33.6 KB/s). Modems in 386s and 486s can be at either extreme or fall anywhere in between. The important cut-off number, 14.4 KB/s, is known as a *fourteen four,* and this is the minimum speed for a modem to achieve acceptable performance on the World Wide Web. Fourteen-four internal modems cost about $30, 28.8 KB/s modems around $50, and 33.6 KB/s modems go for under $100. Most modems are also capable of sending and receiving faxes, but people with a serious amount of faxing to do will find a regular paper fax far more convenient.

Modems that work at 56 KB/s are now available, and many brand-name 33.6 KB/s modems can be inexpensively upgraded to work at 56 KB/s. The 56-KB/s technology works in one direction only on regular phone lines, from a digital server to your PC. Your PC will still only be able to send information the other direction at 33.6 KB/s. Internet Service

Providers (ISPs) are shooting for the end of 1997 or early 1998 to have the technology in place on their end to transmit at 56 KB/s. As of early 1997, most ISPs were limited to 28.8 KB/s connections, and some still had large numbers of 14.4 KB/s lines. So before you invest in a new modem, make sure that the computers you'll be calling are capable of transmitting information at your top receive speed.

Sound Cards

Sound cards are adapters that perform at least three functions. Two of those functions are complementary: converting analog sound from a microphone or stereo jack into digital computer codes (A/D) and converting the computer's digital codes for sound back into voice or music that is played back through speakers (D/A). They provide enough amplification so that a CD drive played through the sound card will provide enough power to drive speakers. Most sound cards also have a ribbon connector for connecting CD drives that can't be connected to a different adapter. Newer cards also support the musical instrument digital interface (MIDI) and wave tables, which allow the card to create instrumental sound based on "cues." These take less than 1% of the storage space of actual recorded music.

Figure 3-5
A sound card with connectors for 4 types of CD drives.

Sound cards, like everything else, have evolved since their introduction in the early 1990s. The original successful card was the Sound Blaster from Creative Labs, and most sound cards manufactured since guarantee "Sound Blaster" compatibility. The oldest generation, called "8-bit" cards, are better than nothing but should not be purchased. The next generation, "16-bit" cards are capable of recording and reproducing sound as accurately as your stereo CD player. However, high-fidelity recording also depends on having a system fast enough to take the recorded sound from the sound card and move it to the hard drive without any interruptions. A "16-bit Sound Blaster Compatible" goes for around $30, while a real Sound Blaster from Creative Labs cost about $60. More expensive sound cards with recording-studio-type software can cost hundreds of dollars.

Network Adapters

Few of us have LANs (Local Area Networks) in our homes, but cost is no longer the reason. Early network adapters cost hundreds of dollars apiece, but while some brand names still hover around the $100 mark, reliable network adapters for all types of networks can be purchased

Figure 3-6
Combo network
card, Thin Ethernet,
and 10Base-T.

in the $30 to $40 range. Special network software which once had to be purchased separately for hundreds or thousands of dollars now comes as part of the Windows for Workgroups or Windows 95 software. LANs allow information to be passed from computer to computer about 1,000 times faster than by a modem connection. There are at least a half dozen types of LANs in use, with names like Token Ring, Ethernet, and Arcnet. The most common LANs in use outside of big corporations are variations on the Ethernet standard; 10Base "T," which uses twisted-pair telephone-type wire, and Thin Ethernet, which uses coaxial cable. The $30 to $40 adapters mentioned earlier support both types of LANs.

Small Computer System Interface (SCSI) Adapters

SCSI adapters, pronounced "scuzzy," are high-performance, general-purpose adapters for connecting the motherboard to a variety of drives and devices. Most high-performance hard drives are SCSI drives, along with CD Recorders (CDRs), some CD players, and quality tape drives.

Figure 3-7
Adaptec EISA SCSI adapter.

SCSI adapters also support connection to external devices, including portable versions of all of the above-mentioned drives, and other devices like scanners, which digitize (change into digital computer codes) documents and photographs. A single SCSI adapter can support up to seven different drives and devices simultaneously. Low-performance SCSI adapters start around $50, while the best adapters with controlling software cost up to $500. SCSI adapters also support floppy drives, so some systems will have a SCSI adapter and an I/O adapter instead of a SIDE adapter.

Video Capture Cards

These special adapters are used to capture single frames or real motion video from a VCR, video camera, or other video source. Prices for *frame grabbers*, which capture a single picture, start under $100, while decent motion video capture cards start at a few hundred dollars. Capturing quality motion video is extremely dependent on the system. A fast 486 with a special A/V (Audio/Visual) hard drive is the minimum requirement and probably won't produce anything good enough to be used in a commercial product. High-end video capture cards cost thousands of dollars and include on-board processing for compressing the video information in real time before passing it along to the PC. Video capture and edit workstations used by professionals may be based on PCs but typically cost well over $10,000.

CHAPTER 4

Things Outside the System Box

There are two things that must be attached to every system box to make it a working PC: a keyboard and a monitor. Modern software employs a Graphical User Interface (GUI), which is easier to work with if we add a third item for pointing at things on the monitor screen, a mouse. The next most common thing to attach to the system box is a printer, followed by external modems, joysticks, external drives, scanners, digitizers, and other special purpose accessories. Things that get plugged into communications ports on the system box are called "peripherals," and are almost never manufactured by the same company whose name goes on the system box. Sometimes the same company name appears on the peripherals because that company pays the real manufacturer to put it there. As with clothing, mattresses, and other purchases, you can often buy the exact same part without the brand name for a fraction of the cost.

Keyboards

The keyboard is an area where preference for "feel" varies greatly from person to person. Most people will be comfortable with the first keyboard they work on and feel there is something wrong with any subsequent keyboard, until they get used to it. Most keyboards sell in the $15 to $20 dollar range, including my personal favorite for reliability and feel from Mitsumi Electronics, over 1000 sold without a single failure. In my experience, the extremely expensive keyboards (almost $200 retail) manufactured by one of the world's largest computer companies have the terrible failure rate of about five percent per year. Keyboards receive power from the motherboard, so there is only one connection to make. Wrist rests and other devices to combat repetitive use injuries are available for people who work at typing for extended periods of time every day.

The newest keyboards on the market feature "V" shapes for supposed ergonomic positioning of the hands. Other options include a wireless keyboard that communicates keystrokes to the system with a small radio transmitter so you can type on your lap, though a keyboard extension cord for five dollars makes a lot more sense. Keyboards are also available in small-footprint, space-saving designs, which mainly do away with the extra bezel that surrounds the keypad areas.

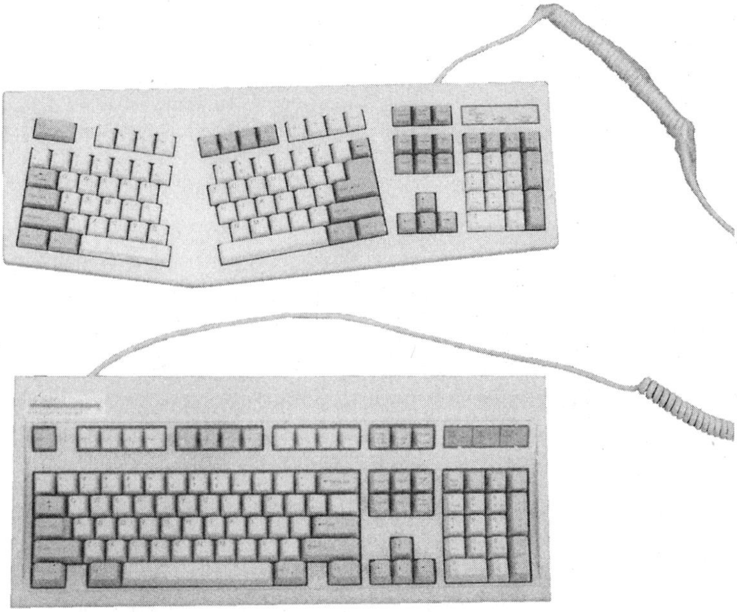

Figure 4-1
Ergonomic
"V"-shaped keyboard
(top) with regular
101-key enhanced
keyboard.

Some keyboards feature a built in trackball or pointing pad, but these come at a premium compared to the cost of buying the items separately.

Monitors

Monitors come in a dizzying array of sizes, capability, and prices. To simplify the discussion, we will stick to VGA monitors and better. Information about old "TTL"-type monitors is contained in the troubleshooting section. The least expensive SVGA monitors start at around $170. Many 386s and some early 486s were shipped with VGA (not SVGA) monitors, not capable of displaying higher resolutions even with a more expensive video adapter. Unfortunately, the manufacturer's labels on the back of the monitor rarely identify the capabilities of the monitor, beyond giving a model number. Try to obtain the instruction booklet with any second-hand monitor purchase, otherwise you'll have to observe it functioning in SVGA mode or trust the seller. Monitors that display VGA resolution only, and "paper-white" VGA monitors are no longer sold and are rarely worth repairing. If you already own a monitor and are happy with it, you might want to skip the next section which unavoidably gets a little technical.

Screen Size

Monitors, like television sets, are measured diagonally, from two opposing corners of the picture tube. The standard monitor size is 14", and prices rise rapidly with increasing screen size. Very large monitors can measure 21" diagonal or greater, weigh over 80 pounds and cost more than $2000. Manufacturers of monitors, like manufacturers of some clothing items, are not entirely consistent with their measuring schemes. Some measure parts of the picture tube that are hidden behind the plastic bezel of the monitor's casing, and others simply don't allow the screen size to be adjusted to anywhere near the edges of the bezel. This has led to an unofficial measurement known as "viewable area," measured diagonally, which describes how large a picture you can actually see. For example, one 17" monitor may have a viewable area of $16^1/2$", while another may have a viewable area of $15^1/2$". One recent innovation is the "flat-screen" monitor, which doesn't have the curved face of the standard picture tubes in most monitors and televisions. Flat screens look a little better and suffer less from glare than standard monitors, but they cost a good deal more.

Interlace and Horizontal Frequency

Two factors that control how "solid" or "flicker free" your monitor is: whether the display is "interlaced" or "noninterlaced," and the horizontal frequency, which controls how many times per second the screen is redrawn. Monitors, like televisions and movie projectors, flash a rapid series of pictures at us, which our eyes and brain merge into a solid image. How many images per second are required to create a really "solid"-looking picture varies from individual to individual, but the minimum number of times per second (frequency) an image is displayed by any modern monitor is 60 per second (60 Hz) at VGA resolution. The cost of the electronic components that control the picture tube go up in price as they go up in speed. One trick that allowed monitors with slower electronics to draw SVGA-resolution images without excessive flicker is "interlacing." When an image is interlaced, the monitor draws the entire image more than 60 times per second, but skipping every other line. On the next redraw, it does only the lines it skipped. The result is that the entire image appears less bright and a little flickery to some people, while others don't notice. For about $20 more, a noninterlaced (NI) monitor will be capable of drawing the whole image every cycle. Interestingly, most clone builders never bothered properly configuring the software and the video adapter to work with the NI monitors, thus buyers didn't get the benefit they paid for.

Even with an NI monitor, some people who stare at monitors all day long, especially under artificial lighting, see flickering or get dizzy by the end of the day. The way to make the picture appear even more "solid" is to run up the horizontal frequency to 72 Hz or 75 Hz. The increase in price to the video adapter is trivial, in fact most 512-K and 1-MB SVGA adapters can already handle 72 Hz, known as the VESA frequency (VESA for the Video Electronics Standards Association). The real challenge for both adapters and monitors is maintaining the higher horizontal frequency at screen resolutions beyond SVGA. Why does it matter? Well, for a VGA screen, the monitor electronics must draw 400 lines each 640 pixels long during each cycle. For each pixel in each line, the video adapter must tell the monitor how much of each primary color (red, green, and blue) to light up for each pixel. At SVGA resolution, 300 lines each 800 pixels long must be drawn in interlaced mode, and 600 lines of the same length in noninterlaced mode. Raise the resolution higher, then tell the electronics they have to redraw the whole image 72 or 75 time per second, and you've got some hardworking transistors on your hands.

Resolution and Dot Pitch (DP)

How "sharp" an image looks is determined by how many pixels (dots) the image comprises and how large the dots are. The best combination to create a really sharp image is a high resolution with a low dot pitch (DP). Resolution depends on the video adapter, software, and monitor all working together; the dot pitch depends on the monitor alone. Manufacturers use a couple of different approaches to defining dot pitch, but it basically defines how large each pixel or dot on the screen ends up being. Fourteen inch monitors should have a .28 DP, while larger monitors range from DPs of .25 to .31. A 14" monitor with a high dot pitch, say .39, is cheaper, but image definition is poor. The trade-off on resolution is a given image displayed at two different resolutions will appear sharper at the higher resolution, but larger at the lower resolution. Most people run their 14″ SVGA monitors at VGA resolution for this reason, although it's nice being able to switch to a higher resolution when you need to. If you want easily readable screen fonts (characters) at SVGA resolution, consider a 17″ monitor.

Mice

Mice can be purchased for anywhere between $5 to $100. The mouse you receive with any system bought as a whole is going to be the $5 model. Unless you do a lot of desktop publishing or other graphics work and want a special "feel" or extra control software with the mouse, the cheap version works fine. A mouse is normally connected to the system box via a Com port, normally Com1, but there are two other methods. The first method, used in brand name machines only, is via a special mouse port. This is normally located next to the keyboard connector. Most new Pentium and Pentium PRO systems are built with a special mouse port. The second approach, popular in the early nineties, is called a "bus mouse." In this approach, the mouse requires its own adapter card, and is plugged into a special port on this card. Other pointing devices include pen pointers, trackballs, touch screens, and joysticks—primarily those used in video games.

Figure 4-2
Serial mice with internal parts.

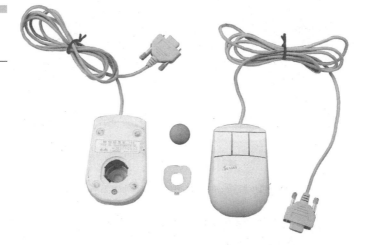

Figure 4-3
Microsoft InPort bus
mouse card and
serial mouse adapter.

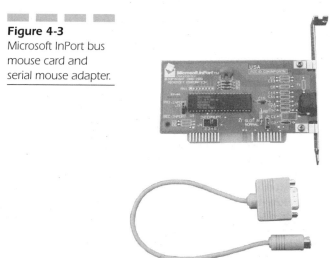

Joysticks

If games figure large in the future of your PC, a joystick is a must. Joysticks are plugged into a special game port, a 15-pin connector on the back of the system box. Mice require a flat, open area, about the size of a hard cover book for operation. A joystick is a self-contained navigation system that can be held in the lap, equipped with between one and four

Figure 4-4
A joystick.

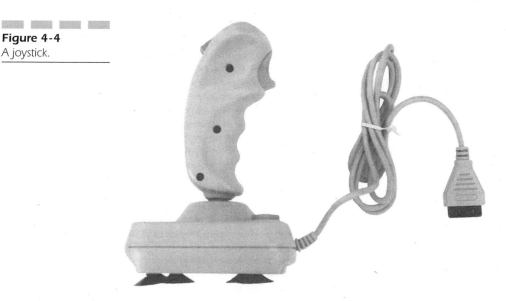

buttons for controlling on-screen action. Joysticks used to come in one variety, analog, which worked pretty well through the first ten years of joysticks' existence. Digital joysticks have been recently introduced, curing such minor woes as cursor wander in the neutral position. Unfortunately, digital joysticks require a special game port, which is only found on high-end sound cards or the newest Pentium systems. Further complicating the issue is the fact that the 15-pin digital port is identical to the standard game port, so if you have a new computer, you'll need to consult your documentation to see if your game port is digital-joystick capable.

Digitizer Tablets

Artists and draftsmen who need to position lines down to the thousandth of an inch or lower often use digitizer pads, which start around $200. The user either draws on this pad with a special instrument like a pen, or uses a mouselike device that sports a cross hair for precise positioning. In either case, the positioning device used on the pad is equipped with two or more buttons, mimicking mouse functionality. In addition, pressing down with the pen point on the graphics tablet performs a selection. Although this approach may seem like the most natural way to manipulate a cursor on the screen, it actually takes more practice to get comfortable with than mice or joysticks. The place where digitizer tablets really excel is in tracing existing artwork or maps, in order to convert them into digital form. Tablets use a magnetic positioning system that works right through the paper or plastic sheet that is placed on the tablet to be traced. The big digitizers used by professional draftspeople can be four or more feet across, are freestanding, and cost thousands of dollars.

Printers

People have been experimenting with ways to reproduce words since Guttenberg printed the Bible over 500 years ago. That's the long way of saying there are at least a dozen technologies that have been widely used at one time or another for computer printers. We'll limit our consideration to the big three: dot matrix, laser, and inkjet. All three types of printers are available as color or black and white, with color inkjets representing the happy medium between price and quality for color printing. Prices range from $100 for a cheap dot matrix to over $10,000 for a production color laser. Each printer has a niche it fills best, but if somebody offers you any one of the above for free, take the laser.

Dot Matrix Printers

Dot matrix printers have been around for over 25 years, so most of the bugs have been worked out. The two characteristics that describe dot matrix printers are the number of pins in the print head, 9 pin or 24 pin, and the width of the carriage—"narrow" or "wide." The cheapest printer is the narrow-carriage 9 pin, and the most expensive is the wide-carriage 24 pin. The width of the carriage simply refers to how wide the paper path is, where the narrow carriage handles the standard 8$\frac{1}{2}$" by 11" paper. The number of pins determines how close to "letter quality" the printing will look. The dots in the individual letters printed by a 9-pin dot matrix will be obvious, while a 24-pin printer on its slow "near letter quality" setting will produce much nicer print.

The print quality of any dot matrix printer can't compete with that of inkjets or lasers, but they maintain a market niche where carbon copies or

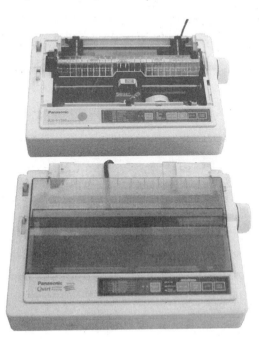

Figure 4-5

Panasonic dot-matrix printer with cover on and off.

labels are used. Dot matrix printers normally come with both tractor and friction feed, chosen by a lever on the side. Tractor feed uses paper with holes along the edges for sprockets to pull the printer, while friction feed works like an old-fashioned typewriter. Dot matrix printers are also rated by their speed in Characters Per Second (CPS). The CPS in draft mode (not very pretty) is always much higher than the CPS in "near letter quality" mode. The consumable (computer lingo for a part which gets used up and requires regular replacement) for dot matrix printers is the ribbon cartridge, which can cost from $3 to $20 or more. Expensive dot matrix printers called "line printers" are used for jobs like addressing hundreds of thousands of bills or making out checks and can cost thousands of dollars.

Inkjet Printers

Inkjet printers are the newest addition to the printer family and operate by shooting a stream of ink drops at the paper where they rapidly dry. Older model black and white inkjets can be had for under $100 while color models start around $125. All inkjets suffer from being slow, often turning out less than one page per minute. The advantages that inkjets hold over dot matrix printers is their ability to turn out good-looking output, including graphics. The more expensive color inkjets can do a pretty good job with photographic images when printing on specially treated paper. The consumable for inkjet printers is the ink cartridge, which averages about $20. The inkjet market, both the printers and the consumables, is dominated by Hewlett Packard, which also has the lion's share of the laser-printer market. Epson makes the best low-cost inkjet for printing photographic images, and Canon Bubble Jets usually offer the best price/performance trade-offs.

Laser Printers

Laser printers operate along the same lines as copying machines, except they have a lot fewer moving parts and are much more reliable. The two measures of performance for a laser printer are the number of dots per inch (dpi) and the number of pages per minute printed (ppm). Older lasers printed 300 dpi, which produces much better print than any dot matrix or inkjet. New lasers can print at 600 and 800 dpi, which is noticeably sharper when viewed through a magnifying glass. A slow laser printer will average about 4 ppm, middle-of-the-road lasers manage 8 ppm, and expensive shared lasers used in office settings often print over 20 ppm. Cheap lasers without paper trays start under $350, but a decent office-quality laser costs about twice that amount.

Options that add to the functionality and expense of a laser are Post-Script compatibility, a software enhancement developed by Adobe that is required by some desktop publishing and graphics software, and additional RAM for temporarily storing the images to be printed. The main consumable for laser printers is the toner cartridge, costing anywhere between $10 and $200 dollars, depending on the life span and print engine. Image drums, which start around $100 for rebuilts to a couple hundred dollars for various new models, have longer lifetimes than toner cartridges, but also require occasional replacement. Pricing and lifetime of laser consumables should be considered when comparison shopping laser printers.

Scanners

Scanners are used to digitize (change into computer codes) photographs, artwork and documents. The resulting digitized image can be used to display the original on a monitor, reproduce it on a printer, or in the case of documents containing letter quality words and numbers, to read them. Changing the image of a document into actual words and numbers that can be used in a word processor or spreadsheet is called Optical Character Recognition (OCR). Scanners see images as either color or "gray scales," which convert the image into shades of gray varying from white to black. Color scanner prices vary from under a hundred dollars for hand-held roller scanners to tens of thousands of dollars for commercial models in the publishing and document-management industries. The most popular models are "flat bed" scanners, where a sheet of paper or photograph is laid flat to be scanned. A decent flat bed color scanner costs between $200 to $500, and comes with software and an adapter card. Inexpensive gray-scale scanners lost out to color scanners when the prices came down, and don't really have any value in the second-hand market. High-end gray-scale scanners, costing from several thousand to almost one hundred thousand dollars, are used for processing large numbers of documents for archiving or OCR. The most expensive of these can scan over 100 pages per minute, compared to the one or two pages per minute achieved by inexpensive flat beds.

Figure 4-6
HP 2P flatbed
scanner with
cover up.

Figure 4-6
HP 2P flatbed
scanner with
cover up.

Scanners use the same "dots per inch" (dpi) figure used by laser printers. Most scanners are capable of scanning at resolutions from 75 to 300 dpi, according to software settings. New scanners, even inexpensive models, can scan up to 600 dpi, and produce images that appear to be 1200 to 2400 dpi using software tricks. High-resolution scanning is important for photographs or artwork that will be reproduced later, but most OCR works fine at 200 dpi. Color scanners also have graded ability to reproduce colors expressed in bits of depth. Any newer scanner will manage 24 bits deep, while 30 bits deep or higher offers more accuracy and control. Most people who aren't professional artists or publishers will be happy with a $200 flatbed scanner that offers 24-bit color and 300 dpi.

Pen Plotters

Plotters are generally used by draftsmen or engineers to produce blueprint-type drawings or to graph measurements taken by scientific instruments. Plotters draw with one color pen at a time but are usually equipped with eight pens of different colors. Desktop plotters draw on standard stationary paper sizes, while free standing floor models can handle all the blueprint sizes (A, B, C...). The only consumables are the pens, which are replaced or refilled one at a time. Plotters are connected to one of the communications ports on the system box, normally Com2, with a serial cable.

Speakers and Microphones

Speakers, which require the presence of a sound card in the system box to be of any use, can be a little different from the speakers on your stereo. In order to play music at a reasonable volume from your sound card, you will need to run the output through an amplifier or purchase amplified speakers. Some amplified speakers require batteries, others come with a transformer that can be plugged into a wall outlet. Good amplified speakers, costing between $50 to $100, can make the CD player in your computer sound like a stereo and add tremendously to the multimedia experience. Cheap speakers often come free with the sound card, but their volume is limited to a level around spoken conversation, and the fidelity is terrible. The microphone supplied with most sound cards works well enough for recording speech and is usually the clip-on type.

Figure 4-7
Inexpensive speakers with microphone and earphone.

External Modems and Drives

A brief discussion of external modems and drives is necessary at this point to highlight some of their limitations, which will be discussed in more detail in the appropriate upgrading sections. For example, external modems will seem like the best way to go for many people, since you don't have to open up the system box or know anything about interrupts to install them. The limitation is that the modem cannot work at a greater speed than the Com port is capable of. The Com ports in most 486 systems, all 386s, and even some early Pentiums, are capable of a top communications speed of only 19.2 KB/s. A 28.8 KB/s or 33.6 KB/s modem will be limited to that 19.2 KB/s speed, unless you buy a new I/O adapter, which you'll have to open up the system box to install.

Many external drives can be configured to work on the printer port, which offers much faster communications than the Com ports, but the overall transfer rate will be much lower than if that same drive were installed in the system box. Some printer-port-connected devices won't work with older printer ports and require the more advanced components available on newer motherboards. External SCSI (Small Computer System Integration) drives work just as fast as their internal counterparts,

Figure 4-8
U.S. Robotics 28.8-K Sportster external modem and transformer.

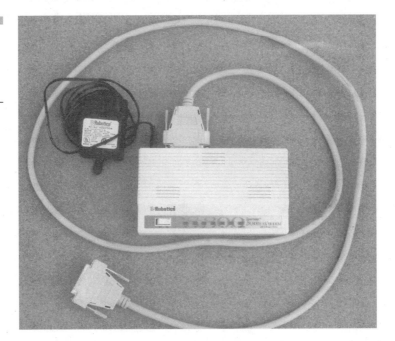

and SCSI drives are generally the highest performance storage devices in a PC. Here again you'll need to open the system box to add a SCSI adapter if you don't already have one installed, and you'll still have to open the system box to reconfigure the terminators if there is a SCSI adapter installed but no other external drives present.

PART

2

A PC for Every Task

CHAPTER **5**

Software Basics

Few of us acquire a PC as a status symbol or try to find one in a color that goes well with our eyes. How much PC you need is entirely dependent on what you want to do with it. Although extensive software reviews are beyond the scope of this book, it is largely the software that sets the minimum hardware requirements. Therefore, we mention some popular software packages by name and discuss the "box" requirements, the minimum suggested hardware configuration. With the exception of some games, compatibility with the Microsoft Windows operating environment is a must for using store-bought software. This excludes PCs older than 386s from our discussion, unless they are already loaded with the software you will use. That doesn't imply that an older PC in working condition should be refused or thrown out, but upgrading a 286 PC to run with Windows essentially involves replacing everything except the case and power supply. PC AT clones (286s) can run Windows in a limited fashion, but only with older, less demanding programs.

For any of the tasks we consider, a new Pentium costing $1,000 would be more than sufficient. In fact, some companies have broken the cycle of buying new computers every two or three years because the 486s or 386s they have are still performing adequately. How much performance you require is pretty much dependent on how patient you are and how much time you spend using the computer each day. For example, when repositioning a picture in a desktop publishing program, a new Pentium may redraw the screen in a half second, while a hand-me-down 486 might take 15 seconds. If you don't think 15 seconds is that bad, try repositioning the picture 20 times to get just the right look. Then imagine formatting 50 pages a day, or paying an employee to sit around idle for over an hour each day in accumulated 15 second increments.

Operating Systems and Environments

Whenever you turn on your PC it loads an operating system, a large software program that controls how any subsequent programs you run get along with the hardware. The operating system market for PCs is dominated by Microsoft, who got their foot in the door by cobbling together the original operating system for the IBM PC. The operating system came to be known by the acronym DOS (Disk Operating System), pronounced like "loss" with a "d." There is actually another layer of software that works even more closely with the hardware than the operating system, called the BIOS (Basic Input Output System), and this software is permanently stored in a special chip on the motherboard. We'll talk more about the BIOS in the upgrading and troubleshooting sections of this book. The DOS operating system provides a number of necessary structures to allow general purpose use of the PC. The organization of files (containers of text and data) on the drives is defined and controlled by DOS. When a file is printed, it's DOS that sends the data to the printer port, and reports back if the printer can't successfully complete the job. One of the most important jobs DOS does is to organize the memory (RAM) into blocks dedicated to housekeeping functions or program use.

The biggest complaint users and developers have about DOS is the rigidity with which it manages memory. Most of the problem stems from history. It didn't occur to creators of the original DOS operating system that PCs would ever have more than 1 MB of RAM, because at the time DOS was being developed, RAM cost more than a hundred times as much as it does today. By the same token, nobody thought the programs would ever get as big as they have. The 512 KB (a half of a megabyte) that shipped with the IBM-AT seemed more than enough for any software challenge. Finally, the whole philosophy of the PC, which does stand for Personal Computer after all, was that only one person would use it at a time. This freed the creators of DOS from worrying about multitasking, the ability of a computer to shuffle memory and jump from task to task, something that multiuser mainframes computers are required to do.

As the years went by and PCs became cheaper and more powerful, programmers wanted to take advantage of memory sizes over 1 MB, and introduce multitasking features to make their software faster and more flexible. Along came a bunch of band-aids, like the Expanded Memory Specification (EMS), which set aside a small block of regular DOS memory to use as a revolving door for accessing RAM on a special adapter. Other fixes involved software products that took over certain memory management functions from DOS and squeezed more room out of the standard block set aside for programs. Competitors of DOS that boasted better memory management and multitasking included IBM's OS/2 and different flavors of the Unix operating system, which was sold by a number of companies. Both OS/2 and Unix continue to have some success in niche markets today, particularly in areas where multitasking is the primary requirement. Microsoft Windows did not eliminate all of the DOS limitations, because it is an operating environment which runs on top of DOS. Microsoft Windows NT, which has been winning market share from OS/2 and Unix, is an operating system in its own right, and the similarities between NT and the other Windows operating systems are superficial.

Windows 3.1 and Windows for Workgroups

Another complaint users had about DOS was that it wasn't easy to learn. The only way to communicate with the operating system was to enter commands on the keyboard, like "PRINT myfile.txt" or "DIR C:", meaning "Show me a DIRectory of the files on the C: drive." Another approach to working with the operating system called the Graphical User Interface (GUI), pronounced "gooey," had been developed at Xerox and popularized by Apple with their Macintosh computers. Microsoft soon had a competing product for the PC, the Windows operating environment, but it wasn't until version 3.0 or 3.1 that it became attractive enough to convince software developers to forget about DOS and begin developing exclusively for Windows. In 1995, Windows 95 was introduced, which supports higher performance software at the cost of requiring higher performance hardware. Most hand-me-down PCs will arrive with Windows 3.1 already installed, and we use this as a baseline for our Windows discussion.

Windows offers several advantages to both software developers and users. The biggest advantage for developers is they don't need to write a new software interface for every new piece of hardware that comes down the pike. For example, a DOS word processor like WordPerfect or Word had to include a special piece of software known as a "printer driver" for every printer that the word processor would work with. This not only required a lot of work for the developer, even if subsidized by the printer manufacturer, but meant the user would have to go through the printer selection step with each new word processor, spreadsheet, or other piece of application software installed. Windows functions as a sort of middleman, so that the user only needs to install a printer driver once, the Windows driver, and the applications developers write printer drivers not for specific printers, but for the Windows interface. The same holds true for all the other hardware components that would otherwise need special software to communicate with each different program, like scanners, video adapters, and sound cards.

Another advantage to the user, which is often taken for granted, is the fact that programs written for Windows all look pretty much alike. Anyone who has used one Windows application can go into a totally new one and already know how and where to save a file, get help, change the fonts, or print. While mice were certainly supported by most later DOS applications, Windows programs are designed from the ground up to take advantage of such pointing devices. The mouse can be used in Windows to do all of the communicating with the operating environment. The only typing the user can't avoid is typing text or entering data. It is possible to work in Windows without a pointing device, using the "Alt," "Ctrl," and "Tab" keys in conjunction with the other keys to navigate and execute menu commands, but it's not a lot of fun.

One feature in Windows which is often ignored by users is that it does support a primitive form of multitasking. Some users learn that they can "minimize" a screen window by clicking on the "down" arrow in the upper right-hand corner, which leaves the application in sort of limbo rather than closing it altogether. Another application can then be started by clicking on the appropriate icon (pictorial representation). The easier way to move from program to program is to hold down the "Ctrl" key and press "Esc." This brings up the "Windows Task List," and allows users to change from one task to the next with a click of the mouse. Using one of Window's other slick features, the "Copy," "Cut," and "Paste" commands included in the "Edit" menu of every Windows program, users can then move text, pictures, and data from one application to another with a few clicks of the mouse.

Windows 95

One of the major complaints about Windows 3.1 and Windows for Workgroups was that you could "lose" things, since there was no real hierarchy to all of the different program groups. Windows 95 retains all of the working characteristics of Windows, such as "cut and paste" and "point and click," but it replaces the basic "Program Manager" screen with a completely new design. Windows 95 features a task bar at the bottom of the screen, which tells you what applications are in use and allows you to move between them with a click of the mouse. The "Programs" option on the "Start" button, gives the user an ordered list of all the applications installed, including Windows Explorer, an updated version of the old Windows File Manager.

One of the features carried over from older Windows is the "Control Panel," now found under the "My Computer" icon or from the "Settings" item under the "Start" button. All of the settings that affect how the computer performs and what you actually see are located here. The most used icon in "Control Panel" is the "Device Manager." Here is where you can find out all those annoying details needed for installing new hardware and software, like what interrupts and I/O addresses are being used. Device Manager can also report on whether or not a piece of hardware is working properly, and if there are any usage conflicts with other installed adapters.

Figure 5-1
Windows 95 Explorer.

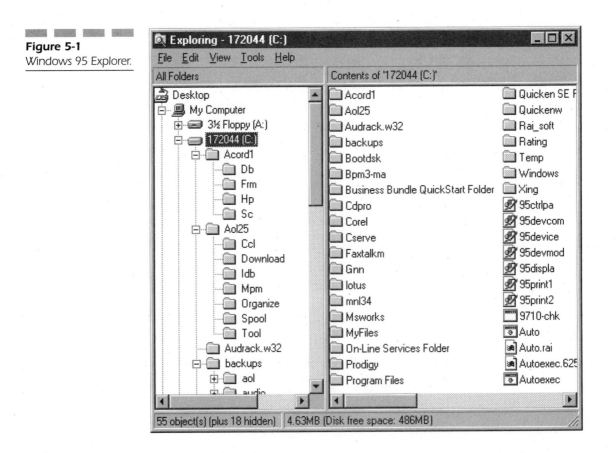

Figure 5-2
Windows 95 control panel.

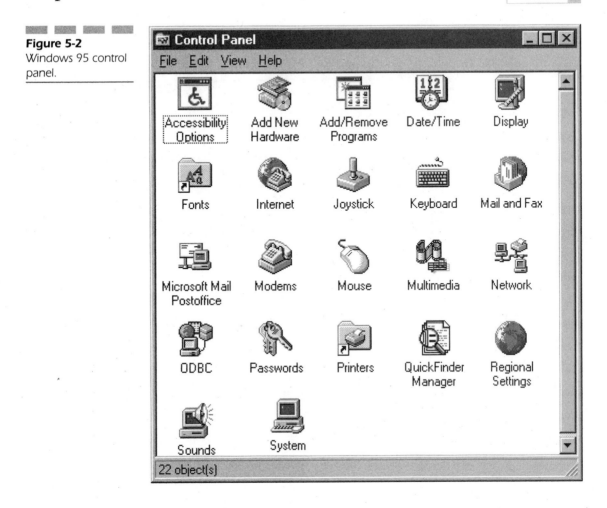

Windows 95 does an excellent job supporting old DOS applications, though you'll notice that the screen often has a compressed look, compared to the traditional full screen appearance of DOS. The old DOS prompt you may have been accustomed to used an ancient character mode, 80 cells horizontally by 25 lines, formed out of visible points of light on a dark screen. The DOS screen in Windows 95 still comes up black, but it's really a VGA screen pretending to be a DOS screen, which will become apparent if you chose to resize the screen. When you scroll a DOS screen in Windows 95, it moves smoothly, rather than flashing from line to line. The important thing is that most applications run just the way they did on an old computer, and can be added to the task bar like any other application.

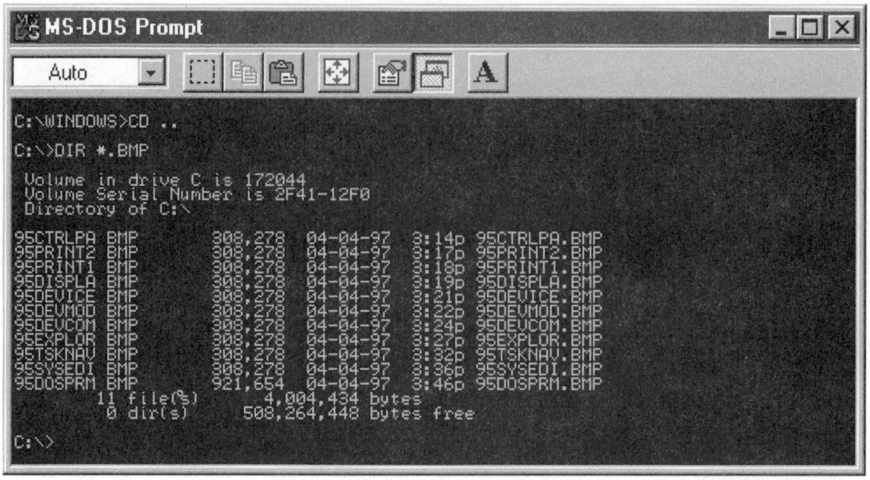

Figure 5-3
Windows 95 DOS
prompt.

In terms of performance, Windows 95 is a 32-bit operating system, compared with 16 bits for DOS, Windows 3.1, and Windows for Workgroups. Due to the increased complexity Windows 95 brings to the table, it actually loads slower than DOS and Windows would on a similar machine. The real performance advantage comes with Windows 95 support for 32-bit application software, which can deal with twice as much information at a time as 16-bit software. Most new software packages are designed for use with Windows 95 or Windows NT only, so if you're sticking with DOS or an older Windows environment, be prepared to stick with old or unsupported software as well.

Windows NT

Windows NT is sold in two basic versions: the client and the server. The Windows NT client, recently released in version 4.0, now uses the Windows 95 interface and looks almost identical to Windows 95. Looks are deceiving, in this case, as the underlying software is very different. Whether Windows 95 or Windows NT is the better operating system is a moot point for most people, since computer manufacturers almost exclusively ship the less expensive Windows 95. Windows NT Server competes primarily with the different flavors of Unix, offering a stable, multitasking network operating system for back office support. As PCs become increasingly powerful, high-end Windows NT systems are replacing minicomputers, often running on the superfast DEC Alpha CPU, which has a basic clock speed about three times faster than the top-of-the-line Pentium.

OS/2

OS/2 was once seen as the heir-apparent of the Windows operating system. Originally codeveloped by Microsoft and IBM, OS/2 was designed for advanced memory management and multitasking from the start. OS/2 achieved acclaim as a stable platform, rarely "locking up" or reacting badly to unpredictable input. When the IBM/Microsoft partnership came to an end, in part over a squabble about Microsoft's continued development of the Windows operating environment, OS/2 ran into the law of supply and demand. There were far more Windows-based PCs in use than OS/2-based PCs, so it made sense for software developers with limited resources to ship their products for Windows first. This, of course, increased the desirability of Windows over OS/2 to the consumer, creating a positive feedback loop for the increasing domination of Windows.

IBM tried to overcome the marketing problem by licensing Windows from Microsoft and building support for it into OS/2, and this product has had quiet success in the corporate world. Unfortunately for the OS/2 group at IBM, the other product groups within the company tend to follow the free market, which these days means developing for Windows 95 first. OS/2 is occasionally balky to set up with older peripherals, and the graphical interface falls somewhere between that of Windows 3.1 and that of Windows 95. Enough copies of OS/2 were sold that you may come across it on a hand-me-down PC, but it will likely be an older version

Unix

Unix is the favored operating system of computer scientists, hard-core programmers, and people who can't stand Microsoft's domination of the software world. Some of the selling points of Unix include stability, the existence of standards, extremely strong support for multitasking, multiuser, and terminal-based systems. If you work in a small office where the employees use dumb terminals, rather than PCs, there's a good chance they are connected to a Unix-based PC. Unix also scales up to much larger computers, and is popular on college campuses, in government installations, and in certain industries. There is a small chance you might inherit a PC with Unix installed.

CHAPTER **6**

PC Application Software

Before we look at the hardware/software configurations for different tasks, we need to discuss some of the software components that will be common to many users. Accountants, students, office workers, and entrepreneurs are all likely to use spreadsheets, and almost everybody needs a word processor. Databases are used in every type of business operation, and most people will want to get on the Internet at least for e-mail. Computer networks are also introduced here, although in functionality they are more closely related to operating systems than applications software. Once we've summarized the common application software, we'll move on to discussing how the PC, software, and peripherals combine to make a powerful, task-specific tool.

Our discussion of applications software focuses on brand-name shrink-wrap packages. This software is usually an evolved product that has been developing new features and improving usability for years. Brand-name software is extensively tested for bugs, which are errors in the program's logical construction. Undetected bugs can make usage quirky or even cause data loss. Perhaps the most important point is that big software companies offer many kinds of technical support, often free, to licensed users of their software. If the database you've been using for three years suddenly refuses to accept any new customers, or your accounting package stops printing invoices during months with even numbers of days, you can count on support, even if it requires a credit card number. Most software companies release upgrades to their applications at least once a year, and licensed users can buy them at a discount.

The main alternative to brand-name software is shareware. Shareware consists of software applications written by individuals or small companies that are distributed free, or for a nominal fee. Shareware is obtainable on floppy disk at computer fairs and from some stores or can be downloaded from numerous archiving sites on the Internet. Users are invited to register their copy by sending a reasonable fee, normally from $20 to $50, to the creators of the software, in exchange for instruction manuals, enhanced versions, or other goodies. Support is sometimes included, but this doesn't compare to the kind of support a big company can provide. I don't suggest shareware to anybody who can scrape together the $100 to $200 that most brand-name software applications cost, and I especially don't recommend it for the work environment. The two exceptions I make are for software addicts, people who need to try out as many programs as possible, and people looking for very specific items, like a Windows application for running the office football pool.

A brief note about computer viruses. Computer viruses are self-replicating, malicious little programs that are put into circulation by destructive individuals. Viruses are spread by contact, through sharing infected floppy disks, by downloading compromised software from the Internet, through running infected programs on a network, or any other procedure that allows the virus to enter your PC's memory. You can protect your PC from viruses by purchasing virus-shield software. Infected PCs can be cured after the fact by virus doctor software, although damaged files may be lost permanently. The important thing to remember here is that viruses affect software only; your investment in hardware is not threatened. In the worst-case scenario, virus damage can be repaired by wiping the hard drive clean and reinstalling all of your software from the original disks.

Hardware/Software Requirements

The first thing you need to do when you pull a box of shrink-wrapped software off of a store shelve is to read the system requirements printed on the spine of the box. The hardware requirements are usually pretty straightforward, defining the minimum or recommended CPU type acceptable, the minimum amount of total RAM in the PC, and the minimum amount of free space required on the hard drive to install the product. In all cases, you want to keep at least 10 percent of your hard-drive space free at all times for temporary use by the operating system, so subtract this 10 percent from your total free space before deciding how much room for new applications you have. A mouse is also a must for most applications.

Almost all applications today require a video card capable of displaying 256 colors, which is sometimes a plain VGA adapter, but many have begun specifying SVGA. Games, multimedia applications, and newer operating systems are most likely to require an SVGA adapter, sometimes calling for 32-K (K = 1,024) colors, 64-K colors, or even "millions of colors." You can get up to 64-K colors out of an SVGA adapter with 512 KB RAM, millions of colors require an SVGA adapter with at least 1 MB of RAM. In all cases, you don't get to see the colors unless the card is properly configured in the Windows environment, a situation which creates one of the most frequent tech-support calls multimedia producers receive.

Since the majority of serious software titles are shipped on CD-ROM today, a CD-ROM drive is normally listed in the hardware requirements. For multimedia applications, the requirement may be for a minimum of a 2X (double speed) or 4X (quad speed) CD drive. Multimedia applications will also require a sound card, usually a 16-bit SoundBlaster compatible, with external speakers. Some games will recommend a joystick, although you can normally get by with the keyboard and a mouse.

The software requirements refer to either the operating system, or the application you must already own to legally purchase an upgrade. The vast majority of software applications are forward-compatible, meaning a program requiring DOS 5.0 will run under DOS 6.0, DOS 6.2, Windows 95, and Windows NT. Windows 3.1 and Windows for Workgroups were omitted in the previous example, because if you are using 3.1 or Workgroups, you must have DOS loaded also. Applications software is never backwards-compatible, meaning an application requiring Windows 3.1 will not run unless you have Windows 3.1 or better, and an application requiring Windows 95 will not run on Windows for Workgroups or Windows 3.1. While many programs are compatible between Windows 95 and Windows NT, some are written in different versions for each, and you should make sure that your operating system is listed as compatible.

Spreadsheets

Spreadsheets were the first application that made people stand up and take notice of PCs, and they originally defined the term "killer app" in industry parlance. The IBM PC was primarily a business tool when first introduced, and Lotus 1-2-3 was the spreadsheet product that convinced managers to spend several thousand dollars on these otherwise uninspiring paperweights. Spreadsheets are chiefly used for doing financial analysis due to their ability to easily produce "What if..." scenarios that can involve multiple interdependent calculations. A family might use a spreadsheet to manage a monthly budget, while a real estate tycoon could use a spreadsheet to determine whether or not to invest in a new development. The spreadsheet used by the family might involve nothing more complicated than addition and subtraction of income and expenses, while the tycoon's calculations would depend on factors like interest rates, taxes, utilities, rental rates and occupancy projections, construction costs, and of course, profit. The power of the spreadsheet becomes apparent when the tycoon says to himself, "What happens to my investment if rents drop from $18/sf to $17.50/sf?" A couple of keystrokes to change the rent figure, and his formula for construction variables reworks the other numbers to tell him what interest rate from the bank and cost of construction he'll need. Or, a couple keystrokes to change the cost of construction with everything but the interest rate held fixed, and he learns that the scenario requires an 8.82 percent bank loan for the profit he desires. Spreadsheets are also the worst abuser of the GIGO rule (garbage in, garbage out). Get your formulas wrong or use unrealistic rental projections and you'll find yourself building skyscrapers in downtown Houston in the late eighties.

We considered the spreadsheet task first for one reason. The spreadsheet obviously worked well enough on the IBM PC for it to have been declared the "killer app." Why not use a 15-year-old PC to run a 15-year-old copy of Lotus 1-2-3 today? The answer is, you can! Even though the original PC had a monochrome monitor, no hard drive, and predated the first good version of Windows by about 10 years, it made some real-estate tycoons very happy. Now, go out to the local store and look for a copy of Lotus 1-2-3 or Microsoft Excel, the two most popular spreadsheets in use today. On the spine of the box are listed the minimum requirements: 4 MB of RAM, 386 or higher, requires Windows 3.1 or Windows 95. You can't buy a modern spreadsheet that will run on the original IBM PC. Are the software makers in collusion with the computer manufacturers to make us buy a new computer every year? Probably not.

Software makers traditionally try to differentiate themselves from their competitors by offering more options. One of the first enhancements to the basic spreadsheet was a feature that would automatically produce color graphs from the numbers. This isn't such a big deal, but it definitely requires a color monitor to be effective. Another feature was support for more numbers and calculations of the sort that would bring an old PC to its knees. The programs got bigger as they included on-line help (on-screen help on demand), conversion of data from competing products, 3-D (three-dimensional) graphing, and so on. Pretty soon, the programs became too big to be run from floppy disk and required a hard drive. Next, they ran too slow for anything less than a 286 with a math coprocessor. Extra memory goes a long way to compensate for poor programming rushed out under competitive pressure. Finally, the software producer gets tired of paying for new code to guarantee compatibility with every new printer and video adapter that comes along, and the product is moved from DOS to Windows. In another year or two or it may be impossible to find a spreadsheet that works with Windows 3.1.

Word Processors

Equipped with a letter-quality printer and a software package for word processing, a PC is a lot more than a replacement for a typewriter. Basic features supported by word processors include font control, style sheets (for quickly formatting similar documents), spell checkers, footnotes, page numbers, and anything else you can imagine that's useful for creating documents from correspondence to books. More advanced features include support for tables, mail merge (for sending the same letter to a whole list of addressees), and grammar checkers. Features that were once the exclusive domain of desktop publishing programs are now common in word processors: frames (for precise positioning of pictures), tables, graphics; and tagging words to create a dynamic index that always gets the page number right.

Box requirements for word processing software began to explode a few years ago. Even WordPerfect for DOS began to demand 6 MB of memory just to run the spell checker! Microsoft Word 2.0 ran pretty well under Windows 3.1 with just 4 MB of memory, but the Windows 95 version obviously needs Windows 95, which requires at least 8 MB of memory, a 486, and a big hard drive, just to get out of the starting blocks. Word processors always include a "Search" or "Find File" function buried in their "File" menu. The reason becomes apparent to anyone who has used a word processor for a year or two. You simply forget the names of your documents (files) and where you put them. Word processor search functions will search all of your drives for a file name, author name, documents saved in a range of dates, or even a random bit of text you know was in the document, like an addressee name or the odd ingredient in a recipe. There are lots of schemes for intelligently naming and organizing files in order not to lose them, but most of us won't bother organizing until the cow's left the barn.

Desktop Publishing System

Desktop publishing software can produce output for typeset-quality printers to create camera-ready galleys for offset printing. With the advent of digital presses, typeset documents can be created directly from software, without an intermediate photographic step. While it's primarily the ability to create printing-press-ready documents that separates desktop publishing software from word processors, the software can also be used with regular laser printers for producing very professional-looking documents. The market is currently dominated by QuarkXPress and Adobe Pagemaker, but Ventura Publisher, now owned by Corel, is making a comeback. All of the desktop publishing packages currently run on Windows, but Ventura Publisher, originally a Xerox product, was available for DOS to run on a PC-AT more than 10 years ago.

One of the features that separates desktop publishing packages from word processors is their precision. Placement of objects on a page to within one thousandth of an inch is standard, and a greater range of font sizes and gradations are available. Other features include kerning, color matching, and snap to grid, which automatically aligns objects precisely along existing lines. New desktop-publishing software includes more and more of the features traditionally found in photo-processing packages, like acquisition of images directly from scanners, cropping and drawing tools, and color definitions. Another strength of desktop-publishing packages, even in their earliest incarnation, is true WYSIWYG (What You See Is What You Get) output to the screen. A larger, high resolution monitor is required if you are going to display full pages and still be able to read the text, but it's comforting to know that what you see on the screen is truly what is going to roll out of the printer. About the only thing you can't do with desktop publishing software is simple typing, at least not as easily as you could with a word processor.

Databases

When you call up your credit card company to complain about a bill, the first thing they ask for is your name and social security number. The service representatives type these bits of information into their computer and have instant access to your charges last month, your address and phone numbers, and maybe even the color of your hair! If their computer system has problems, they can't do a thing for you and aren't shy about saying so. This is an example of a powerful database application, the kind that some sectors of the business world, particularly in the service industry, have become utterly reliant upon. Databases on PCs are commonly used to control inventory, produce customer invoicing, simplify purchasing, track sales contacts, and log shipping and receiving transactions. All of these functions are often combined into a networked database/accounting package which can even do payroll and generate up-to-the-minute profit and loss reports.

In some ways, PC databases are as powerful as multimillion dollar systems. While PC databases can't support hundreds or thousands of simultaneous users or fit millions of customer records on a single hard drive, the methodology for entering and retrieving data can be identical. Databases are normally built from information the operator types into special forms. A form consists of a "fill-in-the-blanks" screen, where information like name, address, phone, and social security number are entered via the keyboard. A completed form is stored in the database as a "record," and can be manually updated or have other information automatically added to it by software at intervals, like an employee's cumulative pay for the year. Database programming used to be an arcane skill that forced would-be designers to adapt to the style of the database, but modern databases running under Windows can be quickly built and modified by anyone with a knack for organization.

Retrieving information from databases can be performed through direct query or through report generation. A direct query uses a unique identifier, like a social security number, to retrieve the record or records associated with that individual. This works very quickly because only the field storing the social security numbers must be searched for a match, and then the whole record is retrieved. Reporting, on the other hand, can search every field of every record to generate new information. The database in a credit card company might be used to find all women between the ages of fifty and fifty six, with an income over $50,000 a year, and a monthly credit card balance over $3,000, to target for a special marketing campaign. This sort of reporting where new facts are brought to light is often referred to as "data mining."

The better PC databases support SQL (Structured Query Language), a tiny subset of English that can be used to ask specific questions of the database. For example, the query "Select Group, Title_Track from CDs where Sales > 100,000" would return the names of each group and the title track from their CD, for all groups in the record company's database whose CD had sold over 100,000 copies. Some products go further, adding a "Natural-Language" interface to the SQL database so the same question could be phrased, "Show me which groups have sold over 100,000 CDs and what the title track was for each of them." Natural language interfaces have their limitations and are sometimes balky to use, but they improve with every passing year.

Games

Learning can be a game, and even when it's not, games can be a lot of fun. Game players are usually the people who buy the most advanced PCs, loaded with special features and expensive add-ons. Games that play out in real time, such as a flight simulation or a battle with monsters, often push the operating system completely out of the way to squeeze every last drop of performance they can from the hardware. As PCs become more and more capable, game designers push the envelope ever harder, trying to create "virtual realities" with their software. Fast video adapters and big screens are a must for the serious gamer, along with a quality sound system, a fast CD drive, and a joystick. While game designers have recognized that support for older hardware allows them to sell into a much bigger market, games remain one of the most demanding PC applications. A good gaming PC is a good multimedia PC, which is the next topic discussed.

Multimedia

Multimedia remains a catch-all phrase that means entirely different things to different people. Salesmen think of multimedia as a tool they use to give snazzy sales pitches with rock music thumping in the background and Madison Avenue style camera angles and cuts. Such presentations are normally "canned," that is, they play through from beginning to end like a VHS tape, and often use video footage as their primary "media." A supermarket might contain a multimedia PC inside a touch-screen kiosk for locating grocery items. The popular Microsoft Multimedia Composer series includes an entire symphony per CD, along with on-screen sheet music, commentary, instrumental solos and learning games. CDs from the series, including Beethoven, Mozart, Schubert, Strauss, and Stravinsky can also be played straight through in a normal stereo system.

A multimedia PC requires the presence of several hardware components that are often absent from hand-me-down PCs. These include: a sound card (16 bit or better required for most applications), speakers, a microphone (if you are creating your own multimedia), an SVGA adapter with a minimum of 512 KB of RAM and configured to display 32 K colors or more, and a CD drive (2X or faster). Multimedia PCs built for presentation or games will often contain special video adapters that can display full screen, full motion video from a specially compressed data stream. Adapters following the MPEG (Motion Photographic Experts Group) standard have taken over this field from scores of proprietary competitors. A different approach uses special software extensions to the operating system, such as Intel's Indeo, Cinepak's Quicktime, or the software version of MPEG. The software decompresses specially prepared data into motion video, but the smoothness of the resulting movie is dependent on the overall performance of the PC.

Some of the best multimedia software is not as creative as it is imitative, of books! Multimedia encyclopedias, wildlife guides and photography collections are usually built around an existing successful book, taking from it the text and pictures. The multimedia version is then enhanced with a small number of video clips and audio tracks, like a bird guide including footage of birds in flight and bird calls. The real value of the product remains in the carefully researched text, illustrative drawings and photographs, which are accumulated over many book editions and years. The most valuable addition to the book form that the multimedia version can offer is a search capability that will sort through the voluminous information based on a key word or phrase, or through a logical tree structure.

World Wide Web Browsers

One of the most popular activities for home PC users is "surfing the Web," following links from site to site on the graphics-oriented addition to the Internet known as the World Wide Web. The main limitation for almost all home users is the speed of their connection, a combination on your modem speed, the modem at the other end of the phone line, and the quality of your Internet Service Provider (ISP). A 14.4-K modem is adequate for patient individuals. A 33.6-K modem is capable of transferring information more than twice as fast as the 14.4-K modem, but your ISP is rarely up to steadily supplying data at that speed. Either speed is a snail's crawl compared with a networked connection at the workplace, university, or at your local Internet cafe. Whether you can get by with a 14.4-K modem or need to spent the $100 for a 33.6-K modem also depends on how you want to use the Web.

Users who plan to do only text-based research and fact finding will see little benefit from the higher speed. Most people will want to browse, which involves loading pictures that might take from 15 seconds to a minute each to arrive using the 14.4-K modem, depending on Internet traffic. Downloading a piece of software or a motion video to your hard drive can take from 20 minutes to an hour. The potential to cut these times in half makes a lot of sense, particularly if you are paying by the hour for your Internet access. Faster computer hardware will improve performance for the more graphics-oriented material, but an old PC-XT will do fine in "text-only" mode. Text-mode functions include the ability to send and receive e-mail and to participate in chat groups and news groups. Chapter 17 is devoted to the home and business use of the World Wide Web.

Network Clients

One of the best features of Local Area Networks (LANs) is that they allow low-cost workstations access to fast storage and expensive peripherals. A budget-stretching public school customer was still using Leading Edge XT computers in the mid-Nineties, just one generation removed from the original PC, to give an entire classroom of students access to WordPerfect word-processing software on a 386-based network server. Granted, without hard drives in the workstations, the software took an extra minute to load, and the monitors were old-fashioned amber monochromes, but output looked great on the networked laser printer. At the most basic level, the only thing a PC needs to become a network workstation is a network adapter and the software driver that lets DOS talk to it (must be DOS 3.3 or higher).

Now, onto the real world. Most users, in businesses, schools, anywhere a network is set up, will want to run Windows. Depending on the applications software available, they may have to run Windows. This means saying good-bye to PCs older than 386s. Next, many people will want to run Windows 95. Now we're looking at needing a minimum of a 486 with 8 MB of memory. In other words, the requirement for the hardware investment in each workstation is not set by the network, but by the applications software. Requirements are set by the highest common denominator, meaning if one application needs 16 MB of memory, another requires a Pentium processor, and a third needs a 6X CD drive; the workstation must be equipped with all three.

Network Servers

One of the most common mistakes made in PC purchasing is to reflexively spend megabucks on network servers, and upgrade them as frequently as next generation parts become available. How much muscle is needed in the network server is determined by the NOS (Network Operating System) software, and the model of networking followed. In many schools, offices, and factories, the network server really functions as a print server and post office, and nothing more. A print server is a networked PC with one or more printers attached to it, where the other PCs can send their printing work, known as "print jobs." When the desired printer is free, the print server sends it the next job, according to the order the requests come in, or some other priority-based scheme. The post office function on most networks is a low-demand task, holding and routing e-mail or files to users.

If the client/server model of computing is used, we have a different story altogether. In this case, the server actively processes requests submitted by clients, which may include complex database searches, financial transactions, or updates to shared information as required in an airline reservation system. Since the clients are constantly accessing information from the server's drives and adding the load of processing requests to the server's normal duties of routing information and handling print jobs, a superfast server becomes a necessity. The two easiest ways to judge your server's performance are by checking the utilization percentage, which should be low, or to use the less scientific method of listening to user's complaints. Not even a $10,000 PC on steroids can handle corporate-type traffic, which requires midrange and mainframe-type computers as servers, and utilizes PCs as mere interfacing devices.

CHAPTER 7

Custom Computing

Now that we've reviewed some of the basic applications software, we can move on to a consideration of how several software products can be combined with a hand-me-down PC and peripherals to create a complete working environment. One of the biggest changes to have crept into the industry in just the last couple years is the advent of the cheap software "suite." A suite consists of several applications from a single company, usually a word processor, a spreadsheet, and a database, along with one or two special offerings like a drawing package or multimedia presentation software. The three players in the suites market are Microsoft, Lotus (IBM now owns Lotus), and Corel (Corel now owns WordPerfect). The bundled cost (cost when included with a new computer) of suites run about half of the retail cost in the case of Microsoft, and much lower with Lotus and Corel. That's why the majority of new systems are sold absolutely loaded with software, sometimes taking up as much as 1 GB of space on a new multigigabyte hard drive! Low bundling costs also explain how PCs sold as complete systems can sometimes be cheaper than doing it all yourself and buying the software retail. In each case we'll concentrate on the minimum requirements, from the standpoint of both hardware and software. If a better machine is available through either luck or a good credit rating, both performance and user satisfaction will rise.

Computing for Students

Probably the number one reason (or excuse) for bringing home a computer is for the student in the house. Parents who were just getting used to constant demands for $150 sneakers and other examples of high fashion in the school yard, now have kids clamoring for the latest Pentium. The main reason? Games. For the parents who are genuinely concerned that their children don't get left out of the information age but aren't overly concerned at the speed with which they can play Doom, good news. A 486 PC with 8 MB of RAM, a 340-MB hard drive, an SVGA monitor and a CD drive is still a pretty good platform, and costs around $300 on the second-hand market.

When you buy a second-hand PC, be aware that the only salvage value is in the monitor and the peripherals, like a printer or external modem. The CD drive is necessary both for loading new applications and for the wonderful reference software available, like an encyclopedia or the complete works of Shakespeare. In order to print homework and otherwise use the PC as a typewriter, you'll need a printer. A free printer is the best kind, but if you have to buy one, the choice is a little more difficult. A $100 dot matrix will get the family printing, but a color inkjet for $150 or a $400 personal laser printer will be able to handle all of your family needs for the near future.

There are several pieces of "got-to-have-it" software for any older PC, the first two pieces of which are DOS 5.0 (or higher) and the Windows 3.1 (or higher) operating environment. Make sure you get the original diskettes and manuals when you pick the PC up. A 5-year-old copy of Word or WordPerfect comes with most hand-me-downs; the books and diskettes would be a nice bonus. What can your kids do with this system? Well, the first valuable skill they'll learn is how to use Windows. Kids pick this up incredibly fast compared to adults, because they're used to experimenting with things to find out how they work. Besides word processing skills, which they'll use until computers start taking dictation, they'll be able to run most of the education or "edutainment" software you buy them. While a sound card is a nice feature, it's just not a particularly good investment for an older PC if you are paying for the labor. Besides, the sounds that come out of a PC playing games aren't all that different from the annoying noises generated by a video game that hooks up to the TV.

College PCs

The days when the only college students with PCs were rich kids or technology majors are long forgotten. Universities, which resisted the idea of telephones in dorm rooms, are now wiring the same rooms to give students access to the World Wide Web. Some universities even require students to buy PCs, spreading the cost over four years of attendance. Four years provide an interesting key to this discussion, since four years ago, 486s were just beginning the final push to take the mass market away from 386s. Whatever computer a student brings to college will seem as obsolete as a 486 does today by the time a degree is earned.

The minimum configuration for a college-bound student should be a Windows 95 capable machine. A clock-multiplied 486 (DX2/66 or greater) with 16 MB of memory, a 500-MB hard drive, a CD drive, an SVGA monitor and a modem. Don't pay for a 486 PC if you are university bound;

buy a $1,000 Pentium from the school bookstore on installment if you have to. Software suites are ideal for students, and while the word processor and the spreadsheet will be the most used components, don't be surprised if the database also gets a workout. A printer can make life a lot easier, but students can also print on school networks or put their work on a floppy disk and bring it (sneaker net) to the library or a computer lab for printing. Universities are not in the business of providing free software, except in special cases where the program is an integral part of course material. Internet access is provided free by most schools, and students will receive an e-mail address as part of orientation.

Public School Classroom

The biggest dumping ground for hand-me-down PCs is our public schools. Businesses can choose to donate discarded PCs for a number of reasons:

1. To generate good will in the community.
2. The tax write-off for undepreciated machines is often higher than their resale value.
3. Selling PCs to employees can be problematical.
4. Nobody will buy really old PCs, but schools won't turn them down.

Except in extraordinary cases, schools end up with such a hodgepodge of donated equipment that it takes a serious volunteer effort to sort it all out. Any school receiving donated equipment can save a lot of time and money by following these guidelines:

- Don't count your PCs before they boot!
- Never spend a dime repairing donated equipment.
- Always be prepared to cannibalize, but make sure the eaten PC doesn't work better than the one you're trying to fix.
- A primitive sorting effort by teachers and students, such as trying every monitor on a working PC, will reduce storage space and allow volunteer technical talent to make better use of their time.
- Don't try using old network adapters unless you have enough of the same kind to complete a lab.
- Throw out printers (except lasers) unless they work the first time you try them.

- Don't mix 286s and lesser machines in a room with 386s or higher.
- Ask for the DOS and Windows diskettes and manuals!

The biggest problem in making good use of donated computer equipment in schools is the lack of a uniform operating system and application software. Schools are some of the worst offenders when it comes to software pirating (illegally using copies of software), which doesn't send a good message to the students. Most software companies will sell to schools at a special education price, which is a fraction of retail, and the software can be transferred to the next generation of PCs. If you are a school administrator, make sure that your software vendors are certified as education resellers, because otherwise the pricing they give you (even under competitive bid) is many times what you could be paying.

Classroom computers are often dedicated to a single purpose, due to the way schools organize classroom space. Providing printing for each of the PCs is always a challenge, though some schools start by getting a cheap dot matrix to go with every machine. Some subjects really benefit from a special purpose printer or plotter, like a laser printer for a word processing class, a color inkjet for a business computing class, or a plotter for a CAD lab. There are three basic approaches taken when sharing a central printer or plotter between a large number of PCs. The simplest approach is to hook the printer or plotter up to a single machine and have students carry their work to it on floppy disk for printing. The down side is that this PC usually ends up being dedicated for printing only, though it can often be a cheaper PC that's too slow for normal use. The intermediate solution uses a "smart" printer switch, where each PC is connected to the switch box by a serial or printer cable, and the switch has a single connection to the printer or plotter. The hardware and cables cost a few hundred dollars, but the software comes with the switch, and is easy to set up. Finally, a LAN (Local Area Network) solves the problem, but each PC must have a network adapter installed, cabling must be run. If you aren't using Windows for Workgroups or Windows 95, network software must be purchased and configured.

Classroom Word Processing and Typing

Word processing and typing are normally taught in the same room, with early classes learning typing skills with special tutoring software. Whatever word processing program is chosen, it should be a Windows

Figure 7-1
The buddy system
in learning.

program, since using standard Windows features will enable students to pick up other Windows applications with ease. Educational materials, including course books and lessons on video, can be purchased for all of the major word processors. Older 386 machines will perform adequately in this task, although 8 MB of memory may be required to use some advanced features. Many schools use old 386 PCs with small hard drives (80 MB or less) in these classes, just enough to hold DOS, Windows, the application software, and a little free room necessary for operating system use. All of the work the students do is kept on a floppy disk that is given to them at the beginning of the course. This approach works well with word processing, since the files remain fairly small, and most of the time is spent typing, and not waiting for the computer to work with the information on the floppy.

Classroom CAD (Computer Aided Design)

CAD (Computer Aided Design) is the successor to drafting. Most schools cannot afford the industry standard AutoCAD, even at education pricing, but a variety of look-alike programs are available in the subhundred dollar range. CAD labs are one of the few instances where DOS programs will do as well as Windows applications, and the skills learned can be easily transferred to the Windows environment when it is encountered in the workplace. The minimum realistic hardware platform for a CAD lab is a 486 PC with 4 MB of memory and a several hundred megabyte hard drive. CAD programs will run on older PCs if they have a math coprocessor installed, but don't get involved in upgrading machines this way. Any extra money should be invested in big monitors, which don't become obsolete. A plotter is required for actually printing finished drawings, so provisions for sharing the plotter must be made.

Classroom Business Computing

Business computing is commonly taught in vocational schools, and the focus is preparing students for office jobs in the "real world." Software suites are popular in business computing classes, as they provide boundaries to the curriculum as each one of the applications is studied for a length of time. Spreadsheets are particularly useful for introducing business use of math in a fun way. A color inkjet is handy for printing pie charts, bar graphs, and other visual displays of data a spreadsheet can generate. Learning how to enter and retrieve database information is a good skill that is used in many entry-level jobs, from telemarketing to shipping and receiving. Since the goal of these classes is to prepare students for the modern workplace, the most up-to-date software, namely Windows 95, is desirable.

School Library Computers

School libraries have been under siege for over 20 years to turn themselves into "media centers." The audio/visual learning tools that comprised the "media" of the seventies have been transferred to computers. The first rule for putting multimedia computers into a library is to trade the speakers for headphones. Be prepared to pay real money for good headphones, the cheap ones quickly break. Multimedia products are using more and more video, which requires a minimum of a very fast 486 system to be displayed without skips. CD drives are also a necessity, since most of the software is sold on CD. Libraries often get involved in networks to provide access to electronic card catalogs and reference CDs, which are permanently stored in a CD changer attached to a local server.

Figure 7-2
Computer
headphones for
library or classroom.

The Moonlighting Accountant

Accountants are traditionally cost conscious, and when they do buy a new PC, they're liable to still be calling it "my new PC" well after the three-year rapid depreciation schedule is finished. Two of the most important purchases for an accountant who will complete multiple tax returns are a laser printer and a modem. The IRS will accept the forms generated by computer tax software only if they are printed by laser printers. Tax agencies are also expanding support for electronic filing, which allows the submission of tax returns by modem. The actual speed of the PC isn't terribly important for the one-man accounting office, and most tax software is available in both DOS and Windows versions. The more important issue for most accountants will be protecting against data loss. A cartridge drive or a tape drive is often used to back up data, and copying important files onto floppies is better than nothing. A 17" monitor costs under $400 and is nice for working large spreadsheets or simply seeing numbers more clearly as eyelids droop in the middle of the night. Monitors have also proven to be a pretty good investment, as they are easily transferred from one PC to the next, and their prices drop much more slowly than any other computer component.

Road Warriors

Salespeople love notebook computers. Nothing fills my heart with fear like seeing a harried salesman on his way to an appointment, working away on a notebook computer balanced against the steering wheel of a car traveling in the lane next to mine. Notebook computers let salespeople take their office on the road with them, and stay in touch with faxes or local calls to an Internet access provider. I wouldn't even consider notebooks as hand-me-down computers if not for the fact that salespeople upgrade whenever they can afford it, which means a lot of second-hand notebooks are available. A loaded Pentium-based multimedia notebook often sells for over $5,000, so the notebook it replaces can have some real value left in it. Purchasing second-hand notebooks is largely a matter of comparison shopping, and I wouldn't touch anything under a 486DX2-50 with a color display. Stick with big brand names that haven't bowed out of the notebook business. Be prepared for sticker shock if you need to replace the battery; prices over $200 are common. Some notebooks support standard batteries, like those used in cameras, for emergency backup. If you purchase one of these, at least you'll always have the option to buy some batteries at the airport, and make it through a flight.

Figure 7-3
Notebook computer.

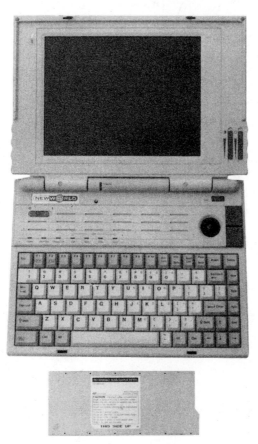

A Drafting (CAD) Workstation

Most CAD workstations will run the industry standard AutoCAD software from AutoDesk. AutoCAD costs almost $3,000, so trying to economize on hardware at this point would be a little silly. CAD computers are normally built with lots of expensive parts, like big fast hard drives, nice tower cases, and lots of memory, so they are one of the most sensible candidates for a motherboard upgrade when a new generation becomes available. A good CAD monitor will run in the $1,500 to $2,000 range, and plotters vary from $500 to over $12,000, depending on the paper size, speed, and quality. One thing that every workstation will need is a digitizer, where the small size (12″ × 12″) starts around $225. Free-standing digitizers in sizes up to 4′ × 5′ cost around $1,500, and are used for tracing drawings and maps. If several workstations running AutoCAD in a drafting department are to share a plotter, a network is necessary. Sneaker net and "smart" printer switches don't cut it for serious CAD drawings.

Desktop Publishing

Earlier we noted some distinctions between word-processing and desktop publishing software. It's also important to draw the distinction between word processor operators and desktop publishers. Desktop publishing is a job for a graphics artist or a person with similar skills, experience in page layout, font selection, and the commercial printing process. A well-equipped desktop-publishing workstation will have two major software applications: the desktop-publishing software (usually QuarkXPress or PageMaker) and Photoshop, about $1,000 in combined software. A scanner is a must for bringing photos and original artwork into the computer, and a laser printer with PostScript is the best choice for creating proofs. Photoshop is often bundled with scanners at a reduced price, so keep this in mind if you're just setting up and don't own either yet.

The basic requirement for a desktop-publishing system is a fast 486 or Pentium, a 1 GB or better hard drive, and the Windows operating environment. Memory is as important as CPU speed for desktop publishing, 16 MBs of RAM are good, but 32 MBs of RAM are better. As with CAD, there's no safer place to put your money than in the monitor. Large-screen (bigger than 17″), high-performance monitors are easy on the eyes, show more detail, and hold their value. Backup is especially important in desktop publishing, and the Syquest cartridges which are commonly used to transfer files and artwork are a better solution than tape drives. CD recorders (CDRs) are becoming more common in desktop publishing because the person who writes the CD can be confident that anyone receiving it will have a CD drive.

Home Office or New Business

The best reason for a home office or a small startup to go the cheap route with a hand-me-down PC is to save the money for new software and peripherals. Remember, a PC is a general purpose computer, but your business is (hopefully) focused on a specific market. For starters, a suite of Windows application software is a must for any business, along with a laser printer. After that, you'll want to look at software applications written specifically for your business. Unless your business is entirely unique, somebody who got into it before you did has written a customized Windows application that they'll be happy to sell you. The best place to find these really specific programs is in trade publications, and if you haven't found a trade publication for your type of business, your business is unique!

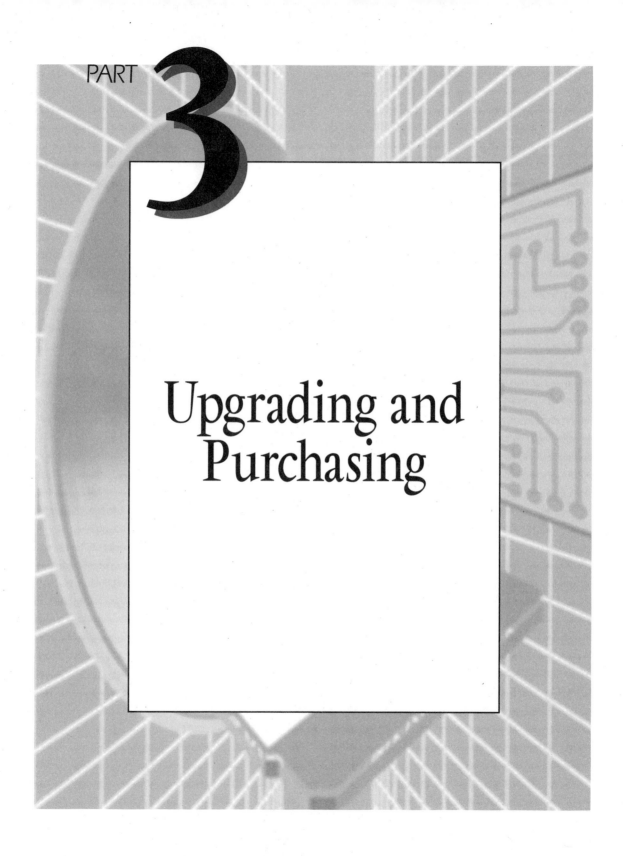

PART

3

Upgrading and Purchasing

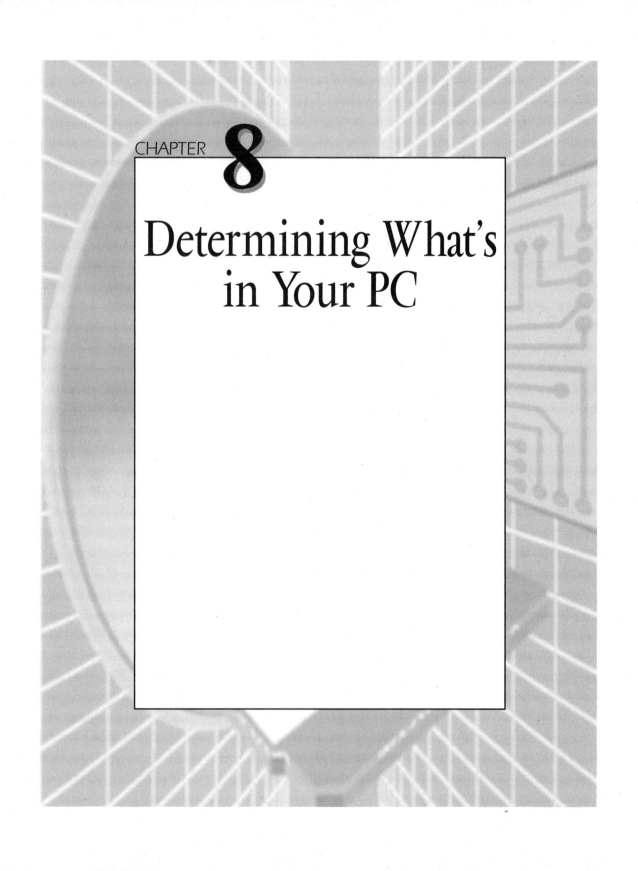

CHAPTER **8**

Determining What's in Your PC

In the first two sections of the book we talked about what components make up a PC, and how the software sets the lower limits on the type and configuration of the parts you need. Most buyers of a hand-me-down PC will know the CPU type, how much memory is installed, and the size of the hard drive. Some lucky readers will receive all of the original documentation that shipped with the computer, but even then, the documentation will cover a whole range of models and configurations. Free PCs will often come with no more information than an off-hand, "I think it had three somethings." In all of these instances, there are four ways to learn about what's really in the system box:

1. Inspection of the ports on the back of the PC and the exposed drives on the front.

2. Reading the system configuration displayed at boot (power on) time.

3. Running a software reporting application, like MSD (Microsoft Diagnostics).

4. Taking the cover off the system box and looking inside.

Visual Inspection of the System Box

The easiest thing to determine, looking at the front of the system box, is whether or not you have a CD drive. A headphone jack, volume dial, large doorway, and the "compact disc" trademark all combine to make it a dead giveaway. You can also determine whether the drive requires a CD caddy (into which the CD is placed before being inserted into the drive), or if it is a permanent-tray type. The caddy type will have a doorway that pulls down or folds inward, while a tray will be visible edge on and remain immoveable until the system is powered on. If you see you're bringing home a caddy type, make sure you get at least one caddy to go with it. You can also see the floppy drives from the outside of the system box and determine whether or not you have both sizes, $3\frac{1}{2}''$ and $5\frac{1}{4}''$, but you can't be sure that they are the newer high-density types until you boot the machine and format a floppy. Systems less than five years old will almost certainly have the newer type.

The back of the system box provides much more information. Two telephone jacks, located in the same slot (you will see eight slots separated

Figure 8-1
Port types on slot blanks.

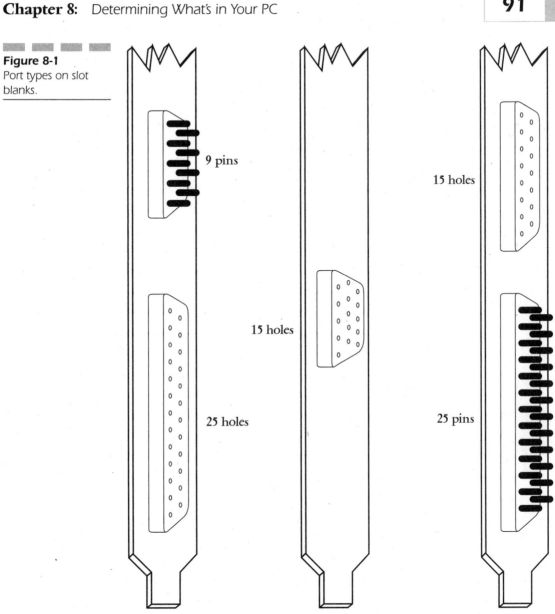

9 pins

15 holes

15 holes

25 holes

15 holes

25 pins

by thin metal strips), indicate the presence of an internal modem. The rest of the ports, which are shaped like thin trapezoids, can be identified by the sex of the receptacle, and the number of gold-plated pins or pin holes you count. The port that your VGA or SVGA monitor is attached to is a female port with 15 pin holes arrayed in three rows. Very expensive cards for big monitors may have five BNC connectors (like on the back of your VCR) instead, but these are rare. Four more ports should be included in all modern PCs, all of which have two rows of pins or holes: a 9-pin male connector (Com1), a 25-pin male connector (Com2), a 25-pin female connector (LPT1), and a 15-pin female connector (Game). These ports may be located in the slots area, or they might be a little closer to the power supply fan. Occasionally they are labeled, but don't be surprised if the labels are wrong.

A sound card can also be easily identified by several audio-jack inputs, for the microphone, speakers, and direct line input, often a volume dial and a 15-pin female feature connector. Some systems will include other ports, for SCSI cables, scanners, video inputs, etc. Don't bother guessing at what these ports are until you boot the PC and see what software are installed. Some SCSI adapters use the same 25-pin female adapter that is used for the printer ports, and some systems include an extra printer port. If you have more than one 25-pin male port on the back of the PC, don't plug in external SCSI devices or printers until you open the system box and determine which port belongs to which adapter. A printer plugged into an SCSI port can damage the printer, the SCSI adapters, and any internal SCSI drives attached.

System Configuration Displayed at Boot

Most systems built since the late eighties will display a "System Configuration" screen when the PC is turned on or rebooted (reset). This is the BIOS (Basic Input Output System) reporting what parts it sees in the computer. System configuration screens appear differently, depending on the BIOS manufacturer, but the following information should always be included:

- CPU Type: The CPU generation—386, 486, Pentium, along with the SX or DX designation.
- Coprocessor: Installed (for all DX chips or systems with a coprocessor) or Not Present.
- CPU Clock: The speed of the CPU in MHz (megahertz).
- Base Memory: This better be 640 K.
- Extended Memory: Add 640 K and divide by 1024 K. This is your total RAM in megabytes.

- Cache Memory: This could be 0 or not installed, 64 K, 128 K, 256 K, or 512 K.

- Diskette Drive A: Can be 360 K or 1.2 MB (5¼") or 720 K or 1.44 MB or 2.88 MB(3½").

- Diskette Drive B: One of the above, or not installed.

- Hard Disk Drive C: A number between 1 and 47, or user type, with the size in megabytes.

- Hard Disk Drive D: One of the above, or not installed. If both drives report not installed, but a hard drive is present and working, it is an SCSI hard drive.

- Display Type: EGA/VGA or PGA/VGA. If it says "Monochrome" or "CGA", ouch!

- Serial Port(s): Lists one or more ports 3F8 = Com1, 2F8 = Com2, 3E8 = Com3, 2E8 = Com4.

- Parallel Port(s): Lists one or more ports 378 = Lpt1: 278 = Lpt2:.

The System Configuration report is the best way to learn about the system, because the BIOS that generates it is also operating the computer. If you believe a component has been reported by the BIOS incorrectly, one of two things is wrong. First, a hardware option could be set wrong, by a jumper in the system box or a software configuration program, and the BIOS is correctly reporting what it sees. Second, an option like floppy drive type could be set incorrectly in the CMOS setup, which can be corrected by hitting the "Delete" key when prompted during boot, and

Figure 8-2
Additional printer
port adapter.

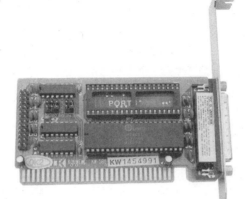

changing the setting. The BIOS has no way of actually determining whether or not a floppy drive is really the type that is entered in the CMOS setup, and a wrong drive type will result in read and write errors.

Software Reporting Application

There are many software utilities for sale that can help you determine what hardware components are in the system box and what their performance is. The most popular is the Norton Utilities, which includes tools for data recovery and other housekeeping tasks. However, you can get almost as much information for free, providing you have Windows 3.1 or a recent version of DOS installed. Just type "MSD" and hit the enter key at the DOS prompt, and the Microsoft Diagnostics program will start. Microsoft Diagnostics reports on the following items:

- Computer: BIOS manufacturer, date (important for compatibility), and CPU type.

- Memory: System RAM and extended memory.

- Video: Video adapter type and video BIOS version (reports DOS mode for VGA adapter, which is normally VGA even for SVGA cards. Video BIOS refers to the software version stored on the adapter, important for troubleshooting video problems).

- Network: Reports on network software drivers installed. Doesn't prove existence of a LAN.

- OS Version: Reports on the MS-DOS version.

- Mouse: Reports on presence of mouse and driver software version.

- Other Adapters: Generally picks up on game ports and little else.

- Disk Drives: Reports on floppies and hard drives. Recognizes CD drive letters, but provides no drive information.

- LPT ports: Reports on printer ports seen by DOS. Some software, especially for multipurpose laser printers, will fool DOS into seeing more than one LPT port, when only one port is actually present.

- Com Ports: Reports on Com ports, including address (3F8 = Com1, etc.), baud rate (useful for modems and serial devices, and port programming).

- IRQ Status: Interrupt request status. Interrupts are the method with which different parts of the computer get the attention of the CPU. You will often need to determine which IRQs are free to install a new adapter.

- TSR Programs: Terminate and Stay Resident Programs. These are programs that are normally loaded at boot time, that once loaded, remain in memory to continue their function. The software that is required to manage SCSI drives and devices is an example of a TSR.

- Device Driver: Device drivers are similar to TSRs and control individual devices, like a CD drive.

The Modern Plug-and-Play BIOS

Almost all PCs built, from the advent of the 386 processor on, incorporate a small amount of CMOS memory maintained by a battery that holds some crucial setup information for the BIOS. This "CMOS Setup" has been greatly expanded and improved over the years, incorporating such features as password protection, auto detection of IDE hard-drive types, and the ability to enable or disable a variety of hardware features for troubleshooting purposes. The newest motherboards feature software upgradable BIOS chips, and PCI slots which are managed from the CMOS settings. PCI adapters, unlike the older ISA and VESA adapters, do not require an interrupt selection on the card. The three or four PCI slots on the motherboard are numbered, and the interrupt to be associated with each slot (and the adapter installed in it) is set in CMOS.

Most new motherboards also incorporate all of the functions previously handled by the SIDE card, including IDE controller (primary and secondary), floppy controller, printer port, game port, and two Com ports. All of these ports are controlled in the CMOS setup, including port types, addresses, interrupts, and whether the controllers are enabled or disabled. This scheme greatly simplifies the installation of new adapters, since port addresses and interrupts can be moved around without recourse to jumpers or documentation. The best BIOS software will report resource conflicts at boot time and prompt the user to enter the CMOS settings screen and remedy the problem.

Plug-and-Play Adapters

These software-controlled adapters, whether ISA, VESA, or PCI, are jumperless, and their settings are controlled by special setup programs or by the operating system. Windows 95 features terrific support for most plug-and-play adapters, suggesting suitable settings for them and configuring the adapter without additional software. When used with older Windows-based systems, plug-and-play adapters are only as good as the software supplied with them. Some come with excellent Windows drivers, others must be set up in DOS. Drivers for older versions of DOS and Windows are generally limited in their ability to identify potential conflicts with other adapters, so be prepared to get out a piece of paper to make a list of your system's resources. A word of caution: some plug-and-play adapters may not accept new settings if their default settings conflict with an already installed adapter. You may have to temporarily remove the nonessential adapters (anything but the video card and SIDE adapter) to change the setting on such a plug-and-play card.

There is a down side to using plug-and-play adapters in older 386 and 486 systems. Sometimes they simply won't work with the BIOS or the other cards installed. If you are considering an inexpensive upgrade to an older PC, like a sound card or a modem, consider buying the older technology versions of these parts that come with on-board jumpers for controlling all of their settings. You can buy these older adapters for well under $50, and since these functions are built into the majority of new systems, there's no point in worrying if you can reuse them when you decide to buy a new PC next year.

Safe Handling of Computer Components

Computer components are shipped in space-age antistatic bags to protect them from the 15,000 to 50,000 Volts of electricity that our bodies can store up in static electricity. The first rule for working on PCs is to avoid rooms where you get zapped every time you touch a doorknob or other metal object. The next rule is not install your PC in such an unfriendly environment if you can avoid it. You should always power a PC from a grounded outlet, and not use a "cheater" that converts the plug to two prongs. The ground not only helps protect against static discharge, it also helps protects your home from electrical fires caused by a short circuit, and reduces RF (Radio Frequency) interference with devices like your portable phone or TV.

Before you open a static-proof bag to handle a part, touch the metal casing of your PC to ground yourself, discharging any static charge you have picked up. Make sure you have enough lighting at your work space before you begin. Do not walk across the room with the part in your hand to examine it more closely under a lamp. If you put the part down without installing it in the computer, put it back in its bag. You can generate static electricity by flipping through a large instruction manual, so remember to touch the case before you pick up the part again. Never touch the gold or silver contacts on the bottom edge of an adapter because the oil from your fingers can create an insulating layer and degrade electrical signals. In spite of all these warnings, computer components are pretty robust on the whole. I have handled tens of thousands of components over the years, and to the best of my knowledge, only once did I damage a part (an SCSI hard drive) with a static discharge, which I clearly felt when it occurred.

Looking in the System Box

Before a hardware upgrade takes place, somebody has to open up the system box. For individuals doing their own work, this is a step that should be taken before buying any hardware. For those who will pay someone else to do the work, make sure a technician looks inside your system box before you walk out of the shop. Most upgrades are dependent on your motherboard and on the other adapters and drives already installed. In some rare cases, even with the system box open and an adapter card in hand, neither you nor an experienced technician will be able to determine what a "mystery" adapter does. These are usually external tape controllers or interface adapters to industrial equipment, which are especially common in PCs that have been sold off shop floors to company employees. Opening up the system box (removing the skin or cover) will be the easiest step of the upgrade process with 90% of PCs, and the hardest part for the remaining 10%. There are three basic variations used to attach the cover for desktops and minitowers, which occasionally involve removing the plastic faceplate or a plastic-back facade first.

Some manufacturers, particularly makers of towers, like to hide all of the screws beneath a plastic facade. This leaves no exposed screw heads on the outside of the case. More frequently, there is no back facade, but the only screw heads showing are the four holding the power supply in place. There are two methods for holding faceplates and facades onto a system box: the first is snap-together plastic fasteners and the second is Velcro. Velcro was rarely used, usually on back facades, and can be easily detected because the facade can be jiggled quite a bit, since the attachment isn't rigid. Cover your ears and rip away. The snap-on faceplates and facades are sometimes a little nerve-racking to remove. A sharp tug at the bottom of the faceplate is the best place to start. Similar to faceplate attached covers, the biggest problem is the fit between the faceplate and the fronts of the exposed drives. Try to keep pressure on the faces of any exposed drives as you pull the case faceplate by them. There are normally four snap-together connectors on these faceplates, one at each corner, though towers may employ six. The male part of the connector can be close to an inch long, so the faceplate needs to be pried out quite a ways before it releases.

Removing a Three-Sided Cover

The three-sided cover is the most common type used for minitowers, and is also used for a good number of desktops. The only difference between the cover as used in minitowers and desktops is the desktop has a broad top and short sides, while the minitower has a narrow top and long sides. The cover, which appears to end flush with the plastic faceplate of either type of case, actually has tabs that extend under the edges of the faceplate, to secure the cover in the front. The screws that actually hold the cover on are usually located along the edges of the back of the case, normally four or six in number, though occasionally three or five are used on some desktops. These are not the four screws grouped around the fan; they hold the power supply in place. In some instances, there will be no screws in the back, but two screws at the bottom of each side of the cover.

Once all of the screws have been removed, you may have to wrestle a little with the cover to get it off. For one thing, there is no way to tell if the cover is really a simple three-sided shell tucked under the faceplate, or if the faceplate is attached. Position your hands against the sides of the case with your fingers against the back, and try pushing back with your fingers, keeping up a steady force with your palms. If that doesn't get the cover started backwards, try lifting a little. The sides of the case usually have a thin strip of metal welded to them to create a channel that fits tightly over the base of the case, and these often fit so tightly that you'll think you missed a screw. Remember to take note of how the cover comes off (slide back and lift, tilt and lift, etc.) because it will have to go back on the same way.

Removing a Faceplate-Attached Cover

Some system boxes, primarily desktops and full towers, are built with the plastic faceplate permanently attached to the three sides of the cover. These covers are attached either with screws at the bottoms of the sides, around the edges of the back, or occasionally by one large-knobbed screw in top center of the back. In all instances, once the screws are removed, the cover and the faceplate will slide forward a couple of inches and then be lifted off. Some brand-name computers use two thumb-activated slide locks on the front of the case to secure it, but no screws at all. These covers often require a strong tug to get moving, because the fit between the drive faceplates (floppies, CD, tape) and the cover faceplate is tight, and the cover faceplate has to move while the drives remain where they are. Floppies are pretty rugged, and if their small plastic faceplates pop off, they can be easily replaced, but try and be gentle if you have a CD drive.

Removing a Back-Attached Cover

These are the rarest of the cover types, and are often accompanied by our fourth variation, which requires prior removal of the faceplate. The screws may be located on the front of the system box and are only exposed once the faceplate is removed. Once the attachment screws are removed, the cover will slide back a few inches, then be lifted off. Unfortunately, this method of attachment often forces you to unplug all of the devices from their ports to get the cover off (keyboard, monitor, mouse, etc.)

Performing or Paying for Upgrades

By this point in the book, you should know what parts are in the PC you own (or are considering buying), and you should know what upgrades are necessary to run the software you want to use. Now we will examine the costs and labor involved in performing the upgrades you need. Even if you intend to pay somebody to make a house call or to bring your PC to a shop, you should read the sections describing the labor involved. For each procedure, we will not only present detailed instructions but also a time range for how long the upgrade should take. Most of these upgrades will take less than a half hour, and many take just a few minutes. If you are paying somebody to do the work, be prepared to pay a minimum hour labor charge regardless. Whenever you plan to open the system box of an older PC for the first time, you should write the hard-drive parameters recorded in the CMOS settings (see motherboard upgrades) before proceeding.

CHAPTER 9

Memory, Motherboard, and CPU Upgrades

Motherboard and CPU upgrades often go hand in hand, and I strongly suggest that you consider upgrading the motherboard if you are considering a faster CPU, providing that you have a standard clone system box. If you have an old 386 or 486 that you want to upgrade from 4 MB RAM to 8 MB RAM, then buying 4 MB of RAM and adding it is probably the most cost-effective route. However, if you want to end up with 16 MB or more in your system, it may be a good time to consider a new motherboard and CPU to go with it. As we'll discuss in detail below, RAM purchased for older systems is generally more expensive per megabyte than RAM used in new systems, and the different types of memory modules are not compatible.

Memory Upgrades

The most common and the easiest upgrade to make is adding more RAM to a system. The price of memory fell more than 90 percent from 1995 to 1997, meaning that the 16 MB that cost $500 for Christmas 1995 will cost less than $50 for Christmas 1997. The pricing for memory is more volatile than for any other PC part, going up as well as down, so you should check the current market price before making any decisions based on the pricing information in this chapter. Before you buy additional memory, or pay for an upgrade, somebody must determine not only how much memory you have, but what kind it is. Also, memory cannot be added in arbitrary amounts, but in fixed increments that depend on the type of CPU you have. If the system was built before 1994, it will likely use 30-pin SIMMs (Single Inline Memory Module). Otherwise, unless you have the original documentation, you will have to look inside the system box and determine what size of memory SIMM you have. In all cases, if you have the motherboard documentation, read the section on adding memory. It may have details about SIMM type and grouping not covered in the following sections.

Single Inline Memory Modules (SIMMs)

A SIMM consists of several memory chips (jargon for encapsulated integrated circuits) mounted on a small circuit board, which in turn is placed

Figure 9-1
72-Pin SIMM (top)
and 30-pin SIMM
(bottom).

into a socket on the motherboard and held in place by spring-loaded clips. There are two different physical sizes of SIMMs, which are described by the number of contacts between the SIMM and the socket. Chapter 14 contains a discussion of the interface between the CPU and memory that explains the logic behind SIMM sizing. Some very old 386s and older computers were not equipped with SIMMs, and in no circumstance is it worthwhile to upgrade the memory in these PCs. Most 386s that use SIMMs, along with older 486s, will use 30-pin SIMMs, which have 30 contact points, and are also known as "8-bit SIMMs." Starting with newer 486s, 72-pin SIMMs were introduced, which are also known as "32-bit SIMMs." These two types of SIMMs appear physically different in three ways. The 30-pin SIMMs are 3 inches long, have a straight bottom edge, and have 30 gold or silver contact points along the bottom. The 72-pin SIMMs are 25 percent longer, have a notch in the middle of the bottom edge, and have 72 contact points on the bottom edge. The newest Pentium motherboards use DIMMs (Dual Inline Memory Modules), often in conjunction with 72-pin SIMMs. DIMM sockets are fractionally longer than SIMM sockets.

After determining what type of SIMMs your system uses, you will want to count how many free (open) SIMM sockets there are on the motherboard for you to add new SIMMs. During the transitional period between 30-pin and 72-pin SIMMs in 1994–1995, some companies manufactured motherboards with both types of SIMM sockets, which is easy to spot since the 72-pin sockets are longer. You will also want to count how many SIMMs are installed, so by comparing the number

to your total amount of memory, you can determine their size in megabytes. Two more details can help prevent problems occurring after the upgrade is completed. With the system power off, remove one of the SIMMs from its socket by gently pushing in the clips securing it with your thumbs, or a screwdriver, while wiggling the SIMM to see which direction it will release. Then, holding the SIMM by its short edges, count the number of chips. SIMMs with an odd number of chips are "parity" SIMMs, and upgrade SIMMs of the same type should be purchased. Also, examine the chips for a number following a dash, like "-100", "-80", "-70" or "-60." This is the speed of the memory chips in nanoseconds (billionths of a second), and the lower the number, the faster they are. SIMMs added during an upgrade should be the same speed or faster.

SIMMs are organized on the motherboard into sets called "banks." Older PCs, like 286s and 386SXs, use a bank size of two, meaning SIMMs are installed in multiples of two. All 486s and 386DXs utilizing 30-pin SIMMs use a bank size of four. A 486 with 72-pin SIMMs has a bank size of one, while a Pentium or 586 has a bank size of two. Finally, SIMMs have different capacities, depending on the chips mounted on them. For 30-pin SIMMs, three standard sizes were used: 256 K (four SIMMs to make 1 MB), 1 MB, and 4 MB. For 72-pin SIMMs, the four sizes you are likely to encounter are 4 MB, 8 MB, 16 MB, and 32 MB, while DIMMs are 16 MB or greater. Using bank size as a guide, we will now go through the upgrade possibilities for each CPU type.

Time and Cost for Upgrades

In 95 percent of hand-me-down PCs, upgrading the memory should take less than five minutes. There are two exceptions, one not quite as irritating as the next. The first exception is if the SIMM sockets are located under something that is removable, like the power supply, or a detachable drive bay. In this case, it takes a few extra minutes to get the part out of the way and to replace it after the upgrade. The really annoying situation comes when the SIMM sockets are located under a welded piece of the case structure. This requires you to remove the motherboard in order to have a look at the memory, turning a simple upgrade into a half hour to an hour job. The cost of generic memory SIMMs is now less than $5 per megabyte, with the price dropping slightly as the size, in megabytes, of the SIMM rises. However, you will pay a premium for low-capacity SIMMs, those under 8 MB, often costing $10 per megabyte or more. Some brand name machines may use proprietary SIMM modules, different from the industry standard parts we have mentioned. Aftermarket replacements for these modules are widely available through mail order, so you can at least learn their prices before going to a store.

Adding Memory to a Pentium or Pentium PRO

The motherboards for these systems have four or eight 72-pin SIMM sockets, and/or one to four DIMM (Dual Inline Memory Module) slots. The bank size for SIMM slots is two, so two SIMMs at a time must be added. DIMMs are 64 bits wide, so the bank size is a single DIMM. We will consider each case based on the amount of memory already installed in the system. We won't consider every mathematical possibility for adding SIMMs, just those to go from 8 MB or 12 MB to 16 MB, or 16 MB to 32 MB. If you go to a shop, always ask for 8 MB or 16 MB to be added; don't simply request the final number you wish to get to, or you may end up losing your old memory. If the SIMMs in your system have an odd number of chips on them, purchase parity SIMMs for upgrades. For double-sided SIMMs, count the number of chips on one side to determine for parity if the number is odd.

Figure 9-3
72-pin SIMM sockets,
the four parallel,
vertical, touching
sockets on the right.

Pentium systems commonly use a type of RAM known as EDO (Extended Data Out). This memory can boost overall RAM throughput by about 20 percent, but it must be supported by the motherboard and BIOS. EDO SIMMs and non-EDO SIMMs should not be mixed on a motherboard, and you certainly won't get the EDO performance boost if you try this. The easiest way to determine if your system supports EDO RAM is to check the documentation or enter CMOS Setup and examine the advanced options. There will be several references to EDO RAM and timing options if it is supported. Some systems with EDO RAM installed will report the fact after counting RAM on boot, as in "16 MB of EDO RAM installed."

8 MB Installed (Pentium)

You have two 4-MB SIMMs installed. Add two 4-MB SIMMs to reach 16 MB, or add one 16-MB DIMM to reach 24 MB. If you have documentation that the motherboard supports 8-MB SIMMs, you can add two 8-MB SIMMs for a total of 24 MB.

16 MB Installed (Pentium and Pentium PRO)

You have either four 4-MB SIMMs installed, two 8-MB SIMMs, or one 16-MB DIMM. If you have four 4-MB SIMMs, and you're out of empty slots, you'll need to remove one bank (two SIMMs) and install two 16-MB SIMMs for a total of 40 MBs. If you have two 8-MB SIMMs installed, you'll want to add two more 8-MB SIMMs for a total of 32 MBs. If you have one 16-MB DIMM installed, you'll add another 16-MB DIMM for a total of 32 MB.

Adding Memory to a 486 with 72-pin SIMMs

The motherboards for these systems have four 72-pin SIMM sockets. The bank size for the 72-pin SIMMs is one, so single SIMMs can be added. We will consider each case based on the amount of memory already installed in the system. We won't consider every mathematical possibility for adding SIMMs, just those up to 8 MB, and then a jump to 16 MB. If you already have 4 MB, don't walk into a shop and ask for an upgrade to 16 MB. Tell them you want to add one 16-MB SIMM, and you will end up with 20 MB for the same price. If the SIMMs in your system have an odd number of chips on them, purchase parity SIMMs for upgrades. For double-sided SIMMs, count the number of chips on one side, to determine for parity if the number is odd.

4 MB Installed (486 with 72-pin SIMMs)

You have one 4-MB SIMM installed. Add one 4-MB SIMM to get to 8 MB, or add one 16-MB SIMM to get to 20 MB. Don't try 8-MB SIMMs unless you have documentation confirming they will work.

8 MB Installed (486 with 72-pin SIMMs)

You have two 4-MB SIMMs installed, or one 8-MB SIMM. Add two 4-MB SIMMs to get to 16 MB, or add one 16-MB SIMM to get to 24 MB. If you have one 8-MB SIMM installed, add one 8-MB SIMM to get to 16 MB.

Adding Memory to a 486 with 30-pin and 72-pin SIMMs

The motherboards for these systems have four 30-pin SIMM sockets, and two or four 72-pin SIMM sockets. The bank size for the 30-pin SIMMs is four, so if 30-pin SIMMs are used, all four sockets must be filled. The bank size for the 72-pin SIMMs is one, so single SIMMs can be added. We will consider each case based on the amount of memory already installed in the system. We won't consider every mathematical possibility for adding SIMMs, just those up to 8 MB, and then a jump to 16 MB. If you already have 4 MB, don't walk into a shop and ask for an upgrade to 16 MB. Tell them you want to add 16 MB, and you will end up with 20 MB for the same price. If the SIMMs in your system have an odd number of chips on them, purchase parity SIMMs for upgrades. For double-sided 72 pin SIMMs, count the number of chips on one side, to determine for parity if the number is odd.

4 MB Installed (486 with 30-pin and 72-pin SIMMs)

You have either four 1-MB, 30-pin SIMMs, or one 4-MB, 72-pin SIMM. The only reason to use 30-pin SIMMs at this point is if you can obtain them for less than the 72-pin SIMMs. If you can get four 4-MB 30-pin SIMMs for free, or cheaper than a single 16-MB, 72-pin SIMM, go ahead and use them for a total of 20 MB (16 MB if you have to remove four 1-MB SIMMs to put them in). Otherwise, you can add a single 4-MB 72-pin SIMM, for a total of 8 MB, or two of these for a total of 12 MB. You can get one 16-MB SIMM for the price of three 4-MB SIMMs, so if you are shooting for 16 MB, just add a 16-MB SIMM and end up with 20 MB. Don't use 8-MB SIMMs unless one is already installed (support varies).

8 MB Installed (486 with 30-pin and 72-pin SIMMs)

You have either four 1-MB 30-pin SIMMs and one 4-MB 72-pin SIMM, two 4-MB 72-pin SIMMs, or one 8-MB SIMM. In either case, to get to

16 MB, add either two 4-MB 72-pin SIMMs, or one 8-MB 72-pin SIMM, if an 8-MB SIMM was already used.

Adding Memory to a 486 or 386DX with 30-pin SIMMs

The motherboards for these systems have either 8, 12, or 16 SIMM sockets, with a bank size of four. We will consider each instance based on the amount of memory already installed in the system. Since larger-capacity SIMMs are cheaper per megabyte than smaller-capacity SIMMs, buy four 4-MB SIMMs for the price of twelve 1-MB SIMMs, and end up with more memory. We won't consider every mathematical possibility for adding SIMMs, just those up to 8 MB, and then a jump to 16 MB. Always install newer SIMMs that have a higher capacity in megabytes than the existing SIMMs in the lowest bank number (usually bank 0), and move any older SIMMs you are keeping to the higher banks. If you already have 4 MB, don't walk in-to a shop and ask for an upgrade to 16 MB. Tell them you want to add 16 MB, and you will end up with 20 MB for the same price. If the SIMMs installed in your system have nine chips mounted on them, use SIMMs with nine chips for the upgrade. If the SIMMs in your system have an odd number of chips on them, purchase parity SIMMs for upgrades.

2 MB Installed (386DX and 486s with 30-pin SIMMs)

Although rare, this means you have eight 256-K SIMMs installed for a total of 2 MB. With a normal eight SIMM socket motherboard, you will want to take out four 256-K SIMMs and add four 1-MB SIMMs to reach 5 MB, or add four 4-MB SIMMs to get to 17 MB. The only remaining option is to ditch all eight 256-K SIMMs, and put in eight 1-MB SIMMs for a total of 8 MB. If you have one of the equally rare motherboards that have more than eight SIMM slots, you can add four 1-MB SIMMs to get to 6 MB, four 4-MB SIMMs, to get to 18 MB, or eight 1-MB SIMMs (on the 16-SIMM-socket motherboard) to get to 10 MB.

4 MB Installed (386DX and 486s with 30-pin SIMMs)

On a normal motherboard with eight SIMM sockets, this means you have four 1-MB SIMMs installed. The only two reasonable options are to add four 4-MB SIMMs for a total of 20 MB, or to add four 1-MB SIMMs for a total of 8 MB. Once, I actually had a 486DX-25 with sixteen 256-K SIMMs installed for a total of 4 MB! If you are in this situation, you can remove four 256-K SIMMs and add four 4-MB SIMMs for a total of 19 MB, or add four 1-MB SIMMs for a total of 7 MB.

6 MB Installed (386DX and 486s with 30-pin SIMMs)

This requires a motherboard with twelve or more SIMM sockets, employing four 1-MB SIMMs and eight 256-K SIMMs. If there are 16 sockets on the motherboard, you can add four 4-MB SIMMs for a total of 22 MB, or four 1-MB SIMMs for 10 MB total. Otherwise, remove four 256-K SIMMs and add four 4-MB SIMMs for a total of 21 MB or four 1-MB SIMMs for a total of 9 MB.

8 MB Installed (386DX and 486s with 30-pin SIMMs)

You have eight 1-MB SIMMs installed. With a normal 8-SIMM-socket motherboard, the only upgrade option is to take four 1-MB SIMMs out and replace them with four 4-MB SIMMs, for a total of 20 MB. On a motherboard with more than eight SIMM sockets, add four 4-MB SIMMs to get to 24 MB, or on a 16-SIMM-socket motherboard, you can add eight 1-MB SIMMs to get to 16 MB.

12 MB Installed (386DX and 486s with 30-pin SIMMs)

You have twelve 1-MB SIMMs installed. If the motherboard has 16 SIMM sockets, add four 1-MB SIMMs to reach 16 MB. Otherwise, remove four 1-MB SIMMs, and add four 4-MB SIMMs to reach 24 MB.

Adding Memory to a 286 or 386SX

The motherboards for these systems have either four or eight SIMM sockets, with a bank size of two. We will consider each case based on the amount of memory already installed in the system. Since larger-capacity SIMMs are cheaper per megabyte than smaller-capacity SIMMs, buy two 4-MB SIMMs for the price of six 1-MB SIMMs, and end up with more memory. We won't consider every mathematical possibility for adding SIMMs, just those up to 8 MB, and then a jump to 16 MB. Always install newer SIMMs, that have a higher capacity in megabytes than the existing SIMMs, in the lowest bank number (usually bank 0), and move any older SIMMs you are keeping to the higher banks. If you already have 6 MB or 8 MB installed, don't walk into a shop and ask for an upgrade to 16 MB. Tell them you want to add 8 MB, and you will end up with either 14 MB or 16 MB, depending on the type of SIMMs already installed, and save about $50. If the SIMMs installed in your system have nine chips mounted on them, use SIMMs with nine chips for the upgrade. If the SIMMs in your system have an odd number of chips on them, purchase parity SIMMs for upgrades.

1 MB installed (286 and 386SX)

This means that there are four 256-K SIMMs in your system. We aren't going to consider adding 256-K SIMMs (a waste of money), so the smallest upgrade you can make is to add two 1-MB SIMMs, bringing your total memory to 3 MB. If your motherboard only has four total SIMM sockets (none available), you must remove one of the banks of existing SIMMs before adding the two new 1-MB SIMMs for a new total of 2.5 MB. To add 4 MB, you must add four 1-MB SIMMs (a single 4-MB SIMM doesn't make the required bank size of two). If the system has eight SIMM sockets, you can simply add the four 1-MB SIMMs for a new total of 5 MB. For systems with just four SIMM sockets, you will have to take out all of the old memory, for a new total of 4 MB. To get to 8 MB, you have two choices. Remove all 256-K SIMMs, and add eight 1-MB SIMMs, or just add two 4-MB SIMMs (cheaper, too). The only way to get to 16 MB is to add four 4-MB SIMMs.

2 MB installed (286 and 386 SX)

Either you have eight 256-K SIMMs installed (so take four out and follow the 1 MB installed example), or you have two 1-MB SIMMs installed. Adding two 1-MB SIMMs gets you to 4 MB, or adding two 4-MB SIMMs gets you to 10 MB. If you have eight SIMM sockets, you can add more memory in two-SIMM increments without taking the two 1-MB SIMMs out, otherwise the only way to get to 16 MBs is to fill all four SIMM sockets with 4-MB SIMMs.

4 MB installed (286 and 386 SX)

You have four 1-MB SIMMs installed. If you have eight SIMM sockets, you can add more memory in two-SIMM increments to get to 6 MB, 8 MB, 10 MB, 14 MB, or 20 MB. If you only have four SIMM sockets, you will have to give up two megabytes to add two 4-MB SIMMs and bring the total to 10 MBs. If you want to get to 16 MB with just four sockets, you must remove all four 1-MB SIMMs installed and add four 4-MB SIMMs.

6 MB installed (286 and 386SX)

You have six 1-MB SIMMs installed. You can add two 1-MB SIMMs to get to 8 MB total, or add two 4-MB SIMMs to get to 14-MB total. You can remove two of the existing 1-MB SIMMs to add four 4-MB SIMMs and get to 20 MBs, but it's rarely worth the expense.

8 MB installed (286 and 386SX)

You have either eight 1-MB SIMMs installed or two 4-MB SIMMs. If you have eight 1-MB SIMMs, take two out, add two 4-MB SIMMs, and settle for 14 MB. If you have two 4-MB SIMMs installed, add two 4-MB SIMMs to get to 16 MB.

CPU

Brand-name machine owners, particularly in businesses, may have a sound financial reason for upgrading their CPU. The machine may not be fully depreciated when performance becomes unacceptably slow, or a new software application demands a faster CPU. Even more importantly, manufacturers test upgrade CPUs in mass-market brand names, so you'll have a good indication before you start if the upgrade can be carried out successfully. CPU upgrades should never be attempted in no-name clones unless you have the original documentation for the motherboard, and then you should stick with the upgrade processors supported by the documentation. The WWW sites of the CPU manufacturers (Intel, AMD, etc.) have great documentation on compatibility information, and FAQs about installation.

Time and Cost for Upgrade

If you have the motherboard documentation and it lists an acceptable upgrade processor, the actual installation will take about five minutes. On most older motherboards, you will need to re-arrange some motherboard jumpers for the upgrade processor, but the most challenging part is normally getting the old CPU out of the socket. Newer motherboards all come with ZIF (Zero Insertion Force) sockets, that use a lever to lock the CPU in place. With these sockets, the only trick is to put the new chip in with the correct orientation. On older motherboards, the CPU was simply pressed into the socket, and you will want to pry it out very gently, so you can reuse it in case the upgrade doesn't work. Upgrade processor prices start around $40 for some of the Cyrix and AMD CPUs, to several hundred dollars for Intel Overdrive Pentium parts.

Do not bring a PC to a computer store for an upgrade processor unless you have the original documentation, or you purchased the sys-

Figure 9-4
Intel Pentium (R).
(Photo courtesy of
Intel Corporation).

tem from that store. Most stores will attempt an upgrade without documentation, and problems may not begin to appear until after the PC is used for hours, or days. At this point, the technician will insist that some other component in your system is too slow for the new CPU, and little by little you'll end up buying a new PC, with the added pain of getting to pay for several hours of labor. All upgrade processors require a heatsink and fan (for dissipating the extra heat generated at the higher operating speed), so make sure you get one, whether the upgrade is done in a shop or you do it yourself from a kit.

Upgrading Pentium CPUs

The earliest Pentium CPUs had clock speeds of 60 MHz and 66 MHz, and the motherboards in these systems may not accept regular higher speed CPUs. However, there is a broad range of upgrade CPUs, led by the Intel Overdrive parts, that may be compatible in these systems. Starting with 75-MHz Pentiums and above, most of the motherboards were designed to work with a broad range of CPUs in the Pentium and 586 family. You'll want to consult the manual, the motherboard manufacturer's Web site, or carefully examine the motherboard itself for small print indicating compatibility settings. Everything else being equal, replacing your 75-MHz Pentium CPU with a 150-MHz Pentium CPU will cost around $200 and double the speed of many applications. If you want to spend $400 or more for the latest Pentium CPU, you should seriously consider purchasing a new motherboard, even if you have documentation that indicates yours will work. For one thing, if the motherboard was manufactured before the CPU was available for sampling, they couldn't have really tested it. For another, the newest CPUs always integrate functionality, like MMX (Multimedia Extension) technology, that only the newest motherboards can take full advantage of. Besides, you can purchase a wide variety of high quality motherboards for less than a third of the cost of the top-speed Pentium or Pentium PRO CPU.

Upgrading 486 CPUs

Upgrading a 486 CPU to a faster 486 CPU should only be considered if the original CPU is a DX40, DX33, or DX25. Fast 486 AMD and Cyrix

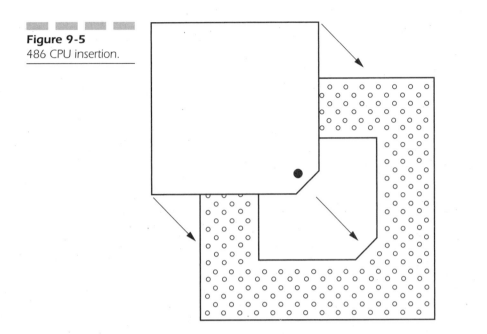

Figure 9-5
486 CPU insertion.

processors are incredibly cheap, but all those currently being manufactured by AMD are 3.3-V (volt) and 3.45-V parts, which will not work on old motherboards that only supported 5-V processors. Cyrix does manufacture a series of clock doubling and tripling 5-V CPUs that will work in many older motherboards. These parts really can double or triple the speed at which your PC does many tasks, but you have to be very stubborn if you want to get confirmation from the vendor that the upgrade will work. You can still find 5-V CPUs from AMD and Intel in the mail order channel, but they are becoming increasingly scarce. Avoid aftermarket parts that allow you to use upgrade CPUs with some otherwise incompatible motherboards; they aren't cost-effective.

Intel no longer manufacturers clock-multiplied 486 CPUs (i.e., 486DX2/66, 486DX4/100), but you can upgrade your 486 with a number of Intel overdrive processors based on the Pentium core. These upgrades really vault you into the current year, but overdrive processors often cost as much as the regular Pentium CPUs of the same speed together with a new motherboard. The positive thing about an overdrive upgrade is that at least in brand-name PCs, you can find out from Intel exactly how much of a performance boost you'll be getting. Overdrive upgrades make the most sense in brand-name machines, particularly those used on networks where they can draw on resources not included in the system box.

Reasons Not to Upgrade a CPU

In many cases, a new motherboard and CPU will cost the same or less than a special-upgrade CPU. A new motherboard will also get you a new, updated BIOS, which will bring you "plug-and-play" compatibility, along with greater compatibility with newer software. A new motherboard means a new system bus and a 64-bit memory interface to take full advantage of Pentium processors, something most upgradable motherboards don't do. Most importantly, a new motherboard and CPU will not be anywhere near as problematical as an old motherboard and an upgrade CPU. The only extra factor to consider in purchasing a new motherboard is whether to use your old memory, which I don't recommend unless you have 16 MB or more.

Figure 9-6
Intel Pentium (R) OverDrive (R) processor. Photo courtesy of Intel Corporation.

Motherboard and CPU Combination Upgrade

Upgrading the motherboard is the one way to turn a hand-me-down PC into a brand-new computer. The only thing that can prevent you from doing a motherboard upgrade is if you have a nonstandard case. Unfortunately, many brand-name systems do have nonstandard cases, either slim desktops, or completely proprietary designs. If you have the

Figure 9-7
486 CPU and
motherboard
socket ruined by
improper insertion.

original documentation, and it states that the old motherboard is a
"standard AT" or "ISA" form factor, then you're okay. One problem with
some older or brand-name system designs is that they used a nonstandard power supply connector. There is actually a simple, inexpensive
solution for dealing with nonstandard cases. Order a new case and
power supply with your new motherboard! For this $40 to $70 extra,
you really will have a new computer. The only extra work entailed will
be transferring over the drives from the old system, which takes a maximum of four screws each. The time lost doing this isn't much longer
than the time it would have taken you to get the old motherboard out
of the old system.

Time and Cost for Upgrades

A motherboard upgrade, using an old case or a new case, will take
between fifteen minutes and an hour, depending on how much experience you have and whether or not you run into any screws with
stripped threads, requiring ingenuity and pliers to remove. The cheapest upgrade worth doing includes a new motherboard and a 100 MHz
or faster 486 from AMD or Cyrix for about $100. Motherboard/CPU

Figure 9-8
Pentium-compatible
motherboard.

combinations in the 120-MHz to 133-MHz range, using 586s (not Pentiums), run around $150 or higher. Motherboards with non-Intel CPUs are especially pushed by small shops for their higher profit margin. Remember that the clock speed (in MHz) is not directly comparable as a measure of performance between 586, 686, and Pentium CPUs, but AMD does offer a "PR" rating that compares the K5 CPU performance directly with Pentium processors.

Motherboards with the Intel Triton Chipset and Pentium processors start around $200 for the P-100, cost around $300 in the middle range (P-150, P-166), and go as high as $500 dollars for the P-200. These prices will probably fall radically in the last quarter of 1997, and you should always check the latest mail-order pricing before making a buying decision. Pentium PRO CPUs still command a premium of several hundred dollars, but the gap will narrow as the new Pentium II processors enter the market. While upgrading motherboards requires taking out and putting in a lot of screws, it's actually a very uncomplicated job when the operating system is DOS or Windows 3.1 or Workgroups. You will have to spend a minute or two in the CMOS setup when the system is first powered up, telling the BIOS what floppy drives are installed, and letting it auto seek the hard drives, but that's all. Windows 95 and Windows NT may present some difficulties when a new motherboard is slid in under them, and you may even have to reconfigure the operating system software.

Figure 9-9
Pentium (R) PRO
(Photo courtesy of
Intel Corporation).

Figure 9-10
Pentium (R) PRO
socket. (Photo
courtesy of Intel
Corporation).

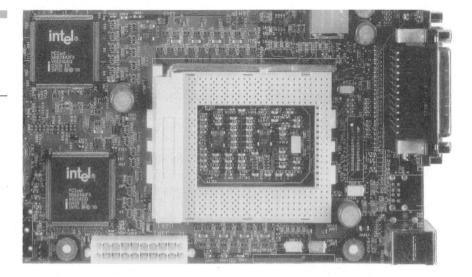

Removing the Old Motherboard

There is one step you should take before you actually remove the old motherboard. Power up the system, enter CMOS setup (hit the "Delete" key after the memory count is finished), and enter the first menu item, normally called "Standard CMOS Setup" or something similar to this. Record the numbers for the hard drive(s) parameters on a piece of paper, and note the floppy drive type(s) also. Now, you can shut down the system, and remove the cover.

To remove the old motherboard, you will first have to remove all of the adapter cards. Each card is held in place by one screw on the back edge of the case and is removed by pulling straight up. If an adapter seems stuck, try lifting one end out first. You should never need to pry an adapter out with a tool, though sometimes you will need to use a bit of force. You can leave any cables running from the adapters to internal drives attached and pile the adapters gently on top of the power supply. Next you will have to remove any cable attached directly to the motherboard, which is normally limited to the two power supply connectors, P8 and P9, and a bunch of small connectors with thin wires that go to the buttons and LEDs on the front of the system box. If the pins they connect to on the old motherboard are labeled and the small connectors aren't, you may want to put little pieces of tape on them with TLED (Turbo Light), TSW (Turbo Switch), KEY (Key Lock), PWR (Power Light, sometimes integral with key lock in a 5-pin connector), HDD (Hard Drive Light), and RST (Reset Switch). If you forget, or get confused, you can always follow the wire back to the faceplate and see where it goes. Besides, the only one that's actually useful for anything is the reset switch, and I rarely bother hooking up the others on systems I build for myself.

The next step is to find and remove all of the screws securing the old motherboard in place, which can number between one and seven. These screws are attached to standoffs, tall nuts made of brass or steel, which are themselves screwed into the case. This is the trickiest part of the job, because if the person who screwed in the standoffs didn't tighten them, they will unscrew from the case when you try to remove the screws. This is bad, because most motherboards are also attached to the case with plastic spacers, which need to be slid an inch or so through a slot to be removed, and the protruding standoff will prevent this. One solution is to retighten the screw, and hope when you loosen it the next time, the standoff will stay attached to the case. Another solution is to use some small wire clippers to cut the heads of the protruding plastic spacers, than lift the motherboard right out. If you have a minitower, the screw ends of the standoffs are often exposed on other side of the case, and can be held from turning with pliers while you extract the screw. On some minitowers, the pan (sheet metal) that the motherboard is attached to isn't welded in place and can itself be removed from the case with just two screws, making the job easier.

Preparing the New Motherboard

There are a few things you should do before you screw the new motherboard into place. First, insert the new CPU in its socket, being careful to match the flattened outside corner of a 486 CPU with the flattened, inside corner of the socket. Pentium CPUs should only be able to fit in the socket in one orientation. Open up the manual that comes with the new motherboard, and make sure that all of the jumpers are set right for CPU type (486, AMD 586, Pentium, etc.) and speed (100 MHz, 133 MHz, etc.). Read the table carefully, and make sure that you find the exact CPU that you have. Even if you bought a motherboard with the new CPU already mounted, you will want to double-check the jumper settings. Next, jumper the turbo switch permanently on if this hasn't already been done. If the clock speed is 40 MHz, 80 MHz, or 120 MHz and the board has VLB slots, check for a bus-speed compatibility jumper and set it according to the manual. Finally, mount the memory SIMMs on the motherboard now, so you won't have to struggle to do it with the motherboard in the case.

Installing the New Motherboard in the System Box

The first step is to carefully note the positions of the existing standoffs screwed into the case. Next, lower the motherboard onto the standoffs, and make sure they all line up with tin ringed holes in the motherboard. If there are any standoffs you can't see (and there are usually one or two), take them out. Count the number of standoffs you use, and when you reach the step of securing the motherboard, make sure the number of screws you put in matches the number of standoffs. If you miss an unused standoff and power up the system, it will short the motherboard to the case and ruin it. Next, if there is only one standoff left screwed into the case, compare the tin-ringed holes in the motherboard with the threaded holes in the case, and see if you can add one or two standoffs back in. If not, it's no big deal. The plastic spacers you put in next and the adapter cards are more then enough to hold the motherboard firmly in place. Tighten the standoffs with a pair of pliers or a socket-end screwdriver.

Now, hold the motherboard near the standoffs, and note which holes (they can be tin ringed or not) line up with the slots in the case, then snap in the plastic spacers from the bottom of the motherboard. Take note at this point if the connector block for the power supply leads ends up in an inaccessible place, like under the power supply. If so, you can connect the power supply leads at this point (see next paragraph). Before you can start putting any screws in, you must insert the round ends of the plastic spacers through the enlarged holes at the ends of the slots, then slide the motherboard over until the tin-ringed holes line up with the standoffs. If you have a very difficult time doing this, try to determine which plastic spacer is causing the problem and remove it (you can cut it off if you have trouble unsnapping it). This is a pretty common problem, since slots that appear to line up are often a fraction of an inch off.

If you have all the plastic spacers well placed in the slots but the motherboard still doesn't want to slide, some of the protruding soldered leads on the bottom of the motherboard are probably stuck on the standoffs. If you can pull up on the motherboard a little (don't use a lot of force) right over the location of the problem standoff, you should be able to slide the motherboard into place. If this doesn't work, take the motherboard back out and remove the problem standoff. Once you have the motherboard in place, secure it with screws to the standoffs. The next step is to connect the two motherboard connectors from the power supply, P8 and P9. Arrange the connectors so that the black wires in each connector are adjacent to one another in the center of the connection block. The little plastic ridges on the power supply leads that face the motherboard connector are sometimes too long and interfere with the connector mating well. Don't hesitate to clip them off.

If your new motherboard has the floppy drive, IDE hard drive, and CD connections on the motherboard, remove these ribbon cables from your old SIDE card, checking as you do so that the red wire in the ribbon is adjacent to the end of the connector labeled with a 1 or 2. Reconnect them to the motherboard, with the red wire adjacent to the 1-2 end of the connector, unless it was done the opposite way on the SIDE card, in which case you want to do it the opposite way on the motherboard. The new motherboard should come with small ribbon cables attached to the port connectors, which are mounted on metal blanks that get attached to the back of the system box the same way as adapters. Connect these ribbon cables to the labeled blocks on the motherboard with the red wire adjacent to the 1-2 end of the connector.

Now you can reinstall all of the adapters onto the motherboard, leaving out the SIDE adapter if it has been superseded by the motherboard. You can hook up all the little wires to lights and switches if you want to, or just hook up the reset switch. If you have a cooling fan mounted on the new CPU, connect it to a power supply drive lead. If all the power supply drive leads are used, remove one from a drive, insert the fan lead in line, then reconnect the other end to the drive. Last, gently turn the whole system box upside down and tilt from side to side to see if any screws fall out or are rolling around under the motherboard. Finally, connect the monitor keyboard and mouse, and power the PC up. If the system doesn't boot, go to the troubleshooting guide in Section four.

The computer should jump into CMOS setup when you turn it on. If it doesn't, hit the reset button, and use the "Delete" key after the memory finishes counting to enter CMOS setup. The first item in every CMOS setup menu is called "standard," "system settings," or something like this. In this menu, you want to set the proper date, time, and the floppy drive type(s). If you remembered to write down the hard drive parameters, you can select "User Defined" for the hard drive type(s) and enter the same parameters. If not, save the settings you have entered (normally with the F10 key), and select "Auto Detect Hard Drive(s)" from the menu. The BIOS will now figure out the parameters for your hard drive(s). There may be several more menu items, with names like "Advanced Setup," "BIOS Setup," and others, but the default settings are probably all fine. You might want to look at each menu and make sure external cache is turned on, if cache is installed on the motherboard. You shouldn't have to change anything else unless you run into problems later or add new adapters whose documentation instructs you to make changes. At this point, you should see your old system running, but it should be many times faster. Shut the system down, put the cover back on, and you're done.

CHAPTER 10

Adapters and PC Communications Devices

Video Adapter

The main reason for upgrading a video adapter is to increase the number of simultaneous colors that can be displayed. Another reason is to get the maximum performance out of a new monitor. Finally, you may want a high-performance video adapter that displays screens faster or includes MPEG hardware decoding for displaying real-motion video. Many older systems that were equipped with motherboards sporting VLB (VESA Local Bus) slots were shipped with ISA (Industry Standard Architecture) adapters. Now that a 1-MB VLB video adapter costs less than an ISA 1-MB video adapter, you may as well buy the VLB adapter if you are upgrading. If you already have an SVGA adapter but cannot display more than 256 colors in VGA mode or 16 colors in SVGA mode, you should investigate whether adding memory to the adapter is an option.

Time and Cost for Upgrade

In 100 percent of hand-me-down PCs, replacing the video adapter should take less than five minutes. Installing and configuring the new video drivers for both DOS and Windows can take up to an additional half hour if several floppies come with the adapter. It's a rare PC shop that will properly configure the adapter for the monitor. This involves checking the monitor manual for the scan frequencies it supports and setting the proper mode with a program included on the utility disk that comes with the video adapter. The install software that comes with the video adapter will copy the program that invokes the mode to your CONFIG.SYS or AUTOEXEC.BAT files, but the mode-setting program will use low-performance defaults until somebody changes them. Windows 95 and the latest Windows NT include not only drivers for the video adapters but also for many "smart" monitors. A software wizard under the "Display" icon in "Control Panel" will guide you through the installation steps.

Some brand-name machines will have the video adapter integrated with the motherboard (not a separate adapter). To upgrade these systems, you will definitely need the manual to locate the jumper that disables the VGA on the motherboard before you can add an adapter. New SVGA cards with 1 MB of memory cost about $30, and I recommend clones using Trident or Cirrus Logic chips. You can pay a lot more for brand names with more memory and higher scan rates, and it becomes a matter of reading reviews and comparison shopping. The $30 adapters are

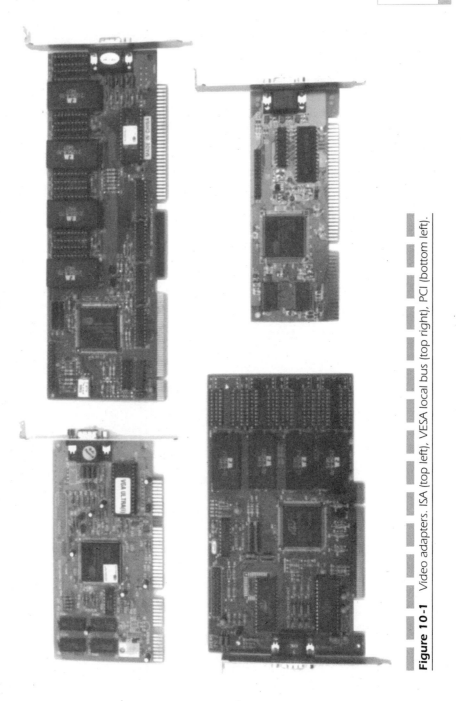

Figure 10-1 Video adapters. ISA (top left), VESA local bus (top right), PCI (bottom left).

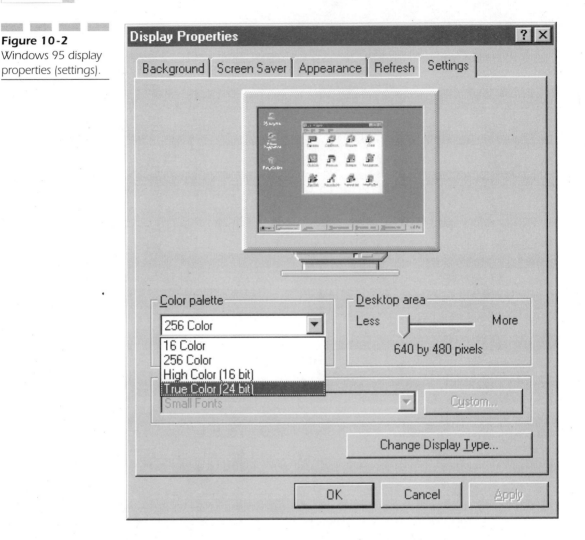

Figure 10-2
Windows 95 display
properties (settings).

more than enough for all but professional CAD designers or desktop
publishing users with $500+ monitors, or for serious game players.

Upgrading Video Memory on an Existing Adapter

Sometimes a SVGA video adapter is installed with less than its full complement of video memory which would enable it to display more colors

Figure 10-3
1-MB PCI SVGA adapter with two empty upgrade sockets.

and higher screen resolutions. This can only be determined by looking at the original documentation that came with the adapter, or taking it out of the system box and looking for empty memory sockets. These sockets usually have the type of memory chip required for an upgrade printed right on the circuit board, but if not, you will have to contact the manufacturer for the correct chip to use. Systems with SVGA integrated on the motherboard may also support more memory, but you will need the motherboard manual to find the correct jumper settings and the video memory type.

Installing a New SVGA Adapter

The first step, before removing the old adapter, is to start Windows 3.X (if you have it), double-click on the "Main" icon, double-click on the "Windows Setup" icon, select "Options" and "Change System Settings" then go to the "Display" list. Scroll up or down until you find "VGA" with nothing else, and select it. The next time you start Windows 3.X, you will have the default 16-color VGA driver that works with every adapter manufactured. If you forget to do this, and the software that comes with the new SVGA adapter isn't smart enough to change the Windows settings for you, you will have to run the Windows Setup program from DOS. You do this by changing to the Windows directory and typing "setup." Then you can change the "Display" type to "VGA" and rerun the adapter installation software. Windows 95 users will start in

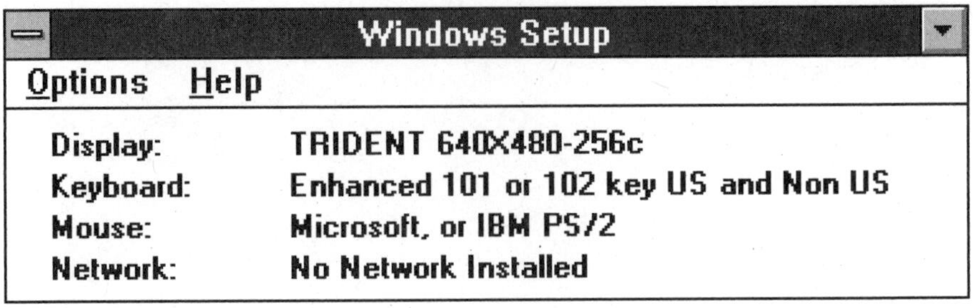

Figure 10-4
Windows 3.1 setup
entry screen.

—	Windows Setup	▼

Options   Help

Display:	TRIDENT 640X480-256c
Keyboard:	Enhanced 101 or 102 key US and Non US
Mouse:	Microsoft, or IBM PS/2
Network:	No Network Installed

"Safe Mode" when the system is first powered up, and will use the "Add New Hardware" wizard to configure the new adapter.

Next, remove the old VGA adapter, and insert the new video adapter in a bus slot. If the new adapter is a VLB adapter, and the CPU speed is some multiple of 40 MHz (ex. 486DX-40, 486DX2-80, 486DX4-120), you will also have to find and set a timing compatibility jumper on the motherboard. The jumper is usually located between the VESA bus slots, and is selectable for <= 33 MHz or > 33 MHz. For CPUs that are a multiple of 40 MHz, or the rare 486DX-50 (not the 486DX2-50), you will change this jumper to > 33 MHz. The only other issue is making sure the adapter is seated well in the bus slot, which is split into two sections. The ISA section is adjacent to the back of the PC, and the VESA section is next to the CPU. The screw that holds the adapter in place will help seat the ISA section of the adapter, but make sure the VESA section, which is farthest from the screw, doesn't pop out when the screw is tightened. Also, if you already have one or more VESA adapters in the system, make sure you can fit a VESA video adapter before purchasing one. Although motherboards usually feature three VESA bus slots, CPU cooling fans and bad motherboard layout sometimes physically prevent more then one of them from being used by most VESA adapters.

The next step is installing the software that comes on floppy disk with the adapter, which can require up to three steps, for those using both DOS and Windows application programs. These steps do not apply to Windows 95 and Windows NT users who will complete the same procedures using the "Add New Hardware" wizard or a vendor-supplied "setup" utility.

1. Install the utilities, which include a program that needs to be informed of the monitor specifications, to take advantage of noninterlaced monitors and high scan rates. Most utilities will allow you to try all of the display modes your monitor

supports with a test pattern, a good way to see if you're getting what you expected. The utilities install program may include a VESA compatibility driver for DOS software.

2. Install the DOS software for each DOS application you are using. This lets older DOS versions of popular applications utilize some of the same screen presentation features as the Windows version. If the only DOS software you use is DOS itself, or games, you can skip this step. Most DOS games have a setup option of their own which supports the popular video adapters. Some games will support the VESA extension (same organization that created the VLB standard, different extension), a software driver that existed as an alternative to Windows for providing a standard interface between video adapters and software. VESA drivers are no longer included with all video adapters, although compatibility is sometimes built into the video BIOS. If you know you will need VESA software compatibility for a specific game or some other DOS software, ask this question specifically before buying the adapter, and make sure they don't think you're talking about VESA local bus drivers.

3. Install the Windows software. Read the instructions carefully, as some install programs need to be executed in rather bizarre manners (the old Trident 9000s from one manufacturer were installed correctly by typing "README" on the A: drive). Some older install programs will require that you have your Windows disks on hand, while others will supply all of the files required.

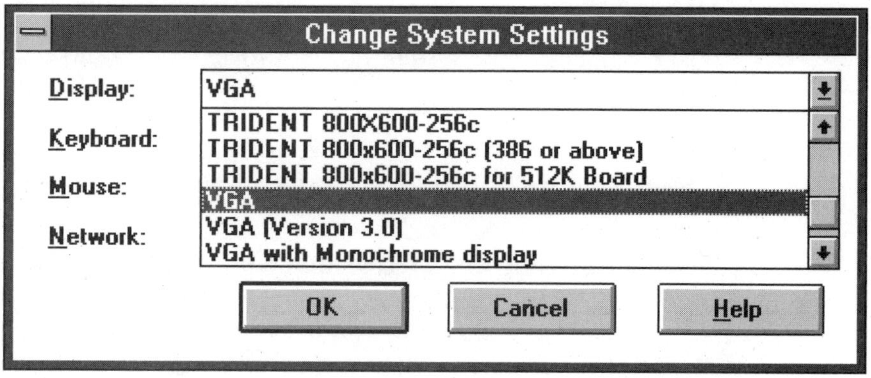

Figure 10-5
Windows 3.1 setup (Options—Change Settings).

Change System Settings	
Display:	VGA
Keyboard:	TRIDENT 800X600-256c
	TRIDENT 800x600-256c (386 or above)
Mouse:	TRIDENT 800x600-256c for 512K Board
	VGA
Network:	VGA (Version 3.0)
	VGA with Monochrome display

OK   Cancel   Help

When installed properly, your system should have a new icon in Windows for the video adapter that lets you change screen resolution and the number of colors displayed in one step. Selecting new settings is carried out by point and click, but remember that the software will always need to restart Windows before the changes take effect. If you find yourself using Windows "Setup" to control the adapter, you've probably installed the driver software incorrectly and should have another look at the instructions.

Modems

There are two choices involved in installing a new modem or upgrading from an old modem. The first choice is modem speed: 14.4 K, 28.8 K, 33.6 K or 56 K. The second choice is whether to buy an internal modem, or to use an external modem, which has its own power supply and is attached to a serial port on your computer. The reason we made modem speed the first choice is that it can have an impact on whether you choose an external modem or not. Most hand-me-down PCs are equipped with serial ports that can handle a maximum speed of 19.2 K. You can check this by running the Microsoft Diagnostic at the DOS prompt by typing MSD, then clicking on "Com Ports". If the UART (Universal Asynchronous Receiver Transmitter) type is an 8250, your maximum speed is 19.2 K. This means that if you want to install a 28.8 K or faster external modem, you'll have to open the computer and install a higher-grade SIDE card with a 16550 UART or purchase an external modem that comes with its own adapter card. Either way, it means that if you were purchasing an external modem to avoid opening the system box, you may have to settle for a 14.4 K.

Time and Cost for Upgrade

Installing an external modem takes about two minutes if you don't need to install a new adapter with a 16550 UART. Installing an internal modem can go as quickly as five minutes but often takes a half an hour or more, depending on your Com port availability and the strength of your documentation. You can buy internal 14.4-K modems for less than $40, internal 28.8-K modems cost less than $60, and internal 33.6-K modems start under $100. Some brand name 33.6-K internal modems are upgradable to 56-K internal modems, which otherwise cost close to $150. External 14.4-K modems start under $60, and external 28.8-K and 33.6-K modems cost around $100. If you buy a 28.8-K or 33.6-K external modem without an adapter and you have a slow (8250) UART, you can buy a SIDE card with a 16550 UART for about $30, but you may have to read a lot of ads to find one. External modems also require a serial cable which costs less than $5, but if you don't get it at the same place as the modem, you will end up paying twice that for shipping and handling.

External modems use one of your system's Com ports. Internal modems add a Com port or replace an existing Com port. For Windows 95 and Windows NT users, adding the modem as Com4 works fine, but for DOS/Windows users, you will have less problems with software applications if you disable your existing Com2 port or change it to Com4, and then set up the internal modem as Com2. If you have trouble getting your plug-and-play internal modem initialized on the port you've chosen for it, don't hesitate to call the manufacturer or vendor you purchased it from. There are always exceptions and updates relating to the use of plug-and-play modems, often due to known conflicts with other cards. Modems all come with software, and your Internet application will also need to be configured for the modem. Follow the instructions that come with the software after completing the hardware installation procedures.

Installing an Internal Modem

The first step, even before you take your new modem out of its protective bag, is to determine the current configuration of your Com ports. Turn on your computer and hit the pause key as soon as the system configuration screen appears, which occurs after the memory count and before the operating system begins to load. The system configuration screen informs you what hardware the BIOS (Basic Input Output System) can detect in your PC. If the BIOS can't see your serial ports (Com ports), they aren't going to work. The serial communications ports are reported in hex as follows: 3F8=Com1, 2F8=Com2, 3E8=Com3, 2E8=Com4. In

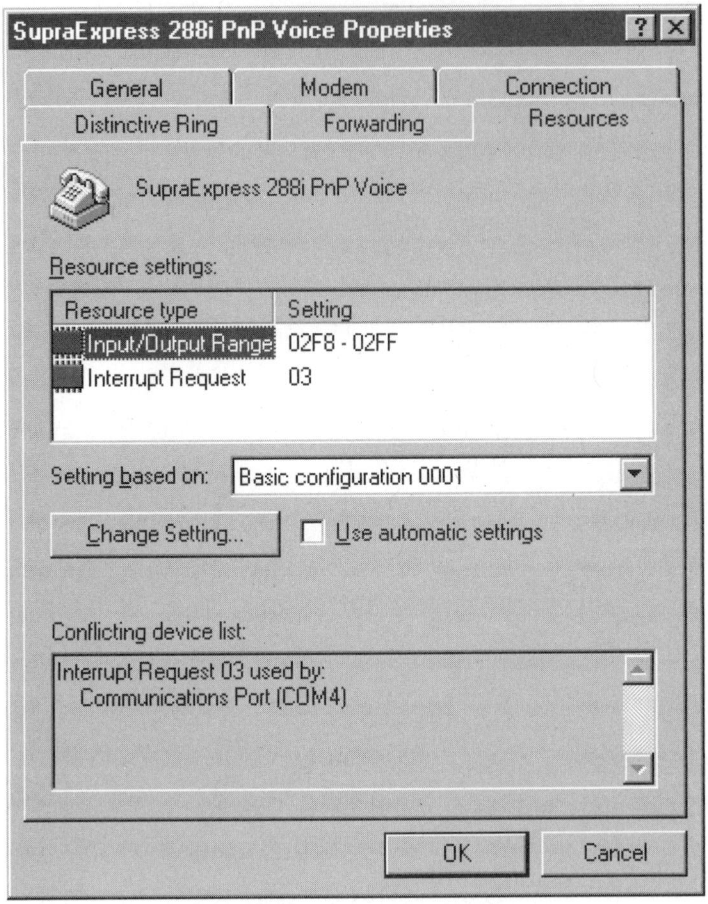

Figure 10-6
Windows 95
(modem selected in
Device Manager).

almost all instances, the basic PC is equipped with Com1 (a 9-pin male connector) and Com2 (a 25-pin male connector). Before actually installing your modem, you'll want to make sure that the Com address you want to use for the modem is open, restarting the PC after any changes are made to make sure the address is not listed on the system configuration screen. Installing an internal modem usually requires you to move or disable a Com port by moving jumpers on your SIDE card. If you have problems configuring the Com ports on a SIDE card, refer to the troubleshooting section. Newer motherboards with integrated Com ports let you change or disable the settings in the CMOS setup.

If your mouse is attached to Com1 or has a separate mouse port, you should set your internal modem to Com2, IRQ = 3, first disabling or moving the existing Com2 port if it exists. Windows 95 will report a modem on Com2 as having conflict with a Com4 port, but this won't create difficulties as long as you don't try to use Com4 for anything. If your mouse is attached to Com2, you should set your modem to Com1, IRQ4, first disabling or moving the existing Com1 port if it exists. After installing the modem, power up the computer again, and make sure that the hex designation for the Com port you installed your modem on now shows up on the system configuration screen. If not, power down, remove the adapter, check the jumpers, and try again. Lastly, the "line" or "telco" connection on the back of your modem card goes to the wall jack, and the "phone" connection is for plugging in a telephone handset.

Installing an External Modem

You will need a serial cable, which is generally not supplied with the modem. The modem manual will specify what kind of cable is required, usually a standard modem cable. The end of the cable that attaches to the modem is generally a 25-pin female connector, but the end that attaches to the system box can be specified for Com1 or Com2. The cable end for Com1 is a 9-pin female, and the connector for Com2 is a 25-pin female. External modems are equipped with their own transformer-type power supply, which requires an AC outlet to plug into. The "line" or "telco" connection on your modem goes to the wall jack, and the "phone" connection is for plugging in a telephone handset.

Installing Modem Software

If you only intend to use your modem for surfing the Web, the Internet provider will supply software that works directly with the modem, so it's not necessary to install the software that comes with the modem. When you run the Internet software setup, one of the modem options will be "pulse" or "tone." This depends on the type of phone service you have, not the modem. If you have push button telephones that make short beeps of different pitches when you dial, you have a tone connection. If on your first try to make your Internet connection you can hear the modem dialing but then hear a dial tone instead of ringing (until the recording comes on asking you to hang up), you installed the modem as tone, but have a pulse connection.

If you have purchased a fax/modem, the software adds another "printer" to your installed printers list in Windows 3.1 or Windows for Workgroups, where the printing device is your fax. Windows 95 and Windows NT not only offer enhanced fax support, but also provide a service called "dial-up networking," which lets your modem act like a (slow) network connection to a modem-equipped network server. If you are using Windows 95 for a dial-up server, you must also have Microsoft Plus for Windows 95 loaded. When you select a document in any of the Windows environments and click on Print, you can select the "Fax Printer," at which point you will be prompted for the phone number of the fax you are sending to, along with cover sheet information. In order to receive faxes, your computer must be turned on and in Windows, and the fax receiving software must be loaded. I do not recommend having this software loaded every time you boot unless you have a separate phone number for your fax. Otherwise, your computer will pick up your house phone and whistle every time the phone rings when you're in Windows. Almost all modems have fax capability, but they are a poor replacement for a fax machine, since they can only fax out documents created and saved on the PC.

Sound Card

The sound card upgrade is easiest if you have Windows 95 or NT and a PnP (Plug-and-Play) BIOS because possible hardware conflicts can be detected and corrected through the operating system or CMOS setup software. The second best case is a PnP sound card without a PnP BIOS, which means while the sound card might not work the first time you plug it in, you can adjust the settings in software rather than pulling the card back out and changing jumpers. The usual hand-me-down PC candidate for a sound card upgrade is DOS/Windows running on a 386 or 486 system, without a PnP BIOS. Windows 95 and Windows NT are much more sound-card friendly than DOS and Windows 3.1, which pre-date the widespread use of multimedia enhancements.

If you have a very basic system with no modem or other extra adapter cards, then installation is a breeze. Most sound cards are

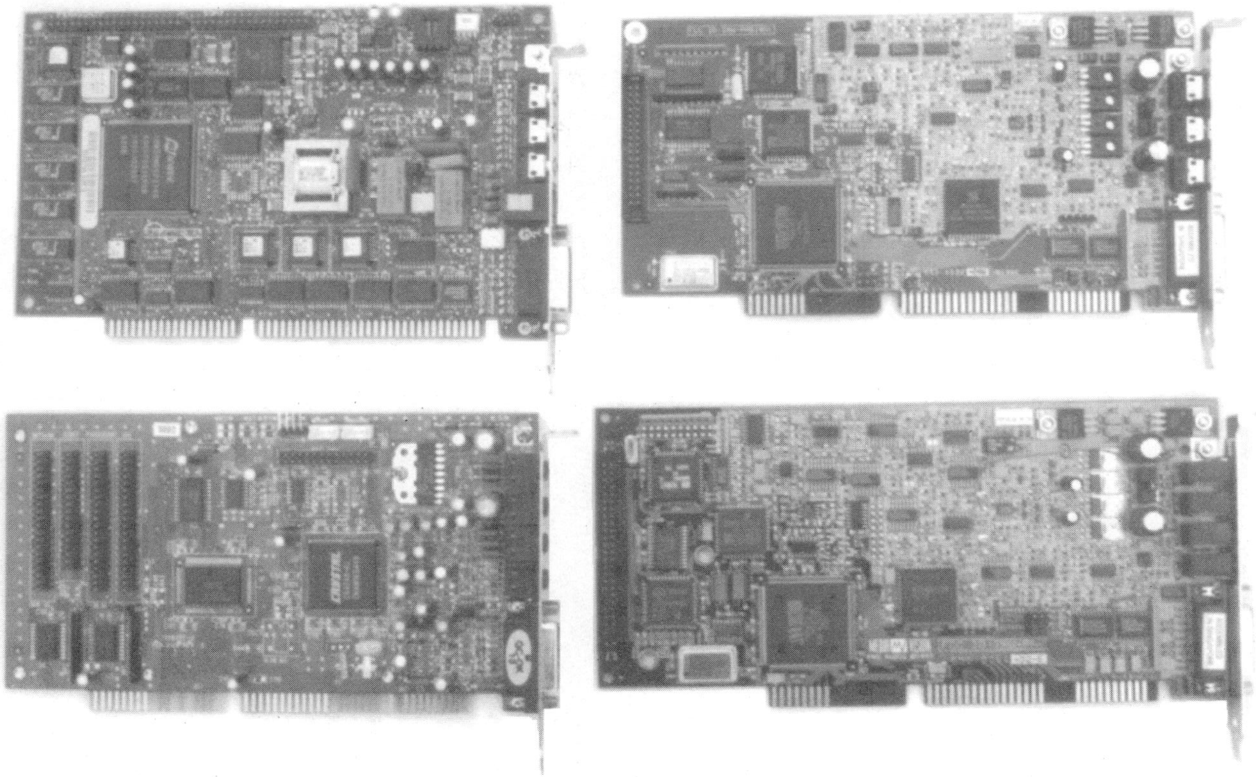

Figure 10-7 Four sound cards.

designed for 16-bit ISA slots. Unlike all other adapter cards, the multiple of eight, as in "8-bit Sound Blaster," "Sound Blaster 16," or "Sound Blaster 32," does not refer to the data path width (in bits) of the bus connection. In fact, the numbering convention doesn't even remain consistent from generation to generation. The "8-bit Sound Blaster" was called such because it had an 8 bit D/A, A/D converter. This means that it could sample only 64 discrete levels of volume (dynamic range), and it had a maximum sample rate of 22 kHz (half the fidelity of a music CD). The "Sound Blaster 16" has 16 bits of D/A, A/D resolution, giving it a dynamic range 64,000 levels. It is also capable of sampling at 44.1 kHz, the same sampling rate used for recording music CDs. When artificially generating music (MIDI or Wave Table), it is capable of 16 simultaneous voices (polyphony). The "Sound Blaster 32" series also has 16 bits of D/A, A/D resolution, but they are capable of 32 channels of polyphony, and support memory expansion for Wave Table sound.

Time and Cost for Upgrade

Sound cards are available in a range of prices from $30 to over $400. The minimum I would recommend is a Sound Blaster 16 compatible, starting around $40. If you invest in a genuine Sound Blaster (around $60 for the basic model) or other brand-name card, you will get better support and access to software upgrades than with a clone card. Creative Labs, the creators of the Sound Blaster, have one of the best tech support sites I've ever seen, at www.creativelabs.com, which includes diagrams and jumper settings for all of their boards. Avoid sound cards from manufacturers who don't maintain a Web site. The time to perform the upgrade should be under a half hour, but occasionally you'll run into a system so riddled with resource conflicts that it can take hours to work it all out. If you have your sound card installed at a PC shop, make them set the system up and give you an opportunity to exercise all functions before you leave. Record your voice, play it back through the speakers, play a test MIDI file, and if you have a CD drive installed, make sure you can play a music CD through the speakers. It's very easy for a shop to accidentally send you away with what they believe is a working sound card upgrade, but you're the one who will have to lug the system box back in again if they missed something.

Installing a Sound Card

You must have the documentation that comes with a sound card to install it properly. If you are using DOS with Windows 3.1 or Windows for Workgroups, the first step is always to run either a special software utility that comes with the sound card or MSD (MicroSoft Diagnostic), to determine what resources are available for the sound card settings. Sound cards come with a number of default settings (IRQ=5, Base Address=330, MIDI Address=220, and DMA=1) that are assumed to be standard for many DOS games. Most sound card manufacturers recommend that you leave the sound card on its default settings and change the settings on any conflicting cards. A plug-and-play sound card in a DOS/Windows system will come with software for changing the card's resource settings. In a very basic system, these resources will all be free. In a system with add-in adapters, it means having to reconfigure some existing software—either the drivers for those adapters whose resources are changed or the programs which expect the sound card to be on the default settings.

Windows 95 and Windows NT 4.0 systems control settings from Device Manager under Control Panel. If your new sound card is plug-and-play (recommended), the operating system should automatically detect it when it is installed and the system is rebooted, and make the proper resource assignments. If the card is not plug-and-play, you should first use Device Manager to determine the available resources for the sound card. In either case, Device Manager will let you know if there are any resource conflicts and flag any nonfunctioning devices with an exclamation mark (!). If you need to change any resource setting under Device Manager and you don't have PnP adapters, remember that you'll have to change the physical jumpers on the cards to agree with the new settings.

Finally, sound cards are delivered with a great deal of software of their own, for playing music CDs, recording and playing WAV and MIDI music, etc., all of which must be installed in Windows. It's a common problem to install a sound card and not realize that one of the software drivers isn't working properly until months later, when you first use a MIDI or Wave Table application. Wave table cards come with upgradable memory modules, often in the form of standard SIMMs. The memory is used to store more and bigger samples of actual instruments, for playing better quality and more complex music.

Figure 10-8
Windows 95 Device
Manager.

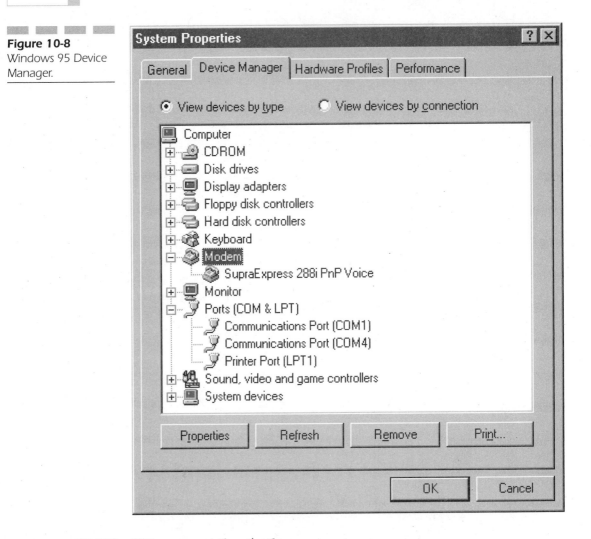

Network Adapter

Most network adapters sold today are PnP (Plug-and-Play) or jumperless,
the predecessor to PnP technology. On older jumperless adapters, rather
than changing resource settings in the CMOS Setup or through Windows 95 or NT, the manufacturer supplies a DOS or Windows program
which sets up the adapter. All the same, this beats having to move a
bunch of jumpers around. The settings for your network adapter
depend on the LAN (Local Area Network) software, which may not support every combination of settings the card can produce. If you have

Windows for Workgroups, Windows 95, or Windows NT, you can create a peer to peer (no dedicated server) network using just the Windows software, network adapters, and cabling. The biggest users of hand-me-down PCs on LANs are probably schools, and in the classroom environment, you should really strive to use the same network adapter, on the same settings, in every PC. Otherwise, the software installation and maintenance becomes a nightmare.

Time and Cost for Upgrade

This is one procedure which is almost never performed in computer shops since the cabling and software installation have to be done at the customer site anyway. There are few parts easier to install in the PC than a PnP network adapter. Even if the adapter is a manual jumper type, only one interrupt and base address must be selected, and most adapters come with software that determines the possible settings for you. Network adapters capable of running thin ethernet (direct wired coaxial cable) and 10base-T (twisted-pair phone wire) start around $30. Don't buy VESA Local Bus network cards. If thin ethernet is run, you can expect to spend about $200 additional in parts (coaxial cable, connectors, two terminators and a crimping tool) in order to wire a classroom of computers. For 10Base-T cabling, the wire (four twisted pairs in a sheath) and the connectors (RJ-45 plugs) are a little cheaper, but you need to buy one or more active hubs for hundreds of dollars. Hubs are sold by the number of ports (connections) they support, and they can always be connected together to support more users, although you may lose a port doing so. Eight-port clone hubs start under $100, while 24-port name-brand hubs cost over $500. School buyers should always ask for an educational discount on networking software.

Installing a Network Adapter

Installing a network adapter takes about five minutes. Most clone adapters emulate the old Novell NE2000 standard, and will work with your network operating system if you choose NE2000 for the adapter type. Of course, having one PC with a network adapter installed accomplishes nothing. The real work is connecting it to other PCs and getting the software configured. The software configuration will depend on your choice of network operating system, and is beyond the scope of this book. We will provide a brief overview of network cabling for the two most common low-cost LANs—thin ethernet and 10Base-T.

Installing a Thin Ethernet LAN

A thin ethernet LAN consists of a many segments of RG-58U or other 50-ohm coaxial cable, linking together many PCs and terminated at each end with a 50 ohm terminator. Each PC is connected to this segmented cable by a "T" connector, where the vertical member of the "T" is attached directly to the network adapter, and a segment of cable is connected to each side of the cross member. Cable segments are added from "T" to "T" until the last PC in the chain is reached, at which point a terminator is installed on the unused end of the "T." The main disadvantage of thin ethernet is that if one connection is broken, the whole network fails. The only skill you must master for this process is putting BNC connectors on coaxial cable, and you can even avoid this if you buy pre-made lengths. Coaxial cable consists of a central conductor insulated by a thick dielectric cylinder, covered by a conductive braid or foil, and protected with thin plastic sheath.

There are three different types of BNC connectors you can work with. Twist-on connectors are favored by many schools, because they require no tools and can be easily remade if rough handling breaks the connection. Crimp-on connectors are the easiest to make, but they require a special tool ($20) and aren't particularly robust. Solder connectors are rarely used anymore because they are labor intensive to make up, but they offer the best reliability and electrical characteristics. In all cases, you may want to consider buying a special coaxial cable stripping tool that cuts the cable sheathing from the braid and the braid and insulator from the central conductor at the proper distance ($20).

Installing a 10Base-T LAN

A 10Base-T LAN consists of a bunch of PCs, each separately connected to a central hub. The disadvantage is the cost of the hub, but the advantage is that a connector failure affects only the PC on that segment. The wiring used for 10Base-T networks is twisted-pair phone wire, which is normally sold with 4 twisted pairs together in one sheath. The pairs are easily identified by color coding, like green and white with a green stripe, blue and white with a blue stripe, etc. You only need four wires to make 10Base-T cables, but it's important that you use two pairs, since the twists in a pair provide the electrical shielding. Cables are connected straight through using RJ-45 jacks, which look like very wide telephone jacks. RJ-45 jacks can house 8 wires, which is why most cabling is sold with four pairs, but only two pairs are actually needed for 10Base-T.

The first pair is used to connect pin 1 to pin 1 and pin 2 to pin 2, and the second pair to attach pin 3 to pin 3 and pin 6 to pin 6. This is called a "straight-through" connection scheme. You need a special crimping tool to make up these connectors, and you have to squeeze really hard to make a good connection and crush the stress relief into the cable. Before you actually crimp a cable, carefully examine your wiring through the transparent connector to make sure you have the wires ordered correctly, and look at the connector end-on to make sure the copper ends of the wires show up as an even row of orange dots against the connector end. When a good cable is plugged into an adapter and a powered up hub, the green link light on the back of

Figure 10-9
BOCA twisted-pair hub (front and back) with 10Base-T cable.

the adapter should be lit. The red light shows network traffic or is used in diagnostics as described by the documentation. Unless I'm in practice, I end up mistaking the colors and making about one in four cable ends wrong. You can repair a 10Base-T cable by finding the bad end, cutting it off, and replacing it.

CHAPTER **11**

Drives

IDE (Intelligent Drive Electronics) Drives

All modern IDE drives can function in two modes; as the "master" or the "slave." Some drives include a third mode, "single," which is used when the drive is the only IDE drive installed. Your PC can support two separate IDE controllers, each with its own master and slave drives, for a total of four IDE drives per system. The two IDE controllers are referred to as the "primary" and "secondary" controllers, and the boot drive with the operating system software must be the master drive on the primary controller. Newer PCs all come standard with primary and secondary IDE controllers integrated on the motherboard and controlled through CMOS Setup. The mode selection for the hard drives is controlled by a set of jumpers on the individual hard drives. Another variation on the basic scheme is a "slave-present" jumper, which must be set on the drive that is master when a slave is being added. The main problem with older drives is that they rarely labeled the jumpers, neither on the circuit board nor with a diagram pasted to the top of the drive (new drives often have both). Drives are sold with documentation that describes the use of these jumpers, but it rarely stays with the system long enough to reach the new owner of a hand-me-down PC. In this situation, you can obtain the jumper information from the

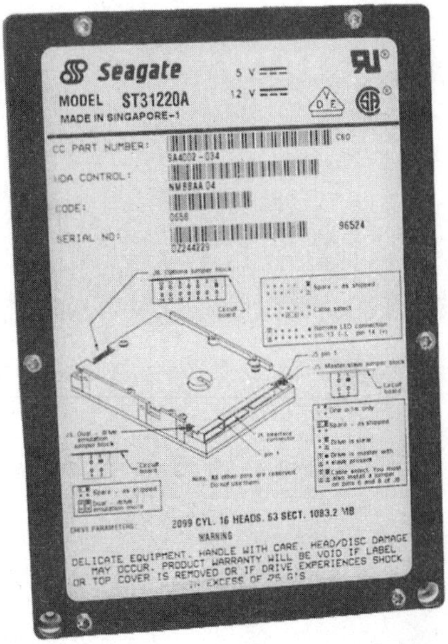

Figure 11-1
Seagate 1-GB IDE hard drive with all drive information on the label.

manufacturer's WWW site, by phone contact with their technical support, or from a fax-back system, which most drive vendors employ.

SCSI (Small Computer System Integration) Devices

A SCSI adapter actually adds an entirely new data bus to your computer, where the adapter serves as the interface to the motherboard. You can install up to seven different SCSI devices on a single adapter, using a multiconnector ribbon cable inside the system box, or daisy-chained (serially connected) SCSI cables outside the system box. There are two important facts to understand about a SCSI bus. First, both ends of the bus must be terminated, which involves using on-board resistors for internal devices, or attaching a SCSI terminator pack to the daisy chain connector on an external device. Second, each device on the bus has a unique ID, a number between zero and six (the adapter itself is number seven). A boot device (normally a hard drive) must be installed as ID zero or one. CD drives and tape drives are usually sold with the default ID set at two, while hard drives are generally shipped with the default ID set at zero.

Figure 11-2
1-GB SCSI drive with wire repair shunts on circuit board.

Hard Drive Upgrade

Almost everybody with a hand-me-down PC will want to consider a hard drive upgrade at some point. Hard drive prices, as measured by dollars/megabyte, have fallen by a factor of at least 20 times over the

Figure 11-3
IDE drive (left) with
MFM drive (right).

past 5 years. A 40 MB IDE hard drive cost about $200 in 1992 and was
often difficult to obtain due to demand. A 800-MB IDE hard drive costs
less than $150 today, and a 1600-MB hard drive sells for about $200. In
the meantime, program sizes have skyrocketed, with some applications
requiring more than 40 MB of free space just to be installed! New hard
drives are also faster than the older models by a factor of two on seek
time (time to find where the information you want resides on the disk),
and several times faster on transfer time (time to move the information
from the disk to the system bus). The discussion of hard drive upgrades
will be divided into two sections: IDE hard drives and SCSI hard drives.
Older types of hard drives with designations like MFM and RLL have
not been manufactured since 1990 and are not covered. There are no
good reasons to upgrade MFM or RLL drives with a rebuilt version of
the same type or to replace or repair their controllers. Replace them
with IDE drives.

Time and Cost for Upgrades

Upgrade cost is dependent on whether you choose a SCSI or IDE drive. If
your existing system already has an IDE drive (most PCs) or a SCSI drive
in it, it's easiest and most cost-effective to upgrade it with the same type.
The price difference between entry level IDE and SCSI drives is minor for

the smaller-sized units, but the difference in controller cost is tremendous. IDE controllers are integrated with all new motherboards, and are otherwise found on SIDE cards, which cost less than $15. SCSI hard drives are available in a number of performance increments. Stick with the cheapest drive unless you are positive that you need the enhanced performance and that you have a SCSI controller that can take full advantage of the drive. For example, a 1.0-GB SCSI drive may cost anywhere from $200 to $400 depending on the exact model. SCSI controllers start around $50 and go as high as $400 or more for enhanced versions with serious support software. IDE controllers are limited to controlling a combined total of two hard drives or CD drives, while a single SCSI controller can also control high quality tape drives and a variety of external peripherals, up to seven in number. Some old system boxes, without provisions for 3$^1/_2$" drives (the same size as your 1.44-MB floppy), will require you to purchase a $5 mounting kit along with the new hard drive. In rare circumstances, the ribbon cable attached to your original hard drive may only have one drive connector on it, and you will have to purchase a new ribbon cable for $5, though if you ask nicely you should get one for free.

There are a few factors impacting the amount of time needed to install a new hard drive. The first is whether or not you need to transfer all of the data from your old drive to your new drive. Another factor is whether you want to change the boot drive (the drive the operating system loads from) to the new drive, which is recommended if the old drive you are keeping is smaller than 340 MB. If you take your PC to a computer shop, you will have to tell them to change the boot drive if you want it done. Changing the drive designations and copying all the data from the old drive to the new drive adds fifteen minutes to the total job. Another factor is whether the drives are mounted in easily accessible bays or in a removable cage. In the space of a couple minutes, a removable cage can be taken out and replaced in the system box, allowing you to secure the new drive with four screws. In some systems the drives are mounted in fixed bays that are located in the front of the case, and you may have to remove other components in order to get screws into both sides of the drive. This can end up taking an additional fifteen minutes.

Hard drives of over 512 MB, which includes all new models, require a software driver for DOS and Windows 3.1 to utilize all of the drive capacity in a single partition. If the drive is broken into multiple partitions, you will end up with a new drive letter (C:, D:, E:, etc.) for each additional 512 MB, which isn't desirable for most people. Windows 95 and

Windows NT users don't need to worry about this unless their BIOS (basic input output system) is so old that it needs software assistance in recognizing large drives. By 1994, most PCs were built with a BIOS capable of supporting large hard drives. Installing this software is sometimes a frustrating process, depending on the quality of documentation, and can add yet another fifteen minutes to the job. If you are simply adding a second hard drive under 512 MB to your system and are continuing to boot from your original hard drive, the whole upgrade should take less than 15 minutes. If you are changing the boot drive, have obstructed access to the mounting screws, and are adding a drive over 512 MB to a DOS/Windows system, the job can take upwards of an hour.

Adding a Second IDE Hard Drive

There are two scenarios for adding a second IDE hard drive. The first is adding the new drive as the new boot drive (master), and the second is adding the new drive as the slave. The simplest way to get your new drive to function as the master sounds a little involved but works out pretty easily. First, install the new drive as a slave by setting the jumper on it to slave, and making sure the jumper(s) on the old drive are on master and slave present, if slave present is supported on the old drive. Connect the ribbon cable to both hard drives, making sure the red wire in the ribbon cable is adjacent to the end of the connector labeled 1 or 2 (normally the end next to the power connector), and connect a power lead, which is keyed to mate the proper way. If there are no drive leads from the power supply available, you will have to get a "Y" power splitter, another free or sub $5 part.

Next, lay the new drive in a stable position on top of the case (note to minitower owners—it's perfectly okay to do this with the system box laying on its side), using a book to create a flat surface if none is available. Power up the computer, enter CMOS setup, and either add the parameters for the new "D:" drive in the "Standard" menu, or use "Autodetect Hard Drive" to let the BIOS determine the parameters. Save the new settings, and let the system boot. If the system hangs or reports an error, shut down, check your jumpers and cables, and try again. Windows 95 and NT users will go through the operating systems "New Hardware Setup" at this point, and can then use "Windows Explorer" or "File Manager" to copy the contents of the old drive to the new drive, unless they

Figure 11-4
"Y" power splitter.

want to leave the new drive as the slave. If that's the case, Windows 95 and NT users can shut the PC off, secure the hard drives at this point, put the cover on, and be finished. Otherwise, Windows 95 and NT users will also have to create an emergency boot disk, making sure that the "FDISK" utility is included on the disk, and can then skip the next two paragraphs.

If the new hard drive is greater than 512 MB, run the install software included, following the instructions exactly. Some drive manufacturers supply the translation software installed on a temporary hard disk partition and instruct you to install the new drive and copy the program to a floppy before proceeding. Run the install software as per instructions. Next, unless the install software for a greater than 512-MB drive has told you to skip this step, type "FDISK" and pick option "5." Change current fixed disk drive. Choose "2" for the fixed disk number, followed by option "1." Create DOS partition or logical drive, and "1." Create primary partition. Now select "Use all available space for DOS partition," after which FDISK will report the partition has been created and will reboot the system on "Esc." Now, type "FORMAT D: /S", and DOS will prepare the new hard drive for the operating system. This may take a couple minutes, and when the job is completed, you will be asked to enter a volume name. You can do so, or hit return and accept a blank volume name. FORMAT will also report how many free bytes you have. If you only have 500 million or so free bytes (536,870,912), and you have purchased a larger drive, something went wrong with the special driver install software. You can try rereading the instructions and running the install software again, or call them for technical support. This is not a hardware problem; you've done everything else correctly.

You should now be able to type "D:" at the DOS prompt, "C:\>", and the prompt will change to "D:\>". If you want the new hard drive to remain the slave, you can shut the computer down at this point, secure the hard drives, using at least three screws each, put the cover back on, and you're done. Otherwise, type "DIR", and you should see the file "COMMAND.COM" and a huge number of bytes free that roughly equals the size of the drive you've added. Now, type "XCOPY C:*.* D:*.* /S /E". This will copy everything on the C: drive to the D: drive, and may take from five to fifteen minutes, during which time you will see your life accumulation of computer files flashing before your eyes. When it's done, type "DIR" again, and you will see that DOS has ordered the files differently on the D: drive, putting directories first and arranging them by creation date, but everything should be there. Now, you must create a boot floppy by putting a floppy disk in your A: drive and typing "FORMAT A: /S". When the disk is finished, type "COPY C:\DOS\FDISK.EXE A:".

Next (Windows 95 and NT users continue here), turn off the computer and change the jumpers on the hard drives, so the new drive is now the master and the old drive is the slave. Place your boot floppy or emer-

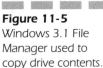

Figure 11-5
Windows 3.1 File
Manager used to
copy drive contents.

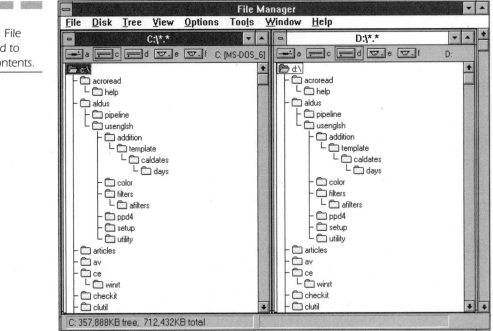

gency boot disk in drive A: and reboot. When you power up the system again it will take longer than usual to boot, because it is loading the operating system from the floppy disk in drive A: instead of from the hard drive. Sometimes, the system does not try to read the floppy drive, and instead merely flashes the drive light, then goes on to report "missing operating system" and freezes. In this case, you must reboot, enter CMOS setup, go to "Advanced Options", or a similarly titled menu choice (normally the second on the list), and change the "Boot Sequence" from "C: A:" to "A: C:". Save and exit, and the system will now boot from the floppy drive.

Type "FDISK" at the "A:>" prompt, and choose option "2. Set active partition." FDISK will report that no partition is set active on fixed disk 1,

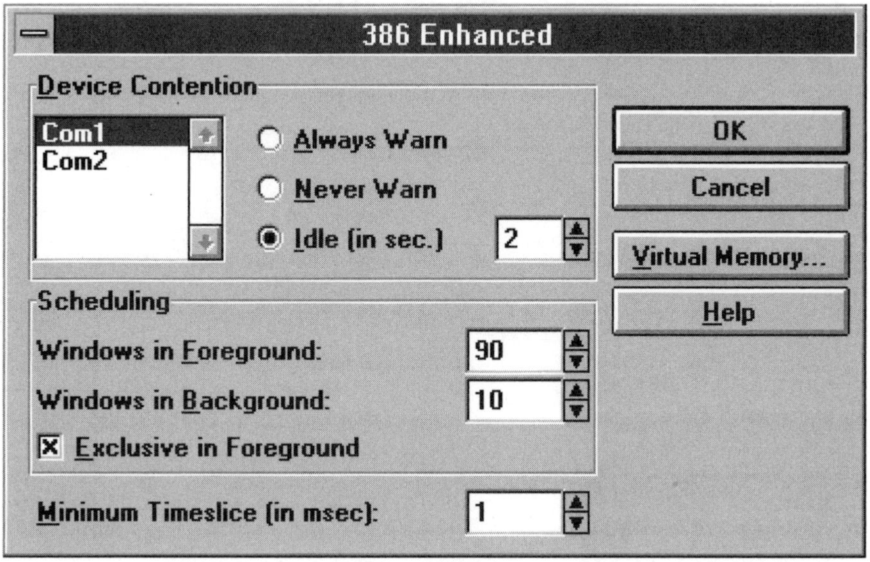

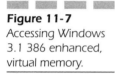

Figure 11-6
Windows 3.1 386 enhanced is found in control panel.

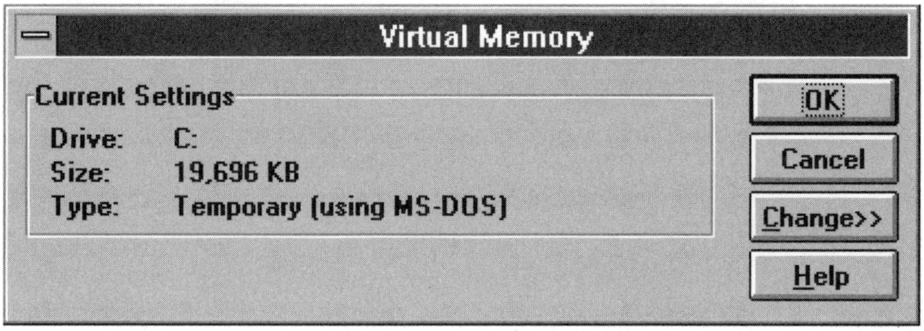

386 Enhanced

Device Contention

Com1
Com2

○ Always Warn

○ Never Warn

◉ Idle (in sec.)   2

OK

Cancel

Virtual Memory...

Help

Scheduling

Windows in Foreground: 90

Windows in Background: 10

☒ Exclusive in Foreground

Minimum Timeslice (in msec):   1

Figure 11-7
Accessing Windows 3.1 386 enhanced, virtual memory.

Virtual Memory

Current Settings

Drive: C:

Size: 19,696 KB

Type: Temporary (using MS-DOS)

OK

Cancel

Change>>

Help

Figure 11-8

Changing swap file
settings in
Windows 3.1.

Virtual Memory

Current Settings

Drive: C:
Size: 19,696 KB
Type: Temporary (using MS-DOS)

OK

Cancel

Change>>

Help

New Settings

Drive: c: [ms-dos_6]

Type: Permanent

Space Available: 388,832 KB
Maximum Size: 278,608 KB
Recommended Size: 51,439 KB

New Size: 51439 KB

[X] Use 32-Bit Disk Access

and will ask you if you want to make the partition active now. Confirm this, and DOS will report that the partition is set active and tell you to hit "Esc" to reboot the machine. Remove the floppy from drive A: and hit "Esc". The PC will reboot and come up just like your old PC, except it will be faster, you will have more free disk space, and you will have a spare hard drive (D:) that you can use for data or backups. Turn the PC off and mount the drives into their bays, making sure to use at least three screws each, replace the cover and you're done.

There is one final task for Windows 3.1 and Windows for Workgroups users. The first time you enter Windows after swapping your boot drive, the system may report that the permanent swap file is corrupt and prompt you to approve setting the file length to zero bytes. This is normal, so go ahead and confirm the prompt. If you get kicked out of Windows or the PC freezes at this point, reboot and start Windows again. Go to "386 Enhanced" which is found under "Control Panel" in the "Main" group, and choose "Virtual Memory." Accept the default settings for the swap file, save the changes and exit.

Replacing an Old Non-IDE Drive with an IDE Drive

If you have a 286 system or older, you can install a small IDE hard drive, like an old 40 MB, but I would recommend upgrading the motherboard and adding a large drive instead. Do not get involved with upgrading the BIOS on a 286 in order to accommodate a larger hard drive. You can buy a much more capable 486 motherboard, complete with CPU, for the cost of the new BIOS chip. You can read this section for tips if you are proceeding with an upgrade to a 286 system or older, but you will have to follow special instructions for jumper settings that are included with the 40-MB hard drive, and you will see minimal performance gain as the end result.

If you are replacing an old non-IDE drive with an IDE drive, you will need to purchase a SIDE controller. IDE drives will usually not work in systems with other hard drives, except for SCSI drives, and if you already have a SCSI controller you should be using a SCSI drive for the upgrade. If you want to transfer all of your old software from the old drive to the new IDE drive, you will have to use an intermediate storage location. The best way to complete this procedure is to use a portable tape backup, or to use a product like Laplink to transfer all of your data to another computer with enough storage space on its hard drive. If the PC is connected to a LAN, copy the drivers and the NETSTART batch file to floppy, than copy your whole hard drive to a temporary directory on the server. Otherwise, you will have to back up any important data on floppy and reinstall all of the operating system and applications software from floppy disks. In any event, before we begin you should create a boot floppy by putting a floppy disk in the A: drive and typing "FORMAT A: /S". Then type "COPY C:\DOS\FDISK.EXE A:" and "COPY C:\DOS\FORMAT.EXE A:". If you have an old version of DOS, and the system reports "File not found", repeat the same step substituting ".COM" in the place of ".EXE".

Remove the old hard disk controller, which may or may not double as a floppy controller. If the ribbon cable from the floppy disk drive(s) connects to a different adapter, remove that component also. If the ribbon cable for the floppy disk drive(s) connects directly to the motherboard, the easiest approach is to leave it there and set a jumper on the SIDE card to "Disable floppy controller". Now you will want to remove the old I/O adapter, unless the small ribbon cables to the "Com" and "LPT" ports are attached to the motherboard. In this instance you should use the jumpers on the SIDE adapter to set the Com port addresses to "Com3" and "Com4" and the LPT address to "LPT2:". Now you can remove the old hard drive and install the new IDE hard drive, checking that the jumpers are set for master or single. Make sure you connect the new ribbon cable with the red stripe to the end of the connector labeled 1 or 2, although the cable should be keyed to fit correctly on the new drive. Connect the power lead that was on the old hard drive to the new hard drive, and connect the two wire HDD LED lead to the new SIDE card, if one was attached to the old drive controller. Use the Com and LPT port connectors that come with the new SIDE card, and mount them in an open slot on the back of the case. Connect the floppy disk drive ribbon cable to the SIDE adapter, if it isn't already attached to the motherboard, and insert the adapter into a bus slot and secure with a screw.

Start up the computer and enter CMOS Setup by hitting Delete after the memory count. If this does not bring you into CMOS Setup and no message like "Crtl-S Now to Enter Setup" is displayed, you have a very old system and will need the original documentation and a special Setup disk to continue. Enter the "Standard Setup" menu choice, or the first menu choice offered, and enter the hard drive parameters provided on the label or in the documentation of the new disk for the C: drive. Save the settings, place your boot floppy in drive A:, and the system will reboot to the "A:\>" prompt. Sometimes, the system does not try to read the floppy drive, and instead merely flashes the drive light, then goes on to report "missing operating system" and freezes. In this case, you must reboot, enter CMOS setup, go to "Advanced Options", or a similarly titled menu choice (normally the second on the list) and change the "Boot Sequence" from "C: A:" to "A: C:". Save and exit, and the system will now boot from the floppy drive.

If the new hard drive is greater than 512 MB, run the install software included, following the instructions carefully. Next, unless the install software for a greater than 512-MB drive has told you to skip this step, type "FDISK" at the "A:\>" prompt, select "1. Create DOS partition or logical drive", and "1. Create primary partition". Next choose "Use all available space for DOS partition," after which FDISK will report the partition has been created and will reboot the system on "Esc." Type "FORMAT C: /S", and DOS will prepare the new hard drive for the operating system. This may take a couple minutes, and when the job is completed, you will be asked to enter a volume name. You can do so, or hit return to accept a blank volume label. FORMAT will also report how many free bytes you have. If you only have 500 million or so free bytes (536,870,912), and you have purchased a larger drive, something went wrong with the special driver install software. You can try running the install software again, or call them for technical support. This is not a hardware problem; you've done everything else correctly.

Now you can reinstall all of your old software. If you used a tape backup, first you will have to re-install the tape software. If you used Laplink with a parallel cable you will have to re-install the Laplink software, while if you used a serial cable, you can execute a "Remote Install" from the other PC. If you backed up onto a network, you will have to re-install the network drivers, log in, and then restore your data. If you had none of these means available, reinstall all of DOS and Windows, following the instructions on the disk labels, reinstall all of your application software, and copy your backed up data from floppies into the proper directories.

Adding a SCSI Drive

Systems that already have a SCSI hard drive were probably high-performance systems when they were built. For that reason, you probably won't want to bother changing the boot drive (the drive the operating system loads from). If you do want to change the boot drive, read the procedure for installing a second IDE hard drive as the master, and follow the same basic steps, except for substituting the SCSI jumper configuration discussed below for the IDE master/slave jumper configuration. If you are adding a SCSI drive(s) and controller to a system that previously had no SCSI devices installed, you will have to follow instructions provided to install the adapter and any accompanying software, before proceeding.

When your computer boots, you will see the SCSI adapter seeking SCSI devices and finding the hard drive, at which point it will report on the type of drive and the SCSI ID (probably zero). When one internal SCSI device is already present, the best way to proceed is to disable termination on your new drive and attach it to the SCSI bus, using a connector on the ribbon cable in the section between the adapter and the existing hard drive. If there are no connectors between the adapter and the existing hard drive, re-arrange the cable connections such that there are. If the ribbon cable only has two connectors on it, you will need to buy a new cable

($10 to $20). If your system has a SCSI adapter and both an internal and an external SCSI device(s), the procedure is exactly the same. However, if you had a SCSI adapter controlling external SCSI devices only, you will have to remove the terminators from the SCSI adapter itself, and leave them installed (usually default) on the new internal SCSI drive.

If you are adding an external SCSI hard drive with an adapter, because there were no SCSI devices in the system, the drive and the adapter must be terminated (default settings). If you are adding an external SCSI drive, and you have no external SCSI devices and one or more internal SCSI device(s) installed, you need to remove the terminators on the SCSI adapter and install a terminator on the new external drive. If you are adding an external SCSI hard drive, and there are already external SCSI devices present, put the hard drive nearest to the system box on the daisy chain, so it is connected directly to the adapter and the next external SCSI device.

Select a SCSI ID not used by any other device for your new drive, and attach a power connector. Then power up your system and note that the SCSI adapter now finds your new drive, along with the existing devices. If you have Windows 95 or NT, you will now go through the "Add new hardware" procedure, after which you will be able to use the new hard drive. If you are using DOS/Windows, you can FDISK and FORMAT the drive at this point. If your new hard drive is larger then 512 MB and the amount of free space reported is around five hun-

Figure 11-9
External SCSI cable
and terminator.

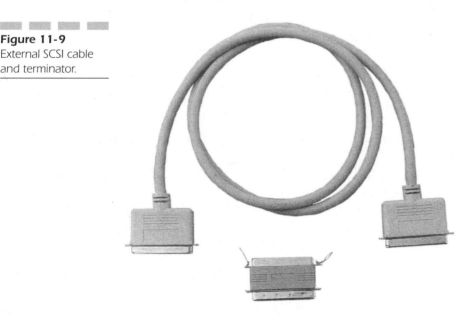

Figure 11-10
Adaptec SCSI card with terminators installed (three 8-pin packs horizontally along the top of the card under the wide SCSI cable connector.

dred million bytes (536,870,912), you need additional SCSI software to support the larger drive. Contact the drive maker and adapter maker, or check their WWW sites for software upgrades or information.

CD-ROM Drives

There are four different routes to go when adding a CD drive to a PC. Most readers will already have a single IDE hard drive in their PC, so the easiest and least expensive route is to buy an IDE CD drive and add it as the slave (see Installing IDE Hard Drives, Chapter 11). The next option is to buy a CD player, IDE or otherwise, that comes with its own controller or can be hooked to an existing sound card. The third route is to buy a multimedia upgrade kit (see Installing a Multimedia Upgrade Kit, Chapter 12), which includes a CD drive, sound card, speakers and several CD titles. The fourth choice is adding a SCSI CD, internal or external, which is easily connected to an existing SCSI bus (see Installing SCSI Hard Drives in the last section). Both SCSI and IDE CD drives are available in multi-CD changer units, like those in more expensive stereos, and SCSI CD drives also come in external versions.

Time and Cost for Upgrade

The majority of CD drives sold today are IDE drives. If you have a system with one IDE hard drive, you can add an IDE CD drive with no extra hardware required. If you have two IDE hard drives in your system, you will need to purchase another SIDE adapter ($15) to use as a secondary controller, unless your motherboard has both the primary and secondary IDE controllers on board. IDE CD drives start under $50 for older 4X speed, cost about $50 for the 6X speed, all the way up to over $150 for the 16X speed. Pricing for CD drives including a proprietary controller runs about $10 higher. SCSI drives range in price from under $80 for old 2X models to over $300 for 8X external multi-CD changers. CD drives that are supported by a proprietary connector on an existing sound card in your machine (Panasonic, Mitsumi, Sony) are often older 2X drives and can be found for under $30. In some instances your PC will be out of free power supply connectors, and you will have to buy a "Y" splitter (less than $5). Adding a CD drive will take between 10 to 15 minutes, including installing the software.

Required Software (All CD Drives)

CD drives require a special software driver to operate, which is usually supplied on a floppy disk with the drive kit. If the CD is being added to a Windows 95 or NT environment, software support will probably be included in the operating system, but follow the instructions that ship with the drive. There are two pieces of software that need to be installed in the DOS/Windows environment. The first program is the low-level driver provided by the manufacturer, which lets the BIOS communicate with the CD like a fixed disk drive. If you are adding a SCSI CD to a PC that already has SCSI drives attached, this support may already be installed. The second piece of software is MSCDEX.EXE (MicroSoft CD Extension), and is normally included both with the drive, and in your DOS and Windows directories. The install program should pick the latest version of MSCDEX to handle the DOS/Windows interface for your CD. Software upgrades are widely available on the Internet.

The software driver installed in the CONFIG.SYS file will use a line looking something like "DEVICE=C:\???\???CD.SYS /D:XXXCD", where the question marks are the name of your specific software driver and "XXXCD" is know as the Device Signature. The installation software will have to add a line to your AUTOEXEC.BAT file that looks like "C:\DOS\MSCDEX.EXE /D:XXXCD", where "XXXCD" is the same device signature used when installing the device driver in the CONFIG.SYS file.

Windows 95 and Windows NT make use of these extra drivers when running in DOS mode, so they are generally installed on these systems also.

Adding an IDE CD Drive to a System with an IDE Hard Drive

The IDE CD drive has a set of master/slave jumpers, just like IDE hard drives. The CD drive must be set as the slave if it is installed on the primary IDE controller. The order of the two drives on the ribbon cable is unimportant, although the CD drive is usually placed on the end connector due to cable length considerations. The red wire in the ribbon cable should be adjacent to pins 1 or 2 on the connector of all the IDE devices (both drives and the controller). If the system reports a hard drive error and won't boot up, check that the hard drive is not an older type that has a Single jumper, and needs a slave-present jumper to be added. Install the software and verify that the drive is functioning before putting the cover back on the system box.

Adding an IDE CD Drive to a System with Two IDE Hard Drives

The master/slave jumper on the CD drive should be set to master. If you have a secondary IDE controller integrated on the motherboard, you can attach the ribbon cable from the CD drive to it and won't need another adapter. If you're unsure whether or not there is a secondary IDE connector on the motherboard and don't want to open up the system box yet, you can check in the CMOS setup. Hit "Del" after memory count during power up, and check the "Advanced Setup" menu or similarly named option, which should be the second or third menu choice. If you can't find setup options for your primary and secondary IDE controllers, they aren't a part of the motherboard, which is normal for most older hand-me-down PCs. If you need to add a secondary IDE controller, it is easiest to buy an IDE "paddle card," which has an IDE and floppy drive controller without all of the extra ports provided on a SIDE card. This way, you only have to set the jumpers for "secondary controller" and "disable floppy controller" on the new adapter, instead of having to disable or reassign all of the existing ports as well. The red wire in the ribbon cable should be adjacent to pins 1 or 2 on the connector of the drive and the controller. Install the software and verify that the drive is functioning before putting the cover back on the system box.

Adding a CD Drive with a Proprietary Adapter

Many of the early CD drives and some later models ship with their own interface adapter. In these cases, you will have to follow the instructions that come with the kit. If you are attaching the drive to the interface on an existing sound card, you will probably need the sound card software and documentation to get it working. Most proprietary adapters and all sound cards come with an extra 3- or 4-pin connector block, for direct connection to the audio output of the CD drive. This is needed when the CD drive is used to play music discs. Install the software and verify the drive works before putting the cover back on the system box.

Figure 11-11
A CD-ROM
only adapter.

Adding a SCSI CD drive

Most people won't want to buy a SCSI CD drive unless they already have a SCSI adapter in their PC or they need a large capacity external CD changer. Another reason for buying a SCSI CD drive is if you own a CD recorder and want the ability to make copies of prerecorded CDs. If you are adding your first SCSI controller to the system, you'll need to install the SCSI peripheral interface manager software that comes with the controller. This is the software you will see at boot time, reporting on the SCSI devices installed in the system. Many SCSI CD drives are sold as "bare" drives, i.e., no cables, no software, limited documentation. You may have to re-run the install software that came with your existing SCSI adapter in order to get the CD working.

You can install up to seven different SCSI devices on a single adapter, using a multiconnector ribbon cable inside the system box, or daisy chained (serially connected) SCSI cables outside the system box. There are two important facts to understand about a SCSI bus. First, both ends of the bus must be terminated, which involves using on-board resistors for internal devices, or attaching a SCSI terminator pack to the daisy chain connector on an external device. Second, each device on the bus has a unique ID, a number between zero and six (the adapter itself is number seven). A boot device (normally a hard drive) must be installed as ID zero or one. CD drives are usually sold with the default ID set at two, but you should note the IDs of your existing SCSI devices and make sure that you have picked a free number for the CD drive before proceeding.

When your computer boots, you will see the SCSI adapter seeking SCSI devices and finding the CD drive, at which point it will report on the type of drive and the SCSI ID. With one internal SCSI device installed, the best way to proceed is to disable termination on your new drive and attach it to the SCSI bus, using a connector on the ribbon cable in the section between the adapter and the existing hard drive. If there are no connectors between the adapter and the existing hard drive, re-arrange the cable connections such that they are. If the ribbon cable only has two connectors on it, you will need to buy a new cable ($10 to $20). If your system has a SCSI adapter, and both an internal and an external SCSI devices, the procedure is exactly the same. However, if you had a SCSI adapter controlling external SCSI devices only, you will have to remove the terminators from the SCSI adapter, and leave them installed (usually default) on the new internal SCSI hard drive.

If you are adding an external SCSI CD drive with an adapter, because there were no preexisting SCSI devices in the system, the drive and the adapter must be terminated (default settings). If you have no external SCSI devices and one internal SCSI device installed are adding an external SCSI CD drive, you need to remove the terminators on the SCSI adapter and install a terminator on the new external drive. If you are adding an external SCSI hard drive and there are already external SCSI devices present, connect the CD drive directly to the adapter, and connect the next SCSI device in line to the CD drive. Test the drive before putting the cover back on the system box.

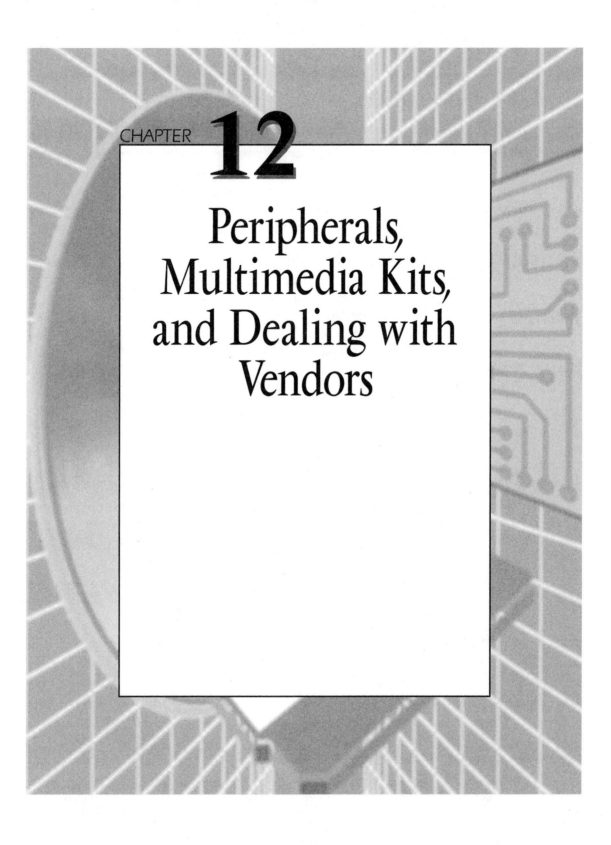

CHAPTER **12**

Peripherals, Multimedia Kits, and Dealing with Vendors

Joysticks

Joysticks are used almost exclusively for game playing, and therefore you should consult your game documentation before picking a joystick. There are two main types of joysticks: analog and digital. Analog joysticks have been in use since the beginning of time and are supported on the standard game port you will find on all but the oldest PCs. Digital joysticks were introduced in just the past two years and require a special game port, found only on some upscale sound cards or the newest PCs. Digital joysticks boast higher precision, reliability, and "drift" elimination, the tendency of the cursor to wander with the stick in neutral position. In most cases, you can add an analog joystick to an existing computer without having to open the system box. The challenge comes in trying to learn how to fly an F-15 without crashing into the ground or your wingman at seemingly random intervals.

Time and Cost for Upgrades

Joysticks cost between about $20 and $140, depending on the brand, number of buttons, and mechanical design. If you buy a digital joystick but don't have a digital game port installed in your PC, you can spend about $30 on a special game port card or buy a sound card that supports digital joysticks. If you buy an analog joystick and don't have a port conflict, the total installation time will be under five minutes, just long enough to clean all the junk off your PC so you can pull it out and get access to the back.

Adding an Analog Joystick

Your analog joystick gets plugged into the game port on the back of the PC, a 15-pin female port. The most likely problem you'll encounter is not the lack of a game port, but the existence of two of them! Game ports have been standard equipment on SIDE adapters, enhanced motherboards, and sound cards for more than five years. If you have two game ports in your system, try using the one on your sound card first. The sound card is easily identified by the three or four audio jacks on it (and sometimes an external volume dial). If the joystick doesn't work on the sound card, try it on the other game port. If it still doesn't work, you'll have to open up the case and take out the SIDE adapter. If the SIDE adapter provides the only game port in your system, you'll want to make sure that the game port is enabled and that the cable to the actual connector is on properly, with the red or striped wire in the ribbon oriented towards pin 1 or 2 on the connector. If you have a sound card with a game port, you'll want to make sure that the game port on the SIDE adapter is disabled.

The easiest way to test whether or not your joystick is functioning properly is to use the test software included with the joystick, or the Microsoft Diagnostic (MSD). Run MSD by typing "MSD" at the DOS prompt, then select the "Other Adapters" button, which should show "Game Port" next to the button. The diagnostic will show two categories, "Joystick A" and "Joystick B", which is a hangover from the two-button, dual-joystick days. Today, a single joystick incorporates so much functionality that it uses the resources of both "A" and "B." MSD reads the settings only at the moment you select the "Other Adapters" button, after which moving the stick or pressing the buttons will have no effect on the numbers shown. With no joystick connected, or the joystick connected to the wrong game port, the "X" and "Y" rows will all be zero, and the "Button" rows will all be "ON."

If MSD sees a joystick, with no buttons pressed and the stick in the neutral position, the "X" and "Y" values for "Joystick A" will be numbers in the range from 30 to 50, and the "X" and "Y" values for "Joystick B" may be zeros or 2-digit numbers, depending on whether or not there are any dials on the base of the joystick, and where they are set. If you want to test the joystick further, you can do so by exiting back to the main MSD menu, holding the stick or a dial all the way in one direction and pressing a button, then selecting "Other Adapters" again. Any button that is pressed should then show up as "OFF." When "Other Adapters" is selected with the joystick pushed all the way forward, the "Y" value for "Joystick A" should be zero, and the "X" value should remain unchanged. When the joystick is pulled all the way back, "Y" will have its maximum value, and "X" will be unchanged. When the joystick is pushed to the right, "X" will be maximum and "Y" will be unchanged, and when the joystick is pushed to the left, "X" will be zero and "Y" will be unchanged. If the zero values mentioned above aren't exactly zero, or the "unchanged values" changes a little, don't worry about it. This is just an example of the drift inherent in the analog system. The "X" and "Y" values for "Joystick B" vary in the same way with any dials on the base of the joystick, or with the second joystick on a dual system.

Adding a Digital Joystick

There are two types of digital joysticks. There are real digital joysticks, which will almost certainly require you to also buy a new game controller for your hand-me-down PC, and there are fake or "software" digital joysticks. The way to tell the difference is in whether or not they require a digital game port. If the joystick will work on the same game port as an analog joystick, it isn't truly a digital joystick. Digital joysticks and the associated controller you'll probably need to connect them may run over $100, so they are for the serious gamer only.

Multimedia Upgrade Kit

A multimedia upgrade kit includes a CD drive, sound card, speakers, microphone, control and application software, and normally has a bunch of CD titles bundled with it. One advantage that purchasing a multimedia kit has over acquiring the parts separately is you are guaranteed simple hookup of the CD drive. There will be two custom cables supplied to connect the CD drive to the sound card: a ribbon cable for data and a stereo connection for music CDs to be played. The only cost benefit of buying a multimedia kit is the bundled software. This is something that must be examined according to the titles included. Many CD titles are so-called "shovelware," collections of clip-art, out-of-copyright text, warmed-over shareware, and three-year-old versions of current titles. These same CDs can be purchased in quantity packs for two dollars each. Other bundles may include reference works, edutainment software, and games that would cost from $10 to $50 each if purchased separately.

Time and Cost for Upgrade

Installing a multimedia kit takes no longer than installing a sound card, which is the main part of the job. A half hour should suffice for most people. The titles that come with the kit should not be installed as applications unless you actually intend to use them. They take up some space on the hard drive for the executable section of the program, and they often make modifications to your system files that alter the memory usage and performance in ways you might not like. Multimedia kits cost between $150 to $450, depending on the speed of the CD drive, the quality of the sound card and software, and the quantity and quality of titles.

Installing a Multimedia Upgrade Kit

The procedure for installing a multimedia upgrade kit is identical to installing a sound card and a CD-ROM, which mainly means carefully following the instructions. Because any additional components are connected to the sound card, and not the motherboard, the multimedia kit is essentially a system within a system. The only part you may need that is not necessarily included in the kit is a power splitter, required for the CD drive if all of the power supply leads are already in use. The sound card included in a multimedia kit is actually several adapters in one, so don't be surprised by the number of jumpers that must be selected, or the number of options you must confirm with a PnP (Plug-and-Play) adapter. See the sections on installing a sound card or installing a CD drive if the instructions with the upgrade kit are incomplete.

Adding a New Printer to Your System

Most printers will be capable of printing simple text pages in the DOS environment immediately after being connected to an active printer port. To print graphics, special fonts, and colors, or to take advantage of any of the advanced features, you have to install the accompanying software driver. To use a printer in the Windows environment, you must always install a driver. New printers are normally shipped with the latest release of their software driver for DOS/Windows, as well as Windows 95 and Windows NT. All of the Windows operating environments include a library of printer drivers on their basic installation disks. Always use the latest release from the manufacturer when prompted by Windows for the disk with the printer driver. Use the "Add New Hardware" option in "Control Panel" when adding a printer to Windows 95 or Windows NT, and click the "Printers" icon under "Control Panel" to add a printer in Windows 3.1 or Windows for Workgroups.

Figure 12-1
Windows 3.1 control
panel.

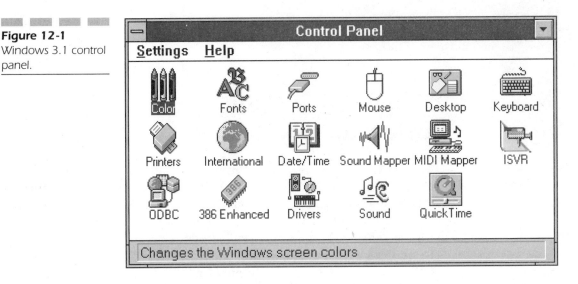

You may run into situations where you don't receive Windows driver software with your printer (perhaps a hand-me-down printer), and
Windows does not list your exact printer model as an option. Pick the
printer closest to the one you have. For example, if you've inherited a

Figure 12-2
Adding a printer to
Windows 3.1.

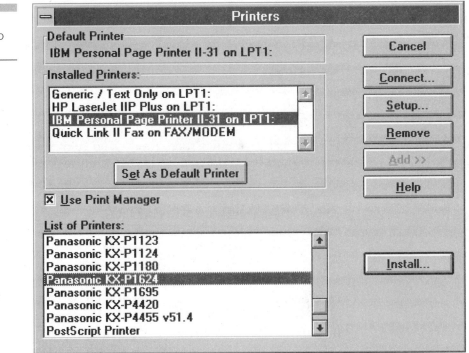

Panasonic KXP-2624, and your original Windows disks only list a KXP-1624, pick this printer. If the choice isn't this obvious, you may have to experiment with a couple of drivers to find which works best. Most Postscript printers will work pretty well with the generic Postscript driver, independent of the brand, though you should certainly use the exact manufacturer's software if it's available. If you have an ancient dot matrix or a printer that looks like a typewriter, chose "Generic/Text Only" in Windows.

Dealing with PC Shops for Upgrades and Repairs

If you don't want to get involved with upgrading or repairing your PC, and you don't have a friend or moonlighting technician to turn to, your only option is to take your PC to a shop. PC shops come in many flavors, from hundred-million-dollar national chains to the mom-and-pop stores in 1,000 square feet on a side street. Dealing with national chains gets you a certain consistency in parts pricing and labor rates, but if you are willing to be part of the decision-making process, a small store usually has more knowledgeable help. Computer repair is not rocket science. This means that the store employees who speak so glibly about gigabytes and megahertz may have learned everything they know by reading this book a week before you. Never walk into any computer store without already knowing what you want and how much you are willing to pay. An ethical technician is a better find than a skilled one.

There are no rules for pricing parts used in upgrades or repairs, but an average small PC store will mark up parts added to existing systems by 50 percent. The markup on a given part often reflects the value, so that a $10 adapter may be marked up to $25, while a $275 printer will sell for $350. On top of this, there is an hourly labor charge, usually $50 or more, but some shops will charge by the half hour, or they will flat-rate certain procedures. Most small shops are willing to bargain, within limits, and may have used parts that they can use to upgrade your machine at a steep discount. By the same token, don't be shy about asking for all of the original documentation when you pay for an upgrade, even the useless hard drive booklet. This helps prevent stores, both national and local, from selling you second-hand parts as new.

Figure 12-3
The trustworthy
technician.

The labor charge and general inconvenience of dragging your PC in
and out of the car make up a large part of the upgrade cost, so it makes
sense to do all the upgrading you may need in one shot. If you are getting a CD drive or a sound card, think seriously about getting both
at the same time. If you are getting a CD drive or a multimedia kit,
make sure you have a 1-MB video adapter, or buy one at the same time.
If you are upgrading the memory (RAM), and your hard drive is under
200 MB, upgrade the hard drive at the same time. Always buy a new
motherboard with a new CPU, unless you have a brand-name machine

that has a nonstandard motherboard with an upgradable CPU. Always remember to call first and ask if you can leave the keyboard and monitor at home. Never spend more than a couple hundred bucks upgrading a PC unless you simply can't afford $800 for a brand new loaded Pentium, sans monitor. If you're really in a bind, you can usually find a middle-of-the-road 486 on the second-hand market for around $300.

If your PC suffers a complete failure, i.e., you can't get it to work, that's an easy sort of thing for your local shop to fix. However, if you have intermittent problems—like the system freezing or rebooting itself, occasional video failure or drive read errors—the speed and cost of repair are entirely dependent on how much you can tell the technician. Write down any error messages that appear on the screen, and which software programs you are using when lockups occur or error messages appear. Seemingly unimportant factors like whether you keep your word-processing files on floppy disk or the hard drive may help the technician quickly diagnose the problem. Technicians do have diagnostics software, but it's pretty useless for most intermittent problems. If you bring a computer to a shop without supplying a detailed description of the circumstances of the intermittent failure, you will either end up paying for parts you don't really need or paying for the labor of a technician playing with your computer and waiting for the problem to occur.

The single most important thing you can do to educate yourself about current pricing is to go out and buy the current issue of *Computer Shopper*, published by Ziff Davis. It's as thick as a phone book, and the index isn't always useful because many advertisement pages lack page numbers, but don't be intimidated. Open it up at random, flip a few pages in either direction, and you'll find the current pricing for the parts reviewed in this book. Check the price in a couple of different ads, knock off 5 percent, and you will know pretty accurately what your computer store is paying for the part(s) you want.

Dealing with Nationwide Warranty Providers

Most PCs are sold with warranties ranging from one to three years, and this almost always includes at least one year of parts and labor. The brand-name computer manufacturers you buy from are rarely the actual providers of warranty service, even though they may take your phone call and handle the problem report. Warranty repairs are generally handled by national services, who often take a flat fee of around $20 per computer to assume responsibility for the labor involved in the repairs. Some of these warranty service providers really employ large numbers of full-time technicians all over the country, who are often trained to do repair work on many types of electronic equipment. Other warranty providers have no real technical employees at all and simply call a PC shop in your local area and fix a price for the repair.

In both cases, the process goes something like this. You call an 800 number to report a problem and ask for your guaranteed 24-hour or 72-hour repair. The telephone representative tries to get you to troubleshoot the problem over the telephone, leading you through complicated software procedures if the PC is still functioning, or asking you to check connections and listen for certain sounds if the computer won't boot. Eventually, the telephone representative tells you that a technician will be out on a certain day, and if you're lucky, the representative tells you morning or afternoon. The company you bought the computer from then overnights (second day for 72-hour warranties) the part to your home or office, where the technician from the service provider meets it and installs it in your system.

If the telephone troubleshooting session went well, this will probably result in a fixed computer. However, if the problem was of an intermittent nature, the solution isn't always obvious, and the new part may fix nothing. Sometimes, when a certain model of computer is experiencing a high failure rate of a particular component, the manufacturer will try replacing that component first, even if the problem doesn't seem to be related to it. There is nothing the technician who comes to your house can do for you if the computer isn't fixed after the repair, unless the manufacturer has a special deal with the technician to provide parts. You will have to get back on the phone and schedule another repair attempt. One of the reasons repairs are done this way is that the manufacturers often use remanufactured parts, which have come back as defective but have later been verified good or sent overseas for repair. They would lose too much money if they had to start paying a warranty provider for new parts.

One of my favorite anecdotes from working in the computer industry involved a man who had once been the national customer service manager for a major retail computer store chain. While interviewing a potential new service hire, he prompted the technician over and over again with the question, "What does a PC technician fix?" He finally got the answer he was waiting for, "The customer." This attitude is prevalent among many computer manufacturers. What the customer-service representative really wants is to get you to stop calling. This is done by fixing your computer, suggesting a work-around, or transferring the blame to another party (i.e., you or a software company). Which one of these happens is largely dependent on you. Never allow a computer manufacturer to procrastinate a repair based on the approach that it will be easier to troubleshoot when it gets worse. This is comparable to your mechanic telling you not to complain about the brake job until you rear-end somebody.

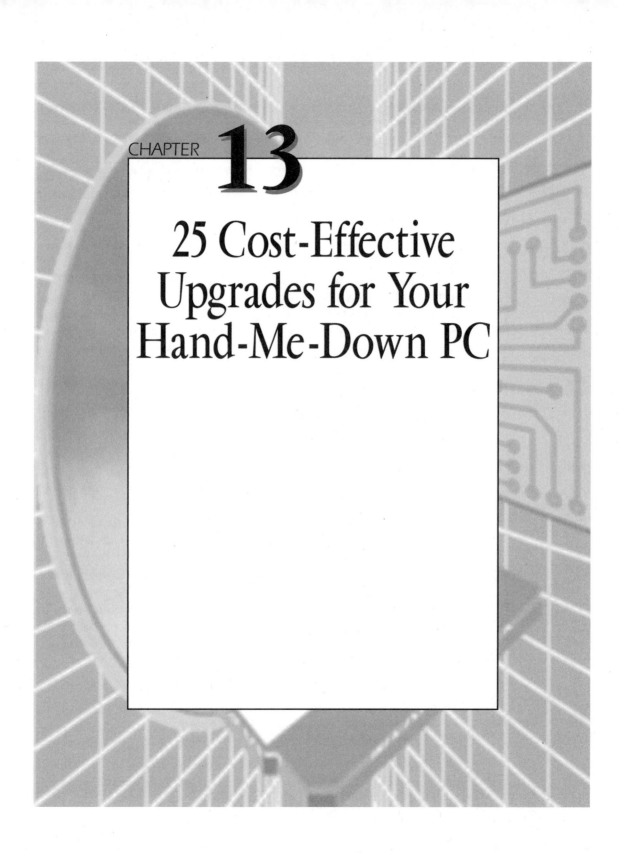

CHAPTER 13

25 Cost-Effective Upgrades for Your Hand-Me-Down PC

Before making any upgrade to your PC, you must first ask yourself, "Where is this going to stop?" If you are happy with the basic performance of your PC and are adding enhancements like a CD recorder or a laser printer, which can later be moved to a new machine, than your investment is safe. However, if you have an older 386 or 486 and you are trying to prepare for an upgrade to Windows 95 or a full multimedia PC, you must compare how much money you will be spending in $50 and $150 increments with the price of a new PC.

For example, $1,000 spent at your local office superstore will buy a brand new 150-MHz Pentium multimedia PC, complete with a 14" monitor and loaded with Windows 95. The PC will come with 16-MB RAM, a 1-MB PCI video adapter, a 33.6-K modem, a 1.2-GB hard drive, and a 10X CD-ROM. The components are all new, preassembled and tested together, and come with a one-year, on-site warranty.

By contrast, if you start with an older 386 or 486 PC with 4 MB or 8 MB Ram, a 300-MB or smaller hard drive, and no multimedia capability, you will need to replace everything except the case, the 1.44 floppy drive, and the monitor to end up with a modern Pentium PC. The case is only worth $30 or $40 dollars, and sports your five-year-old power supply. Even at the best mail-order pricing, you'll have a hard time putting together a machine cheaper than the $1000 special. However, if you keep your monitor, rather than passing your old system on whole to the next victim, you'll cut $200 off the price of the new PC.

On the other hand, if you have a newer 486 and you're happy with the performance and just want to add a CD or a sound card, you can do so for under $100. Next year, when the 200-MHz Pentiums are selling for $1,000, and the 300-MHz Pentium IIs are the rage, you'll be glad you didn't throw good money after bad. The most cost-effective upgrade you can make to your PC is the upgrade that you need, because you're going to have to spend the money somewhere anyway. However, doubling your RAM, getting a faster CD or a bigger hard drive, even replacing the motherboard because you got a nice tax refund, rarely produces the performance gains you expect, and often goes unnoticed.

5 Upgrades under $50

The upgrades you can do for under $50 are likely to have a tremendous impact on your system, because with the exception of adding a joystick, these are upgrades that are only necessary for older PCs. Upgrading to 16 MB of RAM, to a 1-MB video card, adding a CD drive or a modem, will give your PC new capabilities to use software that wouldn't run previously. The sub-$50 upgrade is the most cost-effective upgrade you can make to your system box.

Upgrade to 16-MB RAM

Upgrading your RAM from 4 MB to 16 MB will almost certainly put a smile on your face when using Windows. If you already have 8 MB, upgrading to 16 MB will be less noticeable with older Windows versions, but save a lot of waiting time in Windows 95. The main wild card with this upgrade is what kind of CPU and RAM you already have. The worst scenario is if your PC uses 30-pin SIMMs only, and you have already populated all 8 sockets with 1-MB SIMMs to get to 8 MB. You will have to purchase four new 30-pin 4-MB SIMMs and remove four existing SIMMs to install them. The silver lining is that you'll end up with 20 MB.

The next worse case is if you have a Pentium with 8 MB installed. Because the Pentium requires that 72-pin SIMMs be installed two at a time, this means that you already have two 4-MB SIMMs installed, and would have to add two more 4-MB SIMMs to reach exactly 16 MB. 4-MB SIMMs are the least cost-effective of the 72-pin SIMMs and many Pentium motherboards only have four SIMM sockets, so you will have to start throwing SIMMs away if you upgrade again in the future. Give some serious thought to upgrading to 40 MB instead, buy adding two 16-MB SIMMs.

Upgrade to 1-MB Video (True Color)

This is one of the best upgrades you can perform, whether your current video adapter is a 256-K VGA adapter or a 512-K SVGA adapter. Not only do you end up with the ability to view millions of colors at VGA resolution (640 × 480), but you'll probably end up with faster response time at lower color settings and an improved control over your monitor's electronics. Many leading CD producers still fine-tune their products to display decently at 256 colors, but the difference when viewing a photographic quality image will astound you. In fact, color photographs usually look better on good VGA displays than on prints, because they are much brighter and they scale up to fill the screen.

Add a 4X CD-ROM

This is an upgrade for older PCs that have no CD-ROM, and 4X and 6X drives are the least expensive available. Why should you add the slowest CD drive you can find? Well, if you have more money, spend as much as you like, but it won't make much noticeable difference unless you are running presentation software or games that use large amounts of full-screen video. Music CDs play at 1X speed, and seek time (how long it takes to find the sought-after information on a drive) varies by less than a factor of two from the fastest drive to the slowest. A 4X CD drive (even a 2X for that matter), will give you the ability to load software, play music CDs and games, run interactive encyclopedias, anything you want.

Add a 14.4-K or 28.8-K Modem

Which modem you choose depends strictly on whether or not the $10 difference in price matters to you. The primary reason for adding a modem to a computer is to get on the Internet and the World Wide Web. If your only desire is to send and receive e-mail, the modem speed makes no difference since the transfer time is so short in either case. If you intend to do a lot of Web browsing, you may as well buy the faster modem, but the speed at which images download to your computer is more dependent on the time of day and the quality of your access provider than the speed of the modem. Hopefully, this situation will clear up some time in 1998 and you'll see the speed you pay for, but I wouldn't hold my breath.

Add a Joystick

If you don't play a lot of games, you don't need a joystick. Some people who have joysticks still prefer to use the keyboard for navigating in some games, but that has as much to do with habit as efficiency. The games that benefit the most from joysticks are those where you have to move in three dimensions, like flying a plane. In combat games, some people prefer the joystick buttons for firing weapons, rather than using two hands or stretching fingers around the keyboard. Don't forget to determine whether you need an analog or digital stick before going out to buy one.

5 Upgrades under $100

Four of the suggested upgrades for under $100 are performance upgrades. A faster CD-ROM, 586 motherboard and CPU, 32 MB of RAM, or a 33.6-K modem, are rarely necessary to meet the minimum requirements of a new software package. What they can do, especially the 586 motherboard and CPU, is speed up your computer so much that you or your children can be happy using it for another couple years, rather than going out and spending $1,000 or more on a new box.

Upgrade to a 10X CD-ROM

If you want to buy the fastest CD-ROM available at any given time, you'll have to pay a premium of an extra $100 to $200, which at press time will bring you a 16X player. The wiser choice for most people is to set an upper limit, $100 in this case, and buy the fastest CD-ROM that matches the price. A 10X CD-ROM is capable of transferring movies, pictures, sound, and other data from the CD to the computer five times faster than the 2X players which set the multimedia standard until mid-1995, or two and a half times faster than the 4X players that replaced them. With very few exceptions, software developers make sure their applications will run with 4X players, in order not to lose out on potential market share. The advantage of the faster CD comes into play with transfer intensive applications, like a CD loaded with pictures, video, or large database files. While the performance gain from a $50 CD drive to a $100 CD drive is several fold, the performance gain from the $100 CD drive to the $250 CD drive is barely over 50 percent. This relationship will continue to hold as transfer rates approach 20X and beyond.

Upgrade to 32-MB RAM

If you work with large images, keep many programs open at once in Windows, or have purchased software that recommends more than 16 MB of RAM, this is an inexpensive way to extend the life of your PC. When you switch between Windows and your hard drive light flashes merrily away for 30 or more seconds, it means that your operating system is using the hard drive as "virtual memory." Upgrading your PC to 32-MB RAM should make most of these window swaps instantaneously. Many professional software packages are now suggesting 24 MB as the minimum amount of installed RAM, and at today's RAM prices, you can get to 32 MB for less than $100 on newer PCs, even if you have to throw all of your old RAM away.

Upgrade to a 33.6-K Modem

This is the fastest standard modem available, and integrates the latest in hardware compression technology to squeeze out even higher apparent speeds where supported. U.S. Robotics, the world's largest modem manufacturer, introduced 56-K modems in early 1997, but these only work with a digital downstream link. Most 33.6-K modems sold by US Robotics are upgradable to 56 K, check their Web site at www.usr.com for details. The same caution applies here as with 14.4-K and 28.8-K modems. If you want fast surfing on the World Wide Web, be aware that most of the delays are due to high traffic, oversubscribed service providers, and overtaxed servers. The increasing adoption of streaming audio and video on the Web should make this problem worse before it gets better.

Upgrade to 586 Motherboard and CPU

This may seem like a strange upgrade to be suggesting, but for under $100 you can buy a high clock speed (133 MHz or better) clone 586 complete with motherboard. While not a true Pentium, this is a cheap way to really double or quadruple the speed of old 486 systems. If you have an old 386 or 286 case you really love, this is a great way to keep it around as something other than a paperweight. The hardest part about making this upgrade is deciding when enough is enough. Will you continue to limp by on 4 MB of RAM and your 200-MB hard drive? Is it a good time to get a PCI video adapter? At least all the SIDE adapter functions will be integrated on the motherboard along with a plug-and-play BIOS. Just make sure you aren't going to get within a couple hundred bucks of the cost of a new Pentium system before you start.

Add 16-bit Sound with Speakers

The least-expensive 16-bit sound card is just as good as the most expensive for most purposes, but play it safe and get a brand-name Creative Labs Sound Blaster unless you need to save a few bucks. Installing a sound card is one of the highest impact upgrades you can make. You'll get music and spoken narration with any applications or games that include sound, and that includes most products these days. You'll also be able to record your own voice, or rig up an Internet telephone. Sound is playing an increasing role on the Web, including music, sound effects, and news from foreign countries (in their native language). You can also get software to read computer screens, ideal for the visually impaired.

5 Upgrades under $150

The upgrades suggested for under $150 are generally aimed at dragging your hand-me-down PC into the present. Because the cost of the upgrade itself has risen over the $100 level, I wouldn't suggest doing any of these upgrades on a system slower than a 486DX 2/66. All five of these upgrades could be later migrated to a newer hand-me-down PC, but a brand new system will already incorporate a multimedia kit, Windows 95, and a multigigabyte hard drive, so think about these upgrades twice if you are considering eventually buying new.

Upgrade to an MPEG Video Adapter

This upgrade is strictly for the serious multimedia buff, since it is only useful for playing full screen, full motion video on your PC. If you have a newer Pentium PC, you can get pretty good performance out of MPEG software, which uses the CPU to decompress the video stream.

MPEG (Motion PEG) video came out of the evolution of the Joint Photographic Experts Group (JPEG), which is still a commonly used standard for photographic compression.

Upgrade to a Multimedia PC

A multimedia upgrade kit consists of a CD drive, a sound card (normally 16 bit), a microphone, speakers (usually in the 20-W to 60-W range), and a few CD titles, often an interactive encyclopedia and a few slightly out-of-date games. If you already have one or more of the above components, you may be better off buying the rest individually. However, if your sound card is 8 bit or if your CD drive is 2X or under, you're better off replacing these components while you have the case open. A multimedia PC will give you the ability to play music CDs on your system while you work, record your own music, play videos, listen to live streaming sound on the Web, even set up an Internet telephone. You'll need a minimum of a 486DX/33 to make this upgrade worthwhile, and the faster your CPU, the better any video or streaming-audio applications will work.

Upgrade to Windows 95

If you are new to the world of PCs and your computer is a faster 486 (66 MHz or higher) with at least 8 MB of RAM and a few hundred megabytes of free hard drive space, you should consider upgrading to Windows 95 or its successor immediately. If you don't, you'll be spending a lot of time learning a technology that has already passed out of use. Just make sure that you accept the options which create an emergency boot disk and make a complete backup of your current DOS/Windows system. The "Undo" program which they bury in the "C:\WINDOWS\COMMAND" directory really works, I've used it. If you are already comfortable with Windows 3.1 or Windows for Workgroups, and you already have all the software you need, this isn't a good upgrade to be making. Windows 95 is a full 32-bit operating system, so software properly created for it will run faster than it would in a 16-bit version. However, the overhead incurred in running Windows 95 will make the actual performance to the user seem slower, unless you have a decently powered Pentium PC.

Upgrade to a 1.0-GB Hard Drive

1.0-GB hard drives have become the bottom end of the hard drive market. If you currently have a 200-MB hard drive or (yikes) smaller, this upgrade will contribute as much to your performance as to your storage capacity, because the smaller drives had slower seek times and lower transfer rates. If you have one of these small drives, you'll definitely want to set up the new drive as the IDE master (C:) drive, and either dispense of the old drive or use it for backing up critical files. If your current drive is in the 340-MB and up range, you won't see as much performance gain, but you should still make the new drive the master if you have the patience to transfer all the files over and switch the jumpers back and forth. If you have an older PC, you'll probably have to install translation software which comes with the drive to access its full capacity. Read the instructions carefully before you start. Some drive manufactures ship the software on a temporary partition on the hard drive, which adds several steps to the process, and you'll have to go on the Internet to download new software if you mess it up the first time.

Add a Travan Tape Drive

The problem with very inexpensive tape drives (under $100), is they tend to let you down when you really need them. Tape drives are much less reliable than hard drives, and the tapes they write are often indecipherable if you try to read them in another drive, or even in the drive that wrote them! The smaller Travan drives (800 MB using compression), represent the low end of fairly good backup media; both the tapes and the drives are of improved quality. Travan drives are currently available up to 4-GB capacity, although these tip the scales around $300, and the tapes are expensive also.

5 Upgrades under $250

Upgrades approaching the $250 level add a whole new capability to your PC, and all five of the suggestions listed here are easily portable to a new PC. The best investment of all is probably the 15″ SVGA monitor, since monitor prices have remained remarkably stable over the past 5 years. Color scanners and color inkjets have fallen so far in price that they are unlikely to drop too much further, but beware of the consumable cost (ink cartridges) associated with color inkjets.

Upgrade to Unlimited Internet Access ($19.95/month)

Internet access is generally paid for credit card, making it just another piece of the monthly bill for most of us. Yet, at $19.95/month for unlimited access from the national Internet Service Providers (ISPs), Web access costs most homeowners almost $250 a year. All the same, consider using a local ISP, even if they charge a couple bucks an hour for usage over 20 hours a month. Ask friends or local businesses who they use and what the service is like, then stay under the monthly time limit. Good access from a local ISP means no busy signals and a high-speed connection to the Internet backbone, which makes all the difference in your Internet experience.

Upgrade to 15″ SVGA NI Monitor

There are a couple good reasons to upgrade to a 15″ monitor, especially if your old 14″ is dying, losing colors, focus, screen size, etc. When purchasing any size monitor, pay close attention to the "viewable area", which usually ranges from about 12.5″ to 13.25″ on a 14″ monitor, and from about 13.5″ to 14.5″ on a 15″ monitor. Note that the two ranges almost overlap. Besides the viewing area, the 15″ monitor will probably support higher refresh frequencies than your 14″ monitor did, resulting in a more solid picture, even in a tough lighting environment. Again, what you finally see on any monitor is dependent on properly configuring your video card. If you buy a new video adapter at the same time as the monitor, make sure that it supports at least a 75-Hz refresh rate.

Upgrade to a Color Scanner

Color scanners have come way down in price and are a great way to get everything from photographs to handwritten notes into your computer for display or archiving. Most scanners come bundled with software for refinishing photographs and some include software for Optical Character Recognition (OCR), which transforms a scanned document into text that can be edited in your word processor. Combined with a sound card and text-to-speech software, a scanner can be used to actually read documents out loud.

You will have to open up the PC and install a new adapter, unless you already have a SCSI adapter with an external connector installed. Even if you already have a SCSI adapter, you'll probably have to open up the PC to remove the terminator packs, unless you already have one or more external SCSI devices. If you are considering a scanner strictly to scan photographs for Web publication, consider Kodak Photo CDs or the newer Picture Disks, 27 photos written to floppy at development time.

Upgrade to Portable Drive

For $199, less with discounts or factory rebate, you can buy a Zip drive from Iomega. The Zip drive uses removable 100-MB disks the size of 3.5" floppies and will seamlessly backup larger volumes over a number of disks. The variety of portable drives from Iomega and Syquest, the two leading suppliers, covers a great range of applications, and so you should investigate the cost-effectiveness of their current offerings before purchasing one. Remember to take the cost of the media into account, particularly if you will be delivering work on cartridges or exchanging them with colleagues. Cartridge prices range from about $15 to $100, depending on the model and capacity.

Upgrade to a Color Inkjet

Before you buy a color inkjet, make sure you see an example of its "photo quality" printing. Older color inkjets weren't good for much beyond preparing pie charts or bar-graphs for business presentations. The newest color inkjets do a fair job with both art and photography, at least good enough for a professional to proof work before moving to a multithousand dollar color laser for the final output. If you like printing pictures off the Web, or if you have kids, beware of the cost of inkjet cartridges or you'll soon be spending more for ink than for phone bills.

5 Upgrades under $400

Spending $400 on a hand-me-down PC makes very little sense, unless the item purchased can be transferred to your next PC or extend indefinitely the life of your current model. Upgrading your motherboard and CPU to one of the latest Pentium models essentially gives you a new PC. A CD recorder, an office suite, or a 17″ monitor, are all valuable tools for the professional and can be easily migrated to a new PC if necessary. The toughest call here is adding a superlarge hard drive. If you are happy with your PC but simply need that much more space, go ahead, but be aware that more space is all that this upgrade buys you, and your next PC is likely to come with an even larger hard drive as standard equipment.

Upgrade to a CD Recorder

CD Recorders (CDR) provide the ultimate in removable media drives, because almost everybody has a CD-ROM drive that will be able to read what you record. CDRs can also be used to create music CDs that will play in your stereo, although you'll want a decent sound card to get the music into your computer to start with. For under $400, the CDR you purchase will likely be capable of recording at double speed (2X), and playback at quad speed (4X). The record speed is pretty unimportant unless you are producing large quantities of CDs. Personally, I record everything at single speed and take an hour break from the PC. Playback speed is even less important, when you consider that you can pick up a "throw-away" drive for under $100 that will playback several times faster than the best recorder. Don't buy a CDR unless you have at least a 486 PC.

Upgrade to Pentium Motherboard and CPU

Exactly what clock speed Pentium you can get with a motherboard for under $400 depends entirely on Intel, the sole source supplier. At least a 166 MHz, perhaps a 200 MHz. Who should make this upgrade? First and foremost, anybody with a 486 CPU or lower, of any clock speed. Next, anybody with a 586 who is running into performance problems. Some new software requires Pentium processors with MMX technology. If the motherboard you are upgrading from had no PCI slots, you'll want to at least buy a PCI video adapter, and these start as cheap as $30. If your old system was full of older ISA adapters, pick a motherboard that supports four ISA slots. The new motherboard will have a plug-and-play BIOS, integrated IDE and floppy controllers, serial, printer and game ports, so you can throw away your SIDE adapter. Don't be taken in by expensive motherboards with lifetime warranties; in three or four years it will be following your 486 into the trash.

Upgrade to an Office Suite

If you are using your PC for a business, you will want to own an office suite. Suites are available from Microsoft, Corel (Word Perfect) and Lotus. An office suite includes at the minimum: a word processor, a spreadsheet, and a database. Prices on suites are all over the place, and they are sold in a variety of upgrade versions. In many cases, you can buy the competitive upgrade and a legitimate stepping-stone package (a software product recognized as an upgrade path by the suite manufacturer) for less than the cost of the "regular" version. In either case, you end up with a legal product entitling you to technical support.

Upgrade to a Large Hard Drive (3.0 GB or Greater)

If you want fast, local storage for your system, hard drives are still the way to go. If you are simply replacing your IDE hard drive or adding a large drive to a system with a small drive (one under 500 MB), then there are no special headaches. However, if you already have a large IDE hard drive in your system, and the drive uses overlay software, you can save yourself a lot of trouble if you buy the same brand drive that you already have. Although almost all the drive manufacturers use overlay software from Ontrack Inc., the versions for the different brands generally don't play together, and you'll have to take a chance on using the old software for both or purchase a full version direct from Ontrack. SCSI hard drives are simple to add to systems with an existing SCSI drive, but generally cost more than IDE drives. Also keep in mind that if your CD-ROM is an IDE drive and currently set to slave on an older system with using a standard IDE adapter, you'll have to purchase another IDE controller to act as a secondary controller for the new drive or the CD.

Upgrade to 17" SVGA Monitor

There are three basic reasons you may want to upgrade to a 17" monitor, or even larger if your budget can stand the strain. The most common reason is to make the text on the screen easier to read. If you don't change any other settings and simply replace your 14" monitor with a 17" monitor, everything on the screen gets almost 50 percent bigger. The next most common reason is the need to run a higher screen resolution, i.e., to change from regular VGA (640 × 480) to 600 × 800, or higher. The higher resolutions will display on a 14" monitor, but the text will be so small that it is difficult for most people to read. The third reason for upgrading to a 17" monitor is for doing artwork or drafting or other image intensive work. The 17" monitor will support higher scan rates than the 14" or 15" monitors, and the viewable area of a 17" monitor is almost half again the viewable area of a 14" screen.

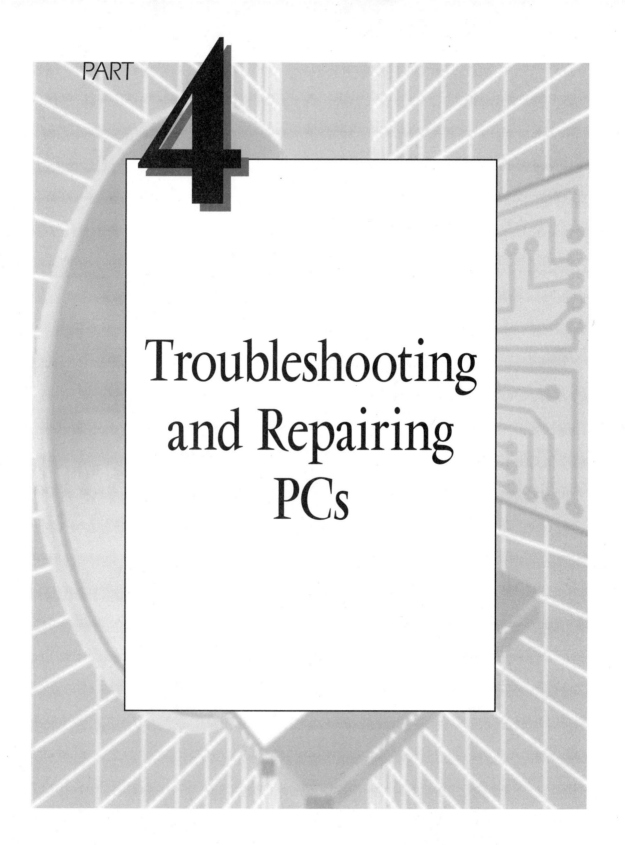

4

Troubleshooting and Repairing PCs

14

Some Basic
Tech Stuff

The whole premise of this book is that you don't have to be an engineer to work on your PC. However, many people will want to know a little more about why there are so many different generations of adapters, or why memory bank size differs with SIMMs and CPUs. The answer requires a quick discussion of how the motherboard connects the CPU with everything else in the system box. None of this information is actually required for fixing your PC, although it can help you understand what you're doing when you order parts. This book also presents a quick tutorial on the DOS startup files, AUTOEXEC.BAT and CONFIG.SYS, because an error in these can mimic some hardware problems.

Computer Buses

A computer bus is a path along which information is passed. Buses are digital, which means the flow of information is not continuous but moves along in lock step with a clock. The bus speed is not the only measure of performance associated with the flow of information on the bus, because some devices require several bus cycles (clock ticks) to respond to a request. For example, most motherboards are equipped with external cache memory, which is about four times faster than the memory SIMMs you install. The external cache memory is also much more expensive, so most computers are equipped with much less than 1 MB of the stuff. When the CPU wants to get some information from memory, it places the address (the location of the byte(s) to be retrieved) on the address bus, and waits for the information to come back on the data bus. If the information has been stashed in the external cache by the cache controller, it is placed on the data bus, and the CPU reads it. If the information is not in the external cache, several data bus cycles (clock ticks) may go by before the slower main memory can supply the information. There are at least two distinct bus routes on every motherboard, one for the memory subsystem and one or more for the I/O bus where the adapters are plugged in.

CPU Speeds and the Memory Bus

On 486 and older PCs, the memory bus is accessed directly by the CPU and shares the CPU clock. This means that memory bus clock speed for a 386SX-16 is 16 MHz, a 486DX-33 bus clock is 33 MHz, and a 486DX-50 bus clock is 50 MHz. These are all examples of traditional, one-speed CPUs. Many hand-me-down PCs will come equipped with a 486DX2-50, 486DX2-66, or 486DX2-80. These are clock-doubled chips whose internal circuitry runs at twice the speed of the CPU clock input. This means that even though the CPU is running at 50 MHz, as in the case of the 486DX2-50, it can only communicate with the outside world at 25 MHz. 486DX CPUs all come equipped with a small amount of internal cache memory that allows them to blaze along at full speed as long as the information they seek is in the cache. If they need to look to external cache, or main memory, they have to sit and wait. The 486DX4-100 and 486DX4-120 are actually clock triplers, despite the "4" designation. These CPUs have internal circuitry that runs at three times the external clock speed.

With the advent of Pentiums, Pentium PROs, and CPUs from AMD and Cyrix that boast clock speeds to 300 MHz, the CPU relies increasingly on internal and secondary cache, which is the new name for external cache. The main memory used in PCs today is only about 30 percent faster than the RAM used five years ago. This comes nowhere near to keeping up with the sixfold increase in CPU speed, and presents a basic bottleneck in the performance of new systems. Extended Data Out (EDO) memory helps a little, but not enough to make it worth replacing regular RAM with EDO RAM in a system that supports both kinds.

The memory bus is also sized according to the CPU's capacity. The 286 CPU (PC-AT) and the 386SX CPUs both see the outside world in 16 bits. With each bus cycle (clock tick), the 286 or 386SX can exchange 16 bits (two bytes) of information with memory, or the I/O bus controller. The 386SX is internally a 32-bit CPU, the same as the 386DX and 486 CPUs, but is restricted in its interface. The 386DX, 486SX, and 486DX CPUs are all full, 32-bit CPUs. They process information internally and exchange it with the outside world, 32 bits at a time. The 386DX had no internal cache and no math coprocessor on board, while the 486SX lacked only the math coprocessor. Clone CPUs with the 586 designation may actually be 32-bit CPUs, depending on the manufacturer and generation. The new generation of CPUs from industry leader Intel are the Pentiums and Pentium PROs, and are full 64-bit CPUs. These CPUs, with clock speeds ranging from 60 MHz to 300 MHz, can access twice as much information from memory in one cycle as the 32-bit CPUs.

Memory Banks and DMA (Direct Memory Access)

In the section about upgrading memory we discussed how there are two physically different sizes of SIMMs, with each size coming in different capacities. The SIMMs that were referred to as 30-pin SIMMs are also called "8-bit" SIMMs because they store information in a format that is eight bits wide. Now that we know that the 286 and 386SX CPUs see the world 16 bits at a time, we can see why the memory bank size used with these CPUs is two 30-pin SIMMs. It takes two 8-bit SIMMs to create a memory bank 16 bits wide. By the same token, the number of 30-pin SIMMs required for a 386DX or 486 CPU memory bank is four. It takes four 8-bit SIMMs to build a bank 32 bits wide. The 72-pin SIMMs that were introduced a few years ago are 32 bits wide. This means that only one 72-pin SIMM is needed to create a memory bank for a 486 CPU. If you have a 586 CPU with a SIMM bank size of four 30-pin SIMMs or one 72-pin SIMM, it has a memory bus limited to 32 bits. The Pentium processors, which see the world in 64-bit clumps, require two 72-pin SIMMs in each memory bank. It takes two 32-bit SIMMs to build a memory bank 64 bits wide. The newest memory modules, DIMMs (Dual Inline Memory Modules) are 64 bits wide, so the bank size for a Pentium CPU is one DIMM.

In the oldest computers, all of the memory management was handled by the CPU. If information that the CPU needed was on the hard drive, a software routine (special housekeeping program) would negotiate with the disk controller, accept the information via the bus controller, and store it in memory for use. Early computer designers saw the value of giving adapters direct access to the memory, to free the CPU from performing this rote chore. The DMA controller is a fairly brainy chip that arbitrates memory access and allows adapters to off-load their information into memory while the CPU is busy doing other things. DMA is a two-way street, and the CPU can also instruct the DMA controller to transfer blocks of memory to an adapter to be written to a hard drive or turned into music by a sound card.

The I/O (Input/Output) Bus

The adapters that add so much functionality to the PC are plugged directly into I/O (Input/Output) bus. This bus has a slower clock than

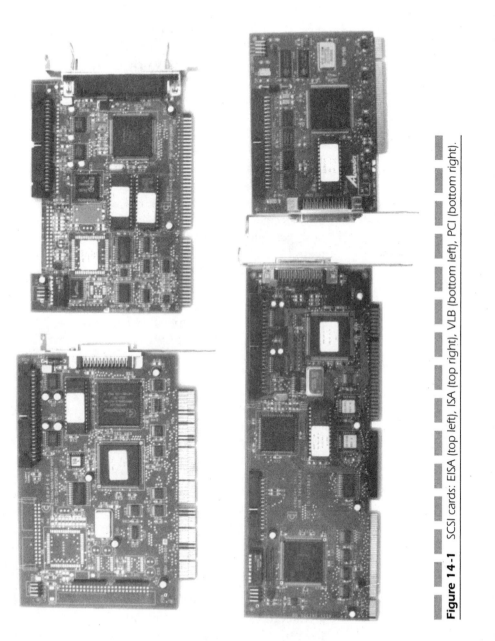

Figure 14-1 SCSI cards: EISA (top left), ISA (top right), VLB (bottom left), PCI (bottom right).

the memory and address buses, no higher than 8 MHz in older PCs. This creates a situation similar to a traffic jam caused by highway construction. If you were the only car on the highway, you could buzz through without hitting the brakes, but when you add a volume of cars, everybody ends up crawling for fifteen minutes. Devices that are attached to the I/O bus may be capable of supplying information at a high speed, and the CPU and memory can certainly work with information at a high speed, but the I/O bus creates a bottleneck that drags everything down to the least common denominator, the I/O bus speed.

Computer designers have always been aware of this issue and have developed a whole slew of work-arounds. The first approach is to simply make the bus wider, the equivalent of adding more lanes to the highway. The bus in the original PC was 8 bits wide, meaning it could pass along 8 bits (1 byte) of data with each bus cycle (clock tick). The next generation of bus, introduced in the IBM PC AT, had a 16-bit-wide bus which passed along twice as much information at the same clock speed. These I/O buses were adopted as the Industry Standard Architecture (ISA). When IBM temporarily pulled out of what had become the clone business, the main selling feature of their new, proprietary PS/2 was its superior Microchannel I/O bus. The clone industry, needing to compete with Big Blue, created the EISA (Extended Industry Standard Architecture) bus, for use in some 386 PCs. The EISA bus increased the clock speed up to 10 MHz, and the bus width to 32 bits. The EISA bus was cleverly designed so that the adapter cards themselves could take over the bus (bus mastering) when they had a lot of information to transfer. Another feature of the EISA bus was backwards compatibility with old adapter cards, which could be used in EISA bus slots. This trick was worked by making the EISA bus connectors twice as deep as normal connectors so that the old ISA adapters didn't reach the extended set of contacts.

The EISA bus suffered from two drawbacks. The first was the expense. Special chips to control the bus, the extra data pathways, and the fancy slots combined to add hundreds of dollars to the cost of a motherboard. Special software was also required to install the new adapters, which themselves cost many times as much as ISA cards. The EISA bus may have overcome these difficulties to become the dominant architecture, if not for the introduction of the VESA local bus. The philosophy of the VESA local bus was simple. Add two or three slots very near the CPU, and let the CPU read and write information directly to

Figure 14-2
PC buses.

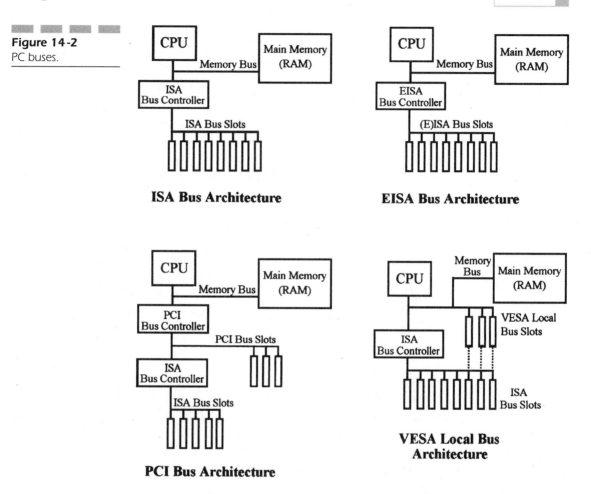

ISA Bus Architecture

EISA Bus Architecture

PCI Bus Architecture

VESA Local Bus
Architecture

them at the same speed as memory. Implementing this is actually a little trickier than it sounds because there are limitations on how much electrical power and noise the CPU can handle, which led to the limitation on the number of slots. However, the net result was a 32-bit-wide bus that operated at the CPU clock speed, when that speed was 33 MHz or under. VESA adapters plug into the regular slots in the ISA bus section of the motherboard for power but have an extended contact area that plugs into the inline VESA slot near the CPU.

With the advent of Pentium systems, the PCI bus was introduced. The PCI bus is another 32-bit bus, which runs at a fixed clock of 33 MHz and supports bus mastering. PCI adapters can transfer data directly to system memory at this clock rate. PCI adapters require their own special slots, which offer no backwards compatibility to ISA family adapters. The PCI bus is a more traditional bus implementation than the VESA local bus, employing full buffering (insulation of the I/O bus from other buses on the motherboard) and sophisticated bus controllers. ISA and EISA buses are isolated from the CPUs memory bus by a bus controller. The VESA local bus shares the memory bus with the CPU for one or two adapters, but the rest are again isolated by a bus controller. Implementation of the PCI bus requires two levels of controllers, a PCI controller which isolates the CPU from the PCI bus, and an ISA or EISA bus controller that buffers the PCI bus from the other buses.

Interrupts

Adapters on the I/O bus and other devices with direct connections to the motherboard all have the ability to generate interrupts. A hardware interrupt is an electrical signal generated by the adapter or device that is wired directly to the interrupt controller. The interrupt controller buffers and prioritizes interrupt requests, then notifies the CPU with another directly wired connection. The CPU then jumps to a memory address associated with the interrupt number and executes the software routine known as the "interrupt handler." Without these interrupts, the CPU would never know when you move the mouse, type a new letter, or when the hard drive has found the requested information.

Interrupts are written in shorthand as IRQs (Interrupt Requests). Early motherboards (pre-AT) supported only eight interrupts, new motherboards support sixteen. The following table presents the mapping of interrupts as they will be set in most systems.

IRQ 0 - Timer	IRQ 8 - Real-Time Clock
IRQ 1 - Keyboard	IRQ 9 - Open (Redirected IRQ 2)
IRQ 2 - Cascade (Triggers IRQs 8 to 15)	IRQ 10 - Open
IRQ 3 - Com 2, Com 4	IRQ 11 - Open
IRQ 4 - Com 1, Com 3	IRQ 12 - Open
IRQ 5 - Open (LPT2;, if present)	IRQ 13 - Math Coprocessor
IRQ 6 - Floppy Disk	IRQ 14 - Fixed Disk
IRQ 7 - LPT1:	IRQ 15 - Open

Although the table shows six open IRQs, they can get used up in a hurry. IRQ 5 is commonly gobbled up by a sound card, and IRQ 9 is used by most SVGA adapters. If any adapter we might want to add could use any of the remaining interrupts, we would be okay, but adapters usually offer a limited number of choices. IRQs 3 and 4 can be shared by two communications ports, or a communications port and a modem, but only if the devices sharing the interrupt won't be functioning at the same time. In other words, a mouse on Com1 (IRQ 4), precludes the use of Com3, because the mouse must be available at all times. Interrupt conflicts are one of the most common problems to be faced in making upgrades.

Quality Control

Quality control is unfortunately a myth in large segments of the PC industry. I once installed a motherboard and powered it up, only to hear a loud pop and smell the aroma of burnt electronics. I was quite irritated with myself, certain that I'd let a stray screw short out the motherboard, but a colleague who had more faith in me insisted we examine the board for damage. I quickly found the blown chip, a part of the buffering circuitry, and noticed that it had been soldered to the motherboard backwards! This motherboard had quality control stickers on it from at least three different "inspectors," yet it had obviously never been powered up. Most of these components are manufactured overseas, competition is fierce, and everyone cuts corners. A SIDE adapter which sells for $10 here in the wholesale market has a couple of dollars worth of chips on it and had to buy a long boat ride to boot. There's just no profit margin in the commodity adapter business, and quality suffers as a consequence.

Electronic devices have a life span that engineers refer to as the "bathtub curve." Lots of parts fail with the first jolt of electrical current, followed by heat-induced failures as they warm up for the first time. Components that weren't manufactured quite as well as they could have been fail next, followed by a long period of relative stability. Near the end of the expected lifetime of the part (the length of time it was designed to last for) failures begin to increase once again. Components with moving parts, like hard drives, have shorter lives than purely electronic parts, because bearing surfaces inevitably wear down, and they are more vulnerable to jolts when you pound the computer in frustration.

All PC vendors promise a "burn-in" period, 24 to 72 hours of diagnostics running on the system, the idea being to get it by the front end of the bathtub curve before they sell it. Some actually do this; many don't. I've personally fixed many DOA (Dead On Arrival) PCs from brand-name vendors, where parts simply weren't hooked up or correctly configured. This has become epidemic as suppliers standardize on models, because they install all of the software by simply putting in a hard drive that's been copied from a master version of the identical system. This leads to lots of misconnections of floppy drives, CDs, sound cards, etc.

A company I worked for once submitted a "standard" PC to a local city, which was bidding a blanket contract for PC purchasing. While I was there, a city employee asked me to take a quick look at a competitor's PC, in which the floppies weren't working. I opened up the system box and saw that they hadn't been hooked up, neither power connectors nor ribbon cables. We won the contract, but I tell the story to illustrate how a reputable PC company was able to screw up on something so simple when they were trying to make an impression. Imagine how their PCs worked when they didn't care!

Troubleshooting 101

The only tool you ever need to fix most PCs is a Phillips-head screwdriver. The first question that jumps into a hobbyist's head is, "How can I fix anything without my soldering iron?" The answer is simple. You find the bad part and replace it. If a part is under warranty, and many expensive adapters and drives are backed by the manufacturer for five years, you can pay for shipping and wait for a replacement. If they don't have a remanufactured part, they'll send you a new one that might be several generations ahead of the failed component. Some computer components actually come with lifetime warranties, based on the idea that you'll never find the paperwork again, and even if you do, the part will be so obsolete you won't want another one anyway. Most computer parts employ surface-mount circuit boards that are assembled by robots. It takes a microscope, micro manipulators, and a highly trained technician working in a hermetically sealed clean room to repair these components.

Where to Start

You probably already know a lot more about troubleshooting a PC than you think you do. Many failures are pretty obvious or are actually reported by the system. For example, if the letters you type on the keyboard don't show up on the screen, the problem could be the connection between the keyboard and the system box. The system might report "HDD/FDD controller failure" when you power up. It's telling you that it can't communicate with the SIDE adapter. The real wild card in troubleshooting is the software. Poor programming, applications used in ways the programmer didn't consider, or unexpected software events can cause a PC to freeze. It could also be any number of hardware problems, but the best approach is to troubleshoot the software first. The way to do this is to get the problem to repeat by trying the same procedure, or to avoid using the same software for a while and see if the problem goes away. Either way, it doesn't mean that you don't have a hardware problem that the software is triggering, but it all helps to narrow down the possibilities. Software-related freezes are often related to improperly configured drivers for peripherals, which should be apparent from the failure occurring when you attempt to access them.

The first step in any "dead PC" troubleshooting job is to open the case to strip the PC down to its bare bones. Remove all of the adapters except for the video card and the SIDE card, than see if the system will boot. If not, remove the SIDE card and try again. You don't have to disconnect all the ribbon cables from the SIDE card when you remove it; just lay it safely out of the way on top of the case or somewhere where it won't accidentally fall in. If you still can't get anything to come up on the screen, the possibilities are reduced to power supply, motherboard and CPU, main memory, or the video adapter.

15

Troubleshooting
PC Parts

Power Supplies

Computer power supplies are among the weaker links in clones. Power supplies suffer from many types of failure: total failure, fan failure, a broken switch, loss of power to one lead, and loss of voltage regulation. Total failure means that no beeps or blinking lights result when the switch is turned on, and the fan on the power supply doesn't rotate. There are a few very basic items that should always be checked first, particularly on PCs that are being installed in a new location for the first time.

1. Make sure that the outlet the computer is plugged into is alive by plugging in a lamp. While house wiring is usually reliable, inexpensive power strips sporting from four to eight outlets often have at least one dead or unreliable outlet.

2. Make sure that the PC end of the power cord is firmly inserted into the PC power supply. These cable ends are an industry-standard female connector which is pushed onto three prongs. Sometimes the cord you are using is not the cord that came with the PC, and the fit is very tight. If you aren't confident that contact is being made, you should try another cord.

3. Check the line voltage switch (110/220 V) on the back of the power supply to make sure it is set on 110 V. This problem rarely comes up anymore because switches are small and taped over, but older power supplies had switches that could be accidentally thrown during transport.

Once you have confirmed that the power supply is plugged in properly, you can check the switch if you have a voltage/continuity meter. A broken power supply switch on the front panel of the system box is probably the second most common type of power supply failure, after fan problems. Switch problems are sometimes obvious, like a push button failing to stay in, but more often you will need to check it with a meter. With the power supply unplugged from the wall, you can remove two of the four connections from the switch and check for continuity with the switch turned on. Then replace the two connectors and check the other pair. The wires chosen for each pair should be on opposite sides of the switch, where the terminals on a side should not show continuity with the switch in either position. Power supplies do have fuses inside the housing that can be checked with a meter, but I've never come across a blown one. There are large capacitors in the power supply, so even with the power cord detached, you can get a bad shock if you remove the power supply cover.

The audible noise from the power supply is normally caused by the fan. A steady squeal or loud hum is caused by failing fan bearings. These noises may come and go in accordance with room temperature, humidity, and other environmental factors. If this problem is present and the PC is still in manufacturer's warranty, change out the supply immediately because it's not going to fix itself. Power supplies can last a long time with noisy fans, but failure of the fan can damage more than just the power supply, which will overheat and malfunction when the fan stops. If you have a noisy power supply fan and you don't want to purchase a new power supply, you can buy a replacement fan and change it out. Before you do so, try vacuuming the power supply out through the fan grating, since a buildup of dust and thread may be the problem. The other key noise produced by the power supply fan is the pitch of the normal droning sound it makes. If the pitch drops greatly when the drives are being accessed, the power supply is not very healthy and should be returned if in warranty.

Power supplies will sometimes appear to be dead if one of the main system components has developed a short circuit. This may be determined by alternately isolating components from the power supply. Unplug all of the power leads to the drives and try to boot the system. If the system comes to life, shut down, and begin plugging the drives back in and rechecking, one at a time, until you find the problem drive. Otherwise, remove the power connectors to the motherboard and try powering up again. Sometimes, one of the power leads from the supply to the drives will fail, but in most instances you can add a power splitter to a working lead and continue using the supply.

When replacing a dead power supply, make sure the replacement is of an identical form, i.e., physical size of supply, location of switch, and connector on switch if it is the front-panel push-button type. If you don't mind the work of moving all of your parts around, a replacement system box, complete with power supply, is usually cheaper than purchasing a power supply by itself. One of the few universal truths in the world of clones is the color coding of the motherboard connectors, P8 and P9. Connect these to the motherboard so that the black leads in either connector are adjacent to one another in the middle of the connection block.

Power supplies can also be responsible for a variety of oddball failures. If a machine reboots itself when the table is jarred or when someone walks across the room, there is a good chance that the short is in the power supply and not elsewhere in the system. Systems which occasionally freeze up and don't want to power up for a few minutes after being shut off may have a power supply problem, the other likelihood being an overheated CPU. Systems that boot and run for a very short period of time before freezing may also be blamed on poor power supply voltage regulation. A power supply with a faulty ground can cause strange problems, particularly with drives that use the frame of the system box for ground. If a known-good floppy or tape drive experiences consistent failures in a system, try demounting it and running it insulated from the case by a book or static-proof bag. In addition, power supplies can be afflicted by whistling capacitors, which produce a high-pitched tone that can irritate the dog and the children. Before fixing the blame for the sound, you should try temporarily disconnecting any hard drives and removing a modem if one is present. High-frequency sound is highly directional, so reorienting the system box in a room or on a desk may save you from having to replace the power supply.

Keyboards

Keyboards are pretty reliable on the whole, given that they are one of the least expensive and lowest-tech parts of a system. Stuck keys, keys that repeat (bounce), and keys that just don't work at all are pretty easy to spot, and the problem normally gets worse in a hurry. If you spill a beverage on your keyboard, unplug it, rinse it with warm water, than let it dry out overnight. Shake it out real good before plugging it back in, and if you even think you see any drops of water coming out, let it dry another day. Keyboards do have a total failure mode, which occurs when the system hangs on booting and displays a keyboard error message. If the system is being set up at a new location for the first time, make sure that the keyboard is plugged in firmly and that a book or your elbow isn't resting on the keypad. Older keyboards had a switch on the bottom for selecting installation on XT/AT computers. Old XT keyboards can't be used with newer systems at all. Sometimes a keyboard will have its encoder circuitry blown by a static electrical shock, or just be mechanically ruined from one too many spilled cans of Coke. Obviously failures such as these can be easily diagnosed by swapping keyboards.

Some combinations of EEKs (Extremely Enhanced Keyboards) and the computer BIOS will always produce a boot time error unless the "keyboard testing" option is turned off in the CMOS setup. Any keyboard going beyond the 101 key scheme can be considered an EEK. More insidious problems can arise from an intermittent keyboard failure. Sometimes a keyboard failure will suggest a problem with the keyboard controller on the motherboard, often called the keyboard BIOS chip. Some keyboards, due to capacitive buildup or heat-related failure, will cease to work while the computer is in use, giving the user the impression that the system has "hung." A simple test to see if the system is locked up or the problem is in the keyboard input is to check if the mouse still works. If you can make anything happen with the mouse beyond simply moving it, like pull down a menu in a Windows program, neither the software or general system hardware can be faulted. If using another keyboard doesn't fix the problem, the failure is with the keyboard BIOS (controller) chip.

The keyboard BIOS chip is a large DIP (Dual Inline Package) chip, with 20 pins on each side of a package about 2" long by $\frac{3}{8}$" wide. Keyboard BIOS chips are pretty compatible in older systems and were normally mounted in sockets, rather than soldered to the motherboard. Before you hunt around for a replacement chip, try removing and reseating the existing chip in the socket. This sometimes remakes a connection that has been oxidized or otherwise mechanically failed. You can take a keyboard BIOS chip, identified by a label or the letters KB appearing somewhere on the top, off any old motherboard and try it in your system. Just make sure to line up the key, a small notch in the top of one end of the chip, with the similar key in the socket. Also, while you want to straighten the legs on the replacement BIOS chip before trying to insert it in the motherboard, avoid bending any leg more than once or twice, because the thin metal fatigues quickly and will break off flush with the package.

On newer PCs, the Gate-A20 feature used in memory addressing schemes is included on the keyboard controller chip. If this fails, the BIOS should generate a nonfatal error at boot time and inform you of the problem. Other error messages related to the keyboard include: "Keyboard Error," "Keyboard Interface Error," and "Keyboard is Locked." "Keyboard Error" appears when the keyboard BIOS doesn't recognize the keyboard type, like in the case of the EEKs mentioned above. "Keyboard Interface Error" means the BIOS believes the keyboard connector on the motherboard to be faulty. "Keyboard Locked" occurs when the circular keyhole on the front of the CPU has been turned to the locked position, or the lock lead hasn't been attached to the pins on the motherboard, and a jumper is required.

Motherboards

Today's motherboards use a lot of surface mount technology and could practically be labeled "no user serviceable parts." For this reason, many of the beep codes generated by the motherboard during POST (Power On Self Test) are just an anachronism. For example, one beep code informs us that the memory refresh circuitry is dead, but there's nothing we can do to replace it. The two most commonly encountered beep codes that remain useful are for the memory and the video adapter. Three beeps, normally slow, indicate that there is a failure in the first bank of RAM installed. Reasons can include a poorly seated SIMM, a dead SIMM, or unsupported SIMM types installed in bank zero. If you have more than one bank of memory installed, try swapping out a higher bank for bank zero. Eight fast beeps means either the VGA adapter is not present or the memory on the adapter has failed. With newly installed VGA adapters, or systems that have been recently worked on, the most common reason for this failure is poor seating of the adapter in the slot.

Most motherboards have the system BIOS, keyboard BIOS, cache memory, and main memory socketed. An onboard battery with some type of replacement option is used to power the permanent CMOS memory and clock/calendar. The system BIOS, which we have broadly referred to throughout the text, is stored on a ROM (Read-Only Memory) chip, which is a permanent, if slow, memory storage device. Newer motherboards may store the BIOS code in flash memory chips, which can be upgraded in place using software downloaded from the Internet or provided on floppy disk. The system BIOS is motherboard specific, which means you can't arbitrarily take any system BIOS chip off a dead motherboard and use it in your PC.

On old motherboards, a socketed clock crystal will very rarely cause boot failure or intermittent lockups, and should be swapped only before replacing the CPU. On systems with a ZIF (Zero Insertion Force) socket, I'd try swapping the CPU first. Since their normal failure mechanism is excessive heat, a bad BIOS chip, system, or keyboard, can often be visually identified by a burnt spot on the label over the center of the chip. System BIOS chips fail even less often then keyboard controllers and are not suspect in intermittent failures unrelated to booting. Problems with recently assembled systems can sometimes be caused by partially inserted CPUs, especially as the larger chips can be difficult to insert in older non-ZIF sockets. Diagnostic failures involving address lines are an indication of this problem, which is easy to spot with the motherboard removed from the case.

The most common problem related to the motherboard that occurs during the upgrading or repair process is inadvertent loss of the CMOS settings. A brief short on the battery backup circuit or too much flexing of the motherboard can cause this problem. When the system is booted, a "CMOS Checksum Error" or "CMOS Memory Failure" will be generated. Enter CMOS setup and restore all of the settings for your floppy drives, hard drives, date, and time. Other CMOS-related errors like "CMOS Display Type Doesn't Match" or "CMOS Memory Size Mismatch" are the normal results of some upgrades, and are corrected by entering CMOS setup and saving the new settings, which the BIOS will automatically generate.

Another common motherboard-related problem is mechanical connector failure. This can occur in the bus slots, with the keyboard connector, or with any of the ribbon connectors that may be attached to an enhanced motherboard. Failure in bus slots is normally due to one of the gold-plated "fingers" that make spring-loaded electrical contact with the adapter being crushed inwards or pulled outwards. Careful visual inspection can detect this problem, which is often repairable by carefully bending the finger back into position. The easiest fix is to simply try the adapter in another slot, but first check to make sure that the bottom edge of the adapter has been nicely beveled to make the insertion smooth. This is sometimes not the case on really cheap adapter cards, but you can take a little off the edge with a file. Be gentle, so as not to cause the gold contact to lift from the adapter surface, which ruins the part.

Motherboards with one or more VESA local bus adapters installed are probably the most prone to failure out of all the different motherboard technologies. After two or three years of normal operation, the PC may cease to boot, and swapping the video adapter or memory, or pulling out all of the adapters except the video adapter may still fail to revive it. Try removing all local bus adapters, replacing the local bus video adapter with a plain ISA video adapter. If the system then works properly, rebuild it using ISA video and SIDE cards. The years of carrying the extra load have worn down the CPU.

The mounting of keyboard connectors sometimes fails so that the connector rocks back on the motherboard, preventing proper insertion of the keyboard lead or breaking a contact point. This is also detectable by visual inspection and is occasionally repairable with a little imagination. Ribbon connectors on highly integrated motherboards rarely fail, but the ribbons are often connected incorrectly. Double-check that all of the pins have entered the connector, since the ribbons will go on missing an entire row of pins without having to be forced. Also check that the red, or other specially marked wire in the ribbon cable, goes to the pin-1 and pin-2 end of the connector at both ends of its length. I've often been fooled when installing new drives or controllers by ribbon cables that were attached backwards at both ends of the connector, and therefore worked properly until I came along and changed one end.

Old motherboards are also prone to mechanical failure due to a loss of flexibility over time, and they may refuse to boot in a new case. If you determine that a motherboard only works when installed in a certain geometry, be creative in using electrically insulating, nonflammable materials to fix it in place. I once salvaged a 486 motherboard displaying this behavior by forcing a small stone under the motherboard, and it's still working today.

Battery

The usual harbinger of a failing battery is a "CMOS battery state low" being displayed by the BIOS at boot time. Often, this message appears only after some of the settings have been lost from the battery backed CMOS memory, but the real-time clock (date and time) is usually still functioning. Schemes for battery backup of the CMOS settings abound, with the most common one on older motherboards being a soldered, rechargeable battery on the motherboard. Newer systems often employ a socketed, real-time clock and battery unit from Dallas Semiconductor, which is sometimes held in place by a tie wrap. In all cases, the onboard battery can be replaced with one of the same kind, or it can be disabled so you can substitute an external battery or battery pack. Replacement batteries come in a great range of sizes and voltages (from 3 V to 6 V), so you should try to determine from the old battery or motherboard documentation what voltage is required.

When replacing a battery of the first type with an external battery, you often have to move a jumper on a 3-pin block on the motherboard from "internal" to "external." If no documentation is available, this jumper block is normally the one closest to the battery connection. It usually takes the form of a 2-pin block to be jumpered or left open, or a 3-pin block to be jumpered on one side or the other. You must find and set this jumper on most motherboards to enable the 4-pin connector for external battery connection. Replacing an onboard battery with one of the same type requires no changes in settings. External batteries come equipped with a 4-pin hole connector, where one hole is usually plugged with a blank to key the plus terminal of the battery to the correct side of the motherboard connector. If a blank is present and there are four pins on the external battery connection pad, you have two choices. You can work the blank out of the connector-pin hole, then connect the red wire side of the connector to the "+" side of the connector block, or you can bend the interfering pin out of the way.

If a replacement battery fails in a few days or weeks, there's still a good chance the fault was in the battery and not the motherboard. If another replacement fails, you can try a higher voltage or try moving a different jumper if your system board was undocumented. Finally, you can try cutting a lead on the onboard battery and remounting the motherboard to ensure that there are no electrical shorts on the bottom. If the problem persists, consider trying to live with it by simply

Figure 15-1
Replacement batteries.

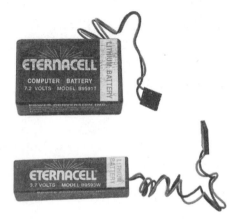

re-entering the system configuration information in the CMOS setup each time you boot. With one hard drive, one floppy, and the date and time, this actually takes less than a minute in most cases. Your only other options are to leave the machine on all of the time, or upgrade the motherboard. If you do go this route and have a 486 whose performance you were happy with, you can pick up a motherboard for under $50 and use your old CPU and memory.

Cache Memory

Cache memory can be responsible for intermittent lockups and errors, conflicts with software caching programs, and system lockups immediately after or during the boot process. Many cache problems will be recognized by the BIOS at boot time, and the message "Cache Memory Bad" will appear. The system will freeze at this point, and you will have to reboot, enter CMOS setup, and select "Disable External Cache" in one of the advanced menus. This is also the best way to quickly determine if a problem with the external cache is responsible for run-time lockups. If the system functions properly with the external cache disabled, the cache is indeed the problem.

Pentium, Pentium PRO, and clone CPUs with clock speeds over 100 MHz are highly dependent on external cache, also known as secondary cache, pipeline burst cache or L2 (level 2) cache, to achieve optimal performance. Cache on these new motherboards usually comes in the form of a single 160-pin module, carrying 256-K or 512-K SRAM (Static Random Access Memory). Due to the importance of external cache on high-speed motherboards, manufacturers try to tweak proprietary schemes to differentiate themselves from their competition, which results in many incompatibilities. If you determine that your external cache is bad, be sure to replace it with exactly the type specified by the motherboard manufacturer. Don't assume that the cache originally installed on the board was the right kind and simply buy the same thing.

External cache chips on older motherboards are DIP (Dual Inline Package) chips, like the keyboard BIOS only much smaller. They come in a variety of sizes, depending on capacity, and most motherboards support at least two types. All older external cache systems utilize a "tag ram" chip which serves as an index to the data chips, and is often a different speed or type. If this is a newly built system, the most likely problem will be improper jumper settings, as there are often five or six jumpers to set determining total cache size and chip type. This requires the motherboard manual or a lot of guessing. The other likelihood is a leg bending under a chip, or missing the socket completely. The latter is easy to spot, while the former may require taking the chips out and inspecting them. Like all DIP chips, the metal legs fatigue rapidly with bending and will only tolerate being straightened out once or twice before breaking off.

If after determining that all the chips have been inserted properly, which includes lining up the key (indentation) on the top of the chip with the key in the socket, the only option is to try replacing chips. If you have 256-K cache installed, using eight data chips, you will be able to reset the jumpers for 128-K cache and use the leftover four chips for troubleshooting. If not, you will have to obtain at least one new chip, two if the tag ram is different, before proceeding. Try replacing the single tag-ram chip first, since it's often the problem. After that, you can replace the four data chips one at a time to isolate the bad egg, or all at once, if you have enough cache on hand. Some software caching programs, particularly those used by some of the older and off-brand network operating systems, will not operate with external cache enabled. Try getting a software upgrade or live with the external cache disabled.

Cache chips don't follow any standard nomenclature, so here is a brief list to help you figure out what you have. All chips are presented as 20nS (nanosecond) versions; they may exist as 15nS or 25nS chips as well.

8K X 8 SRAM	32K X 8 SRAM
AS7C164-20PC	AS7C256-20PC
CY7C185-20	CY7c199-20
IDT7164-S20	IS61C256-20
IS61C64-20	KM68257BP-20
KM6865BP-20	MCM6206NP20
MCM6264P20	TC55328P-20
TC5588P-20	UM61256K-20
UM61648K-20	W24257AK-20

Internal Cache Memory

Internal cache is the on processor cache on 486 and newer CPUs. 486 CPUs, up to the DX2-66 model, came with 8K of onboard cache. Newer 486s and Pentiums come with 16 K or more of onboard cache. The internal cache memory is actually the single greatest user of real estate on the chip. When a system is taken out of turbo mode, along with a reduction in clock speed, the internal cache is temporarily disabled. This effectively slows the system down to something like the old IBM PC-AT speed. If the internal cache needs to be disabled for the system to function, it's time to get a new CPU, because the performance will be terrible. Accidentally disabled internal cache is the most common problem with PCs that have been upgraded yet perform worse than the old motherboard/CPU combination.

Main Memory

Failures of main memory are the most common cause of intermittent lockups, especially when those lockups occur only in specific programs or only in the programs which are using extended memory. A machine that was used for simple DOS applications for many years might first begin experiencing memory errors when Windows is installed, simply because it wasn't using those memory locations before. The easiest way to determine if intermittent problems are due to memory is to run a diagnostic program that does a slow memory check (the test should take at least a minute or two per megabyte). If you don't have a diagnostic and don't have Internet access to download one, you'll have to find SIMMs to trade out or experiment swapping banks with the RAM you have installed.

For example, if you believe you are experiencing an intermittent memory failure in a 486 with 8 MB of RAM installed, open up the case and remove the four 1-MB SIMMs in Bank 1. Reboot the system and try operating for a while with 4 MB. If the problem persists, swap the four 1-MB SIMMs in Bank 0 with the four 1MB SIMMs you've removed and try running again. If the problem still persists, it's not a main memory issue. If the problem clears up, there is a bad SIMM amongst the four that are currently removed. SIMMs should be reseated in their sockets and retested before being written off. In some instances, inserting a wait state in the advanced CMOS setup will solve the problem, at least temporarily, and the system should then pass the diagnostic.

Memory within a bank on the motherboard (two 30-pin SIMMs on 386SX, four 30-pin SIMMs or one 72-pin SIMM on 486s, and two 72-pin SIMMs on Pentiums) should be kept all the same type of SIMM, speed, and brand. Older SIMMs were all of the fast page RAM type, but many newer, 72-pin SIMMs are of the EDO (Extended Data Out) variety, which increases memory access speed. The vast majority of bad SIMMs I've found in PCs either have a mix of chip speeds and brands mounted on the SIMM, or have been mixed in a bank with dissimilar SIMMs. The hobbyist or home user may be willing to gamble on changing a single SIMM, but in field repairs, the whole bank should be changed. Old unmatched SIMMs are handy for troubleshooting or can be used on caching controllers and some high-end graphics adapters.

Main memory problems are reported by the motherboard three ways. The repeated code of three slow beeps at power up, indicates a bad SIMM in bank zero. A "CMOS Memory Mismatch" error means you have added or changed the SIMMs in the system, or the SIMMs in a bank other then bank zero are no longer recognized. An "On Board Parity Error" means that there is a chip failure on one of the SIMMs, or you have just installed non-parity SIMMs in a parity system. The options are to replace the SIMMs in the problem bank with parity SIMMs, or to disable parity checking in the CMOS setup. Disabling parity, if this is an option, won't reduce data integrity if you've purchased nonparity SIMMs. If you have parity SIMMs in the system and you disable parity, you should definitely run a diagnostic to test memory. Often times, the failure is actually due to the parity chip on the SIMM, and the data chips are still O.K.

Older systems were built with DIP memory socketed or soldered to the motherboard. Systems with soldered memory aren't worth any effort; those with socketed memory might be revived by reseating all of the chips. Bad chips can be exchanged one for one with chips of the same or faster speed, it's not necessary to replace the whole bank. Most 16-bit extended or expanded memory adapters will work in newer machines, some require software drivers, others need to have switches set specifying their start address and the total amount of memory in the computer. Some 386 computers feature a single thirty-two bit slot for one special memory adapter. These adapters are going on ten years old and have been orphaned, so don't invest money in one. Many of the older adapters held 2 MB or 3 MB of memory and can come in handy on an

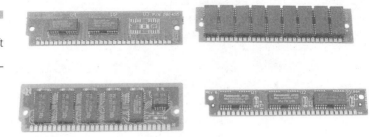

Figure 15-2
30-Pin SIMMs. Top left is no parity.

underpowered machine. An "Off Board Parity Error" is generated by the BIOS if a parity error on an add-in adapter is detected.

Floppy Drives

Floppy drives are among the least reliable and most finicky components in a PC. Part of the problem stems from their low cost, $20 to $35, which just doesn't buy a lot of quality in an electromechanical device. Another problem is due to the lack of quality of the floppy disks themselves. I've often had two floppy disks out of a brand-new box of ten lifetime warranty floppies fail to format to their full capacity. The standard floppy drives, the 1.44 MB 3½″ and the 1.2 MB 5¼″, offer backwards compatibility to the older generation, but they don't always do it very well. Along with all of their other problems, floppy drives get dirty inside, and often suffer from mechanical failures. The most common failure with 5¼″ drives is the handle breaking off on the faceplate. Diskettes for 3½″ drives employ a thin metal shield that occasionally gets a little bent and either sticks in the drive preventing the disk from ejecting, or comes off altogether, jamming the mechanism.

The first category of floppy drive failures are those experienced in new PCs or hand-me-down PCs that you have just upgraded. The most common problems, responsible for at least 75 percent of all floppy problems in this category, are misconnected ribbon cables. If you boot the PC and both floppy drive lights come on and stay on, you've misconnected the ribbon cable. The bad connection can occur at the controller end of the cable or at the 3½″ floppy drive. You don't have to worry about 5¼″ drives because their old-fashioned edge connector is virtually foolproof. At the controller end of the cable, the usual mistake is missing the entire bottom row of pins on the connection block. Looking down at a SIDE adapter from the top, it's nearly impossible to detect that the ribbon cable connector is sitting about an eighth of an inch too high. Take it off to check it, and make sure that the red stripe, or otherwise differentiated side of the ribbon cable, is attached at the connector block end numbered 1 or 2.

At the 3 $\frac{1}{2}$" drive end of the cable, the problem is much tougher to detect. Since the connector block is often recessed into the back of the drive, and the drive is normally mounted in a hard-to-see position, I've often had to take the drive out and reconnect the cable to get it right. When the connector is pushed down on the connector block, it often bends two pins at the end of the block out of the way, but seems to seat properly. If you can get a good look at the connection block, you can often correct the problem by starting the connector at the end with the bent pins and using it to lever them back into place. Sometimes, the problem with older 3 $\frac{1}{2}$" floppy drives is simply determining which end of the connector block is the pin 1 or 2 end. I've even come across a case where only the opposite end of the connector was labeled (pin 33), and you will often need to take the drive out of the system box and examine it to find the markings. A backwards ribbon cable can cause a 3 $\frac{1}{2}$" drive to eat the file allocation table (FAT) on a floppy, so system disks become nonbootable. This can get extremely confusing since now the system won't boot from this floppy with the ribbon cable on either way.

Figure 15-3
Common floppy
drive cabling failures.

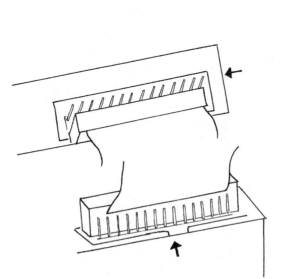

The second most common problem on new machines, or machines that have been worked on, is the wrong drive type (i.e., 360 K, 720 K, 2.88 M, not installed) be selected in the CMOS setup. A drive with the wrong CMOS type will often pass all hardware diagnostic tests and may even properly show the directory of the floppy disk but will fail on extended reads or writes, often resulting in data loss. This problem may not be noticed on a new machine for months after delivery, if the misconnected floppy drive isn't actually used.

The easiest failure to diagnose is when the on-drive LED doesn't come on or the drive doesn't spin up or seek. Try changing the power cable to the drive and reseating the ribbon cable on the drive and the controller card. If the drive still fails to respond, the problem is the drive or the controller. The controller is tested during boot time and will produce a FDD/HDD controller failure message in the case of non-intermittent problems.

Floppy drives are notoriously unreliable, particularly when used in office or school environments that have a large mix of machines with different brands and drive densities. Most strange floppy-drive behavior arises from reading and writing floppies from different PCs and format-ting floppy disks at lower then the maximum drive capacity. As a rule of thumb, if a problem reading and writing a disk occurs on some PCs and not others, the problem is with the disk. The compatibility of new drives with old formats came at a cost. The magnetic read/write heads on a low-capacity drive are twice as wide as the heads on a high-capacity drive and source twice the write current. New drives can make the adjustment for current, but the physical size of the read/write head can't be changed. When formatting lower-capacity disks, the format pro-cedure does not match the media, which is physically different for the high- and low-density disks. In addition, there are always some fiscally conservative individuals who attempt to recycle low-density disks in high-density drives by defeating the mechanical check. This is a bad practice, and failures involving these disks in no way imply a problem with the drive.

In cases where the drive fails to read or write a group of floppies that work fine in a sampling of other machines, the problem is with the drive or controller. The easiest diagnostic is to swap out the drive or con-troller with one borrowed from another PC. Problems with external cache occasionally manifest themselves as floppy errors, so disabling the external cache in the CMOS setup should be on your list of trouble-shooting steps. Don't forget to re-enable cache if the problem doesn't go away. Intermittent read/write failures may be due to the controller or even the motherboard. The former is easy to troubleshoot by swapping out the controller and the latter is very, very rare. Bad chassis ground or memory problems can also produce intermittent floppy problems; refer to power supply and memory sections.

Hard Drives

Modern IDE hard drives are among the more reliable system components. They typically run for many years, then fail with a whimper or a bang. Most of the problems that creep up with a hard drive are actually controller or software issues, particularly corrupted system files or viruses. One easy way to avoid some problems and many complications is to avoid using any type of hard drive compression utility. They reduce overall system performance and create a nightmare for data recovery if you have a problem. The best way to increase hard drive capacity is to purchase a new hard drive. Hard drive performance degrades with time as the information you are seeking gets spread all over the disk, a process called fragmentation. The main symptom is head thrashing, which causes the HDD LED (hard drive light) on the front of the system box flash rapidly for long stretches of time. You can correct the problem with the DEFRAG program that is included in newer versions of DOS, or you can use an aftermarket utility.

The two most common problems encountered with otherwise healthy hard drives are a lack of sufficient free space and lost allocation space caused by turning the PC off while it's in Windows or DOS applications software. As a rule of thumb, you should keep a minimum of 10 percent of your hard drive space free at all times. The main reason is Windows' constant need for virtual memory. When Windows runs out of RAM, the SIMMs installed in your systems, it uses space on the hard drive to swap out chunks of memory. If the hard drive gets too full, the system may lock up in Windows, or files may become corrupted. Many software applications, Windows and otherwise, create temporary files on the hard drive while they are executing. These files are used for backups or for temporary storage. If the PC is turned off while in Windows or these DOS applications, the files aren't closed properly and become lost allocation units on the hard drive. Run CHKDSK on older DOS systems, or SCANDISK on with newer versions of DOS, to free up the lost space.

Physical errors on IDE and SCSI drives are pretty rare, and should be easy to spot with any decent diagnostic program. SCANDISK will test that all of the locations on the drive are usable, while a diagnostic that runs a variety of hard-drive tests (including butterfly read) will spot trouble with read/write head positioning. Another rare problem occurs when the software stored at the very beginning of the hard drive, the MBR (Master Boot Record), gets so corrupted that neither FORMAT nor FDISK can access the drive. Causing this damage is the ultimate goal of several computer viruses. Factory low-level or "rescue" formatters will scrub a drive and prepare it for FDISK no matter how bad the software problems get. If you have a new hard drive that makes excessive noise, a loud hum or high pitched squeal, send it back. Noise is always symptomatic of a mechanical problem.

The most important thing to remember about working with IDE hard drives in older systems is to record the CMOS drive parameters. When you first take possession of your hand-me-down PC, enter CMOS setup and copy the drive parameters onto a piece of tape. Stick it to the side or the back of the system box. These parameters are sometimes incorporated in the drive label, but the person who originally built the PC may have chosen a different set of parameters, yielding a slightly smaller drive size. The parameters for LZ (Landing Zone) and WP (Write Precompensation current) are not used with IDE drives. New systems come with an "Autodetect Hard Drive" option in the CMOS setup, which will restore the drive parameters automatically, and can be used to rediscover parameters for drives from older machines. SCSI drives are set up as "Not Present" in the CMOS setup and are operated through the controller BIOS.

One of the most confusing issues for people installing new hard drives is the size of a megabyte. Drive manufacturers call a megabyte one million bytes, in order to size their drives. Some CMOS setup utilities call a megabyte one million bytes, others use the actual value of 1024 kilobytes. FDISK always calls a megabyte 1024 kilobytes. The difference seems small, but the extra "24s" add up quickly. Hard drives are also sold by their "Unformatted" capacity, which swells the size by another few percent that will never be available to you as storage space. A hard drive sold as 340 megabytes will show up as 325 megabytes in FDISK. A 1080-megabyte hard drive will show up as a 1000-megabyte drive in FDISK.

Hard drives are not worth repairing, due to the availability of faster, larger drives costing the same as the repair. Warranties on hard drives are usually 3 years, sometime 5 years on larger drives. If you pull a bad hard drive out of a system that is a few hundred megabytes or greater and was manufactured after 1994, try calling the manufacturer to see if you can get an exchange. The occasional challenge with old hard drives is trying to recover data that was never backed up before recycling them into bookends. When attempting any of these last-ditch recovery attempts, have your backup media (floppy, tape, or direct computer link) connected and ready, because the drive may get going once, and then not work a second time. Old drives that spin up but don't seek are often stuck in park. Tapping on the drive cover with a screwdriver handle may unstick the heads and get the drive going long enough to get the data off. Drives that hum, or display a lit LED and that don't spin up, may be suffering from failure of the permanent lubrication. Moving the PC to a warm place or even putting it in direct sunlight may get the drive going temporarily.

Video Adapters

The most common problem is for the new VGA adapter not to be seated properly in the bus slot. Sometimes this will cause the POST (Power On Self Test) routine to generate an eight- or nine-beep code, which means the video memory can't be read. Other times the computer will seem to be booting, but the display will never come on. Re-install the video card paying special attention that the end of the card, whether ISA or VESA, is as well seated in the front of the slot as the back section, which is held in place by the screw. In some instances you will have to loosen the screw or to build it up with washers, because it is forcing the adapter to pivot against the edge of the bus connector, lifting the front end. The problem is most common with VESA local bus cards, since the distance of the special VESA connector from the pivot point is very long.

In some cases, a PC won't boot or the screen won't light up, due to the mix of adapters in the bus slots. This isn't supposed to happen, and is probably due to minor timing errors, but I have often seen VGA adapters and SIDE adapters that work fine separately in other PCs simply refuse to work together on the same bus. This is always diagnosed by removing the SIDE adapter, because you can't boot a PC without a video adapter. Another build-time issue involves high end communication adapters for remote terminal support, and other cards requiring frame buffers below the 1-MB boundary. These adapters may produce memory conflicts with the VGA frame buffer area (A000 to C000). Frame buffers on these cards can be moved by switch settings or by a software utility or the EISA configuration in EISA machines.

If the video adapter is well seated, and you still get a beep code, the problem is usually a blown or improperly inserted video memory chip, and this can be easily replaced if it's socketed. On most adapters with more than 256 K installed, the second bank can be substituted for the first, and the first bank can be left out while testing the card. Video memory must be replaced in banks, just like system memory. Some flaky video problems, such as mouse tracks being permanently left on the screen, are due to the wrong video memory being installed on the card. This particular problem may not show up until the card is warm, and only in some applications. There are several different flavors of video memory, so unless you have the original documentation, or the type of video memory required is silk screened on the circuit board, the adapter manufacturer or their WWW site will have to be contacted.

All SVGA adapters have a jumper or software utility for setting inter-laced or noninterlaced operation, and compatibility with monitors sup-porting VESA modes. Windows has no way to take advantage of the new adapters functionality unless you go through all of the configuration software (see Upgrading Video Adapters in Section 3). Never set a card to VESA timing or noninterlaced mode unless you are sure the monitor can support it, or the monitor may be damaged. Failure of an application to display a certain field or text as it does on another PC is usually due to the video driver's being installed incorrectly or not at all. This prob-lem is more likely when working at resolutions higher than standard VGA (640 × 480). Some cards have a jumper for use with monochrome VGA monitors; others may have a 4- or 16-shade monochrome driver.

The vast majority of new systems are built with video cards that are at least downwardly compatible with VGA. When dealing with older TTL cards and pre-VGA high resolution cards, the problem is com-pounded, because it will be hard to find another monitor to use to check whether the problem is the adapter or the monitor. You can find all the old adapters, MGA (Mono Graphics Adapter), Hercules (720 × 350 TTL mono resolution), CGA (Color Graphics Adapter), and EGA (Extend-ed Graphics Adapter), for sale in the $10 range, but it's really a pretty bad investment unless you're dead set on spending the absolute minimum to keep your hand-me-down running. The old monitors themselves are also available as remanufactured units, but I couldn't see buying one under any circumstance.

Monitors

The most common monitor problem is total failure, where power status LED doesn't come on. This can be due to something as simple as a blown fuse, or something serious as a dead flyback transformer or a popped CRT. Repairs on 14″ and under monitors normally cost more than half of the mail order cost of a new monitor, and are backed by only a 30 or 90 day warranty. Simple problems like blown fuses or broken switches can also be repaired at a local appliance shop that does TV work, and you will probably get a better rate than at a monitor repair facility. Monitors over 14″ may well be worth repairing, but this must be decided on a case-by-case basis. Radical changes in screen size or brightness may be compensated for with hidden adjustment pots, but this will normally require working with the monitor live, often with the cover off, around lethal voltages. I don't recommend working inside the monitor case to anyone without proper training. Larger monitors may also come with a degaussing switch, which may clear up some slow developing display problems. Loss of a primary color that can be attributed to the monitor electronics is one of the instances in which out-of-warranty repair may be sensible.

About half the problems I've encountered with new monitors or PCs that have been moved and set up again prove to be connections or electrical environment. A partially mated connector on either end of the cable can result in loss of colors or sync. A bent pin inside the connector shell can cause any problem ranging from no display to missing colors or a continually scrolling screen. The bent-pin problem can be particularly irksome, because the pin may break while being straightened. If the cable is a two-connector type, buy a new cable. If the cable is permanently attached to the monitor, you can remake the adapter end using a 15-pin high-density (3-row) "D-shell" connector, but you will need a superthin soldering iron to make the pin connections in the center row. Long cable extensions result in diminished brightness and loss of focus on VGA and higher monitors.

Monitors that are placed close together will often produce scan-line interference on one another, which manifests itself by a line or set of lines continually moving across the screen. Increasing monitor separation by a few feet or changing their orientation with one another will usually clear up the problem. An oscillating image or loss of a primary color may be due to the VGA card, but often as not it can be a monitor connection or environmental problem. The most common cause for a shaky or oscillating image is the presence of an external magnetic field, such as the power supply for your inkjet, or another small transformer in close proximity to the monitor. Occasionally, high current carrying lines in the walls or location near an air conditioner can be the problem. Troubleshooting these problems is carried out by moving the PC to another location, or experimenting with turning off some of the surrounding electrical equipment.

Some of the older multisync monitors are capable of displaying all of the modes from MDA up to SVGA, so if you are upgrading an old system with a multisync monitor, you may be able to use it on a new PC. Older WYSIWYG (What You See Is What You Get) cards and monitors may be repairable by the manufacturer or by a good repair service, but keep in mind that both the card and the monitor cost over $1,000 each when new and are highly proprietary. Never get involved in paying for old TTL monitors (MDA, CGA, EGA).

I've often run across the situation where the monitor or video adapter has failed on an old PC-XT or 286 system, and the owner just wants to get a file off of the hard drive and copied onto a floppy before throwing the whole PC in the trash. You can do this by typing blindly, if you remember where the files are, along with their exact spelling. Otherwise, you can use the old DOS pipes symbol ">", to send the information that would normally go to the screen to a different device. For example, if you want to print the directory of your root drive, C:, you can type

```
DIR C: > LPT1:
```

Or, if you don't have a printer, but you do have access to another working computer with a compatible floppy drive, you can copy the directory to a floppy by typing

```
DIR D:> A:MYFILE.TXT
```

When the floppy drive light goes out, you can put the floppy disk in the machine with the working monitor and type

```
TYPE A:MYFILE.TXT |MORE
```

and the directory will show on the screen. Whether you use a printer or another system, it's a slow way to navigate through a directory structure, but you'll only have to do it once. You can then copy the important files to floppy and park the PC on the curb.

If your PC always asks for a password on boot or starts off in a menu or in Windows, you will have to get to the DOS prompt by blind typing. Menu exit is normally accomplished through a function key (F1—F12), followed by "Y" or hitting "Enter" to an "Are you sure you want to exit?" question. Windows is exited by holding down the "Alt" key and hitting "F" (for File), then letting up the "Alt" key and hitting "X" (for eXit). Then hit "Enter" to pass the "Are you sure you want to exit Windows" question and return to DOS. This is one of the times where the hard-drive activity LED or a good pair of ears can give you useful clues to your progress.

Drive Controller and I/O Adapters

New PCs integrate all of the I/O functions and IDE controllers on the motherboard. Most upgrade motherboards you buy will also have onboard ports and controllers. These are highly reliable, but in case of failure they can be disabled in the CMOS or with motherboard jumpers, and replaced with standard bus adapters. Most 386 and 486 systems were built with SIDE adapters, which incorporate an IDE drive interface, dual floppy controller, 2 serial ports and 1 parallel port. The default configuration for these adapters is: COM1 on interrupt 4, COM2 on interrupt 3 and LPT1 on interrupt 7. In case of total failure of the drive controllers, the BIOS will notify you at boot time with a "FDD/HDD Controller Failure." The presence of the communications and printer ports can be confirmed by the system configuration screen at boot. Intermittent problems with SIDE adapters are unfortunately fairly common, with hard-drive boot problems leading the pack. Random system lockup while accessing the drives, or failure to consistently recognize a mouse or printer, are also common problems.

SIDE cards are the least expensive components in a PC (under $15), so if you're looking for a place to start spending money on troubleshooting parts, here it is. There is nothing on the adapter itself that can be repaired, but you can make sure your connectors are on good, and you can try reseating jumpers if a port mysteriously disappears after years of use. Some apparent SIDE failures can be attributed to conflicts with other adapters on the bus, a problem which will show up immediately after an upgrade. VESA local bus SIDE controllers are the worst in terms of reliability, and the extra load they present to the CPU often causes the motherboard to appear to be dead. Local bus controllers with hardware cache are problematical and should never be purchased. Compatibility problems with software applications, physical memory errors, and cache bottle-necking are common problems in caching controller installations.

All SCSI controllers and IDE adapters for the EISA or PCI bus are manufactured to higher quality standards and are generally reliable. When adding a SCSI controller during an upgrade, make sure you disable any onboard floppy controller. Make sure that the BIOS on SCSI cards is the current version, as these are upgraded on a regular basis and are available from the manufacturer. EISA controllers must be configured properly using the motherboard EISA utility and configuration files supplied by the controller manufacturer. Both EISA and PCI bus controllers have software-selectable interrupt and DMA settings, either directly available in the CMOS setups, or via an EISA configuration utility. Other EISA settings include support for drives over 1,000 megabytes, bus transfer rate, and options for "standard" or "enhanced" operation. Enhanced operation requires an extra interrupt and must be enabled to take full advantage of the controller.

SCSI controllers which sport an external 25-pin connector should have the connector covered or taped over if not in use, to prevent accidental connection of a printer cable. Systems using IDE disk drives and SCSI CD-ROMs or tape drives may boot somewhat slower that usual, and the controller BIOS may produce a message about the boot device that can be misinterpreted as an error. A common problem with all drive controllers is susceptibility to high heat. If it is over 90 degrees Fahrenheit in the room, you can be sure it's a lot hotter inside the system box, so don't be surprised if drive errors or lockups occur.

Network Adapters

All new network adapters are shipped with software that includes self-diagnostic capabilities. The software not only tests that the card is functional, it also reports on all the jumper settings and allows you to change settings on jumperless versions. Network cards are interrupt driven, occupy I/O space, and may employ memory-mapped transfers, so they are subject to conflicts with other cards if not configured correctly. Network adapters have a pretty high DOA (Dead On Arrival) rate, because intense competition has driven prices so low that quality control has suffered. Most new adapters come with diagnostic LEDs on the

trol has suffered. Most new adapters come with diagnostic LEDs on the back, which indicate the activity of the card.

Nine out of ten network adapter problems will actually be caused by improper software configuration. All network adapters require some sort of driver to be installed when the network boots, and if the driver installs successfully, the adapter is probably functional. Note that the software driver will normally install with the incorrect interrupt specified, or with an interrupt conflict that may prevent reliable operation. Some thin ethernet (coaxial cable type) network cards come with available on-board terminators. These terminators should never be used because they cause a great deal of confusion if network nodes are ever added or rearranged. Many network cards are capable of operating in more than one mode; usually as 10Base-T or Thin Ethernet, and this is often a jumper selectable choice. Make sure you have the adapter jumpered to the type of cabling you are using.

Network Cabling

There are more possible options for network cabling and topology than there are types of cards. All bus-type topologies require a proper terminator at each end of the bus. The terminator resistance must match the characteristic impedance of the cable, which must be the correct impedance for the type of card. Incorrect network cabling may work for some time after installation, or even work consistently until nodes are added to the network. Without expensive equipment, the way to check the impedance of existing coaxial cabling is to pull a little out of the wall or look in the crawl space or drop ceiling and read the casing. Standard coaxial cables used in networking are RG58U (50 ohms), RG59U (93 ohms), and RG62U (75 ohms). The current standard for color coding NC terminators is green for 50 ohms (ethernet) and white for 93 ohms (Arcnet). The 75-ohm coaxial cable used by cable TV and some network topologies is often improperly substituted for either 50 or 93 ohm cable. These networks may limp by with a small number of nodes or over short distances, but if you find out the wrong cable is installed, have it ripped out and replaced immediately.

10Base-T networks utilize twisted-pair cable with RJ45 connectors and require a concentrator, or hub. Cabling is straight through and uses only 4 wires of the eight available in a RJ45 jack (1, 2, 3, and 6).

With both twisted-pair and coaxial-cable networks, the cable and connectors should be the first items checked in case of failure. Unlike small coaxial networks, twisted pair is often already in place or is installed by a separate contractor at a customer site. Intermittent network problems will most often be caused by intermittent hardware failure at the node or server, unrelated to the network. Problems can arise from cabling that is run too close to sources of intermittent electrical noise or that exceeds the segment length limits specified for the equipment. Temperature and humidity can also be factors.

10Base-T connectors are often made up wrong, which is easily determined by substituting a known good cable in place of the questionable length. Other 10Base-T problems include RJ45 connectors that aren't crimped tightly enough, and the wires not being inserted far enough into the connector. Looking at an RJ45 connector end-on, you should always be able to see the copper ends of all four wires in the right positions through the transparent plastic. 10Base-T hubs can also have one or more dead ports, while the rest continue to function normally. If you have problems with a particular workstation, always try moving it to another port on the hub before suspecting the network adapter in the PC. 10Base-T wire can also have a conductor broken after being crushed by a desk or chair, even if the cable sheath remains unbroken.

Coaxial LAN cabling is much more difficult to troubleshoot than 10Base-T LAN cabling because failure of a single connector or segment on a coaxial LAN will usually "down" the whole network. Oddly enough, in the cases where a broken connection doesn't knock all the workstations off the network, it's symptomatic of a worse problem. Coaxial cable is essentially a two-conductor system, with a single-wire central conductor and a braided ground sheath. The information that flows on LANs is transmitted at Radio Frequencies (RF). This means that a radio wave, just like those pulled in by your car antenna, travels down the coaxial cable, trapped between the central conductor and the braided ground shield. The common Thin-Ethernet network utilizes the "T" type connectors that are fastened directly to the network adapter in the computer to tap the RF signal off of the cable. Both ends of the cable must be terminated with a small load (terminator), which turns the remaining power of the RF wave into a tiny amount of heat, preventing it from reflecting back into the cable and setting up interference patterns. If the coaxial cable is broken and some of the network stations continue to be able to communicate with the server, it usually means that the cable is the wrong type or many of the connections suffer from high power loss, such that the leftover RF power is getting attenuated anyway. The most common problem with coaxial cabling is bad contact between the braid and the BNC connector. The second most common are connectors where the central conductor is cut too short, leaving the contact dependent on the exact positioning of the connector and the cable behind it. Never fool around with trying to tape flaky connections into place; just replace the segment or make up a new connector.

Modems

There are a number of setup parameters on a modem, both hardware and software, that can prevent the modem from operating properly. Hardware setup for external modems is done on the modem, normally by an exposed switch block. Since the switches are generally not labeled and follow no convention, troubleshooting the modem requires the manufacturer's documentation. The most common reasons for an external modem failing to operate are the wrong type of serial cable or a bad communications port on the PC. The only way to troubleshoot the cable is to confirm the type from the documentation or try another one. The easiest way to ensure that a Com port is working properly is to temporarily reroute it to the connector that the mouse works off (this means swapping ribbon cables on the SIDE card or motherboard), and then try using the modem with DOS software.

Hardware setup for non-plug-and-play internal modems is done with jumpers on the adapter and requires a knowledge of how the other communications ports are set up. Internal modems often suffer from bad documentation: the settings shown in the book often don't agree with the settings printed on the adapter. Always follow the settings printed on the adapter. Many internal modems allow you to choose a nonstandard interrupt, often IRQ 5 or IRQ 9. If you experience any problems with your modem when using these settings, change back to the communications port and interrupt pair not being used by the mouse (usually Com2, IRQ 3), and disable the existing Com2 port in the system.

The first step in any modem-troubleshooting scenario is to make sure that the phone line you are attempting to call out on is valid by checking it with a telephone handset. Most business phone systems will not support a plain-wired modem and require a special switch or a dedicated line. Modems are more sensitive to connection quality than voice connections. If your modem often disconnects during use, fails to connect, or connects at a low baud rate, try connecting it to a different phone jack in the house. If you can hear cross-talk between separate voice lines in a house, the phone wiring probably has a bad ground. On all modems, the "Line," "Wall," or "Telco" connection on the modem is for connection to the wall jack; the "Phone" connection is for connecting an optional telephone handset.

The software-troubleshooting procedure for both internal and external modems is basically a two-step process. First, ensure that the Com port address or number and interrupt are selected correctly in the software. You should be able to hear the modem go "off hook" (sounds like a phone being picked up) and attempting to dial out at this point. Second, if the modem is dialing out but not making the connection, make sure that you are using the correct parameters for the particular number you are calling, including baud rate, number of data bits, stop bits, parity, etc. The baud rate must be in the range of capability of the modem, and for external modems, within the capability of the UART (see Upgrading Modems in Chapter 10). If the modem clearly picks up the phone to dial, resulting 20 or 30 seconds later in a recorded message from the phone company, you are probably attempting to tone dial on a pulse system. Try changing the modem setup to pulse and dial again. If you are attempting to operate the modem on Com3 or Com4, try reinstalling it on Com1 or Com2. Some software packages will not work on Com3 or Com4 despite having them listed as valid options.

Internal modems tend to be more troublesome than external modems because of a generally lower quality and the need to remove them from the machine to change hardware settings. One of the more annoying tendencies of cheaper internal modems is to pick up RF interference from other components in the system and produce a whistling tone on their piezoelectric speaker. Relocating the card to another slot sometimes lowers the noise level; reorienting the computer can help, as the sound is highly directional. Both internal and external fax/modems often suffer from a lack of fax compatibility. The documentation may help you to change settings to get the fax part of the modem working well with a particular receiving fax, only to lose compatibility with a receiving fax that worked fine the day before. In general, expect problems with sending faxes, and try sending single-page faxes (no cover sheet either) if the connection goes well but page errors follow.

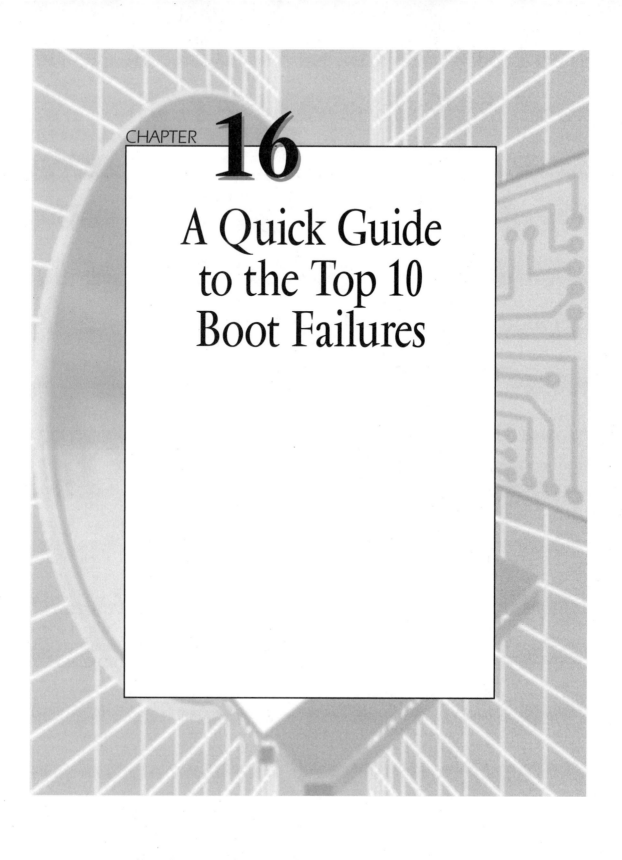

16

A Quick Guide to the Top 10 Boot Failures

SIDE Adapter

The cheapest component in older PCs is also the weakest link. The SIDE adapter incorporates the functions of the IDE drive controller, the floppy controller, two communications ports (Com ports), the printer port and a game port. The failure of any one of these is a reason to replace the entire card, because at less than $15, you won't find a single function adapter to replace the failed function for much less. The most serious failure is the dreaded "HDD controller failure," the hard drive controller failure. When this error appears, the only thing to do is open up the PC, reseat the adapter and all of the connections to the drives, and try again. Often times, this problem will give early warning signs, the error appearing once a month or week, and going away if you just turn the PC off and on again. If you count on your PC for serious use, replace the SIDE adapter as soon as the error appears, unless it turns out to be caused by a poorly seated card or loose connection. If you have a failed local bus SIDE card, replace it with a standard ISA SIDE adapter.

Video Adapter

The PC will normally announce the failure of the video adapter with a series of eight or nine short beeps, besides which nothing will show up on the screen. Before you rush out and buy a new adapter, reseat the card and try it in another slot. If it is a local bus card, pay special attention that the card is seated well throughout its length. Also try temporarily removing the other cards on the bus to see if one of them has failed and is interfering with the video adapter. Sometimes a video adapter will fail without the system knowing. This results in a blank screen, but a normal boot. If your machine normally boots to DOS, you can try typing blindly, something like "DIR" or "CHKDSK", just to see if the hard drive light flashes. If so, you know that the PC is fine, but either the monitor or adapter has failed, but don't forget to check the monitor connector on the back of the PC! The easiest way to determine if the problem is the video adapter or the monitor is to try the monitor on another PC or borrow a monitor to try on your video adapter.

Monitor

The best way to determine if your monitor has failed is to try it on another PC. Most monitors have a status light on the front, often part of the on/off switch, but I wouldn't give up on a monitor just because the status light doesn't come on. A more ominous failure sign is a complete lack of warmth coming from the vented top of a monitor that has been left on. A failed monitor will not prevent the PC from booting normally; you just won't be able to see anything. If your PC boots to DOS and you have a good memory, you can try typing blindly, which is handy for copying important files from the hard drive to a floppy. If you confirm that the monitor is dead, don't try to repair it yourself. The big decision is whether you want to buy a new 14" monitor for around $170, upgrade to a larger monitor, or have it repaired. Out-of-warranty repairs on monitors usually cost a minimum of $75, and most shops have a minimum charge for diagnosing them of $25 to $50. The dilemma is that some failures, such as the picture tube or main logic board, when combined with a labor charge, cost as much or more than a new monitor and carry only a 90-day warranty. Unless you have a personal referral to a monitor repair depot or are desperately short on cash, buy the new monitor.

Power Supply

The first sign of a power supply problem is a complete lack of sound when you turn on the PC. No fans, no drives seeking, no beeps, and no little lights on the front of the box. All power supplies are equipped with a fan that draws the warm air from inside the PC and exhausts it into the room. If the fan is blowing air, the problem is probably on the motherboard. After checking such obvious things like the power cord being firmly plugged in and the wall socket being alive (you can check it with a lamp), you'll need to open the PC to go further. There is still a chance that the power supply is good, but it cannot operate due to a short circuit in one of the devices it supplies. Make sure the switch is off, disconnect the two leads from the motherboard, than try booting again. If the power supply fan and the drives are still quiet, reconnect the motherboard, then disconnect all of the leads to the drives. If the lights on the front of the case still don't come on, the power supply is bad. Otherwise, one of the drives has developed a short, and you can determine which by plugging them back in one at a time.

Memory Failure

The most common memory boot failure occurs when the BIOS POST (power on self test) detects an error in the first 64 KB of RAM, and sounds three beeps. This means that there is a failure in the first bank of RAM, labeled bank 0. The problem is that there can be anywhere from one to four SIMMs in the bank, depending on the CPU and SIMM type (see Memory Banks and DMA). In all cases you should try reseating the SIMM(s) in bank 0 and rebooting. Next, if you have more than one bank of memory installed, try transferring all of the SIMMs from the last bank into bank 0. In most cases this will fix the problem, though you'll have reduced your total amount of memory by the number of SIMMs removed. Always carefully read the markings on the motherboard to see which slots constitute a bank; on some motherboards they will be alternating rather than grouped.

Battery

Battery failure is usually announced by the PC at boot time with the message "CMOS Battery State Low" or "CMOS Checksum Failure." After this message, the PC may further announce, "Insert Boot Disk in Drive A: to Continue," "No System Disk," or something similar. This just means that due to the battery failure, the computer has forgotten all of the settings stored in the battery-backed CMOS memory, including what kind of hard drive is installed. You need to enter CMOS setup and correctly identify the number and type of floppy drives and hard drives, reset the date and time, after which your computer will work fine until you turn it off again. If your setup screen doesn't offer an "Autodetect Hard Drives" option and you don't have the numbers written down somewhere, you'll have to remove the drive(s) to see if the parameters are included on the label. Write down the manufacturer name and drive type if they aren't. The manufacturer, if still in business, will provide the information over the Web, telephone, or fax. Until you replace the battery, the error will repeat each time you boot.

Stuck Key or Keyboard Failure

Keyboard failures are far more common with expensive keyboards than cheap ones. If you have a keyboard failure, don't get it repaired; buy a new one for $20 or less. The most common reason for a "Stuck Key" error, which the BIOS will report at boot, is an actual stuck key which isn't sticking up as far as all of the other keys, or something resting unobtrusively on the keyboard. In either case, when the affected key is freed up, the PC should boot. Other keyboard failures, "Keyboard Failure," or "Keyboard Not Present", can be due to the keyboard cable having popped out of the PC or the keyboard. Unfortunately, cables are often damaged or severed by objects placed on desks, or by drawers and cabinets, especially when the PC resides on the floor or the keyboard on a pull-out tray. You can repair a cable yourself or buy a new keyboard for less than a shop will charge to do the job. Keyboard problems can also be caused by the failure of the controller chip, also known as the keyboard BIOS chip.

Motherboard or CPU Failure

Boot failures due to the motherboard occur most frequently after the system is worked on or moved. The most likely reason for the motherboard to fail is an external short circuit, caused by a loose screw in the case rolling around on top of or under the motherboard and getting into a bad spot. In any case, the best indicator of a dead motherboard is when none of the little lights on the front of the system box come on, but you can definitely hear the drives seeking, and the fan on the power supply is blowing air. Motherboards also fail when flexed after years of stability, not uncommon when a computer with a flimsy case is moved. CPU failures are hard to differentiate from motherboard failures and are most easily diagnosed by trying a different CPU in the motherboard. Systems that employ several VESA local bus adapters put a much greater load on the CPU than other PCs, and a seeming motherboard/CPU failure in an older system may go away if these cards are replaced by regular ISA cards.

Corrupt or Missing Boot Files

One of the leading contenders for the technical support crown is the error message "Missing Operating System." It can be caused by a whole variety of problems, such as the wrong hard drive parameters being entered in the CMOS settings, or the attack of a computer virus, but the most common reason is the accidental deletion or corruption of the system boot files. In any case, the first step is to get the PC to boot from a floppy disk. If you put a known good boot floppy in the A: drive, and the computer continues to report "Missing Operating System", you'll have to go into the CMOS setting and under one of the "Advanced" or "Chipset" screens find the line called "Boot Sequence" and change it from "C: A:" to "A: C:". Once you get the system booted from floppy, you need to make sure that you can read the C: drive, and that the version of the operating system you are booting is the same as the one installed on the hard drive. If the floppy you are using is an emergency boot floppy created when Windows 95 or NT was installed, you don't have to worry. If the computer normally boots to DOS, than use the "DIR" command to take note of the size and date of the file "COMMAND.COM" on both the A: and C: drives. If they aren't the same, you'll have to find a boot disk with the same version, or the original DOS install disk, before you can proceed with the repair.

Bad Startup Files

Eight of the previous nine failures, the exception being a dead monitor, prevent the PC from getting as far as the startup files during the boot process. The startup files, AUTOEXEC.BAT and CONFIG.SYS in DOS, and a variety of registry files in the different Windows versions, can be innocently changed by the user or by a new piece of installed software, such that the computer locks up when the faulty instruction is reached. If you have a DOS version previous to 5.0, than you'll have to use a floppy disk to boot until you resolve the problem, and the following shortcut doesn't apply to you. For all others, tap the <F8> key a few times during the boot process, starting immediately after the computer finishes counting memory. In the case of DOS, you'll be given the option to step through your startup files one command at a time. When you do this, write down each command (the first few words are sufficient) presented before you type "Y" to continue, and the last command you write down is the one causing the problem. Boot the computer the same way, type "N" when you reach the offending line, than use the DOS Editor to remove it from the file. If you are using Windows 95, the <F8> key will give you the option to boot in different modes, including safe mode, after which you can use the "Device Manager" to correct the problem.

DOS System Startup Files and DOS Memory Management

The overwhelming majority of hand-me-down PCs come with DOS installed. Even if you are running Windows 95, the DOS system startup files control how the system functions when DOS mode is invoked. Most of the commands in the startup files, CONFIG.SYS and AUTOEXEC.BAT, are placed there automatically when software applications are installed. Software applications that modify one of these files will usually make a backup copy of the information they are changing, so that you can restore the system to its original condition if the upgrade should fail. These backup copies always keep the same basic file name, but they change the three-letter extension from "BAT" or "SYS" to something like "BAK", "OLD", "SY3", or the like. If you are trying to back out a change to a system file, and the "DIR" command shows that you have many versions of these startup files, you should use the one with the latest date to replace the current "BAT" or "SYS" file.

DOS Memory Management

The main reason for you to start fiddling around with your system startup files is to configure memory. One of the most deceptive errors that DOS can produce in any variation is, "Not enough memory to run program." Messages like this have led many people into upgrading their memory, only to find that the problem is still present. What DOS is really trying to say is that it doesn't have enough free conventional memory to load your program. This refers to the 640 K of program memory that normal DOS programs can access. As long as you have a recent version of DOS (version 5.0 or higher), you can free up program memory by moving some of the system software to other locations. If you don't have a recent-enough version of DOS, you can buy an aftermarket memory manager, but upgrading to DOS 6.2 makes more sense.

DOS classifies memory five different ways. The dividing points are sometimes physical, sometimes logical. Some of the memory locations are reserved for use by the memory that's installed on the adapters, like your VGA card. The ability of DOS to address your memory in accordance with the different schemes depends on the CPU and the amount of memory installed. DOS manages memory beyond the first megabyte via one or more memory managers that are installed as device drivers in your CONFIG.SYS file.

Conventional Memory (or Program Memory)

Conventional memory refers to the first 640 KB of memory installed in the PC. DOS can manage this conventional memory without any additional memory managers being installed. The decision to make exactly 640 KB of memory available for programs was somewhat arbitrary, but when DOS took shape in the early eighties, it seemed like more than anyone would ever need. The actual decimal value, 640, is derived from the hexadecimal addresses between 0000 to 9FFF. The next address, A000, marks the beginning of upper memory.

Upper Memory

Not all hand-me-down PCs come equipped with RAM in the upper memory area, even though DOS is capable of addressing these locations. PCs older than 386s often came with only 512 KB or 640 KB of memory installed. The motherboards in these older systems had no provision for adding more RAM to the memory bus, so any additions had to be made with adapters added to the I/O bus. These adapters took two forms—either expanded memory or extended memory, both of which will be discussed below. Extended memory is present in all new PCs and simply refers to the memory beyond the first megabyte.

The upper memory area comprises the 384 KB (A000 to FFFF, in hex) that DOS sets aside for system use. With older versions of DOS, upper memory could only be used to map access to adapter memory, normally in 64-KB pages. The EMM386.EXE memory manager which can access this memory was added to later versions of DOS, and requires a 386 or higher CPU to run. The main trade-off in using upper memory, is that memory set aside as upper memory by EMM386 can't be co-opted for extended memory by Windows.

High Memory

High memory refers to the first page (64 KB) of memory located immediately after the end of the first megabyte. This translates into addresses 10000 to 10FFF in hexadecimal. DOS can be loaded into high memory, freeing up both conventional and upper memory for more efficient use. You must have more than 1 MB of memory installed to make use of high memory.

Extended Memory

All of the memory installed beyond the first 1 MB is known as XMS (extended memory). The DOS extended memory manager is the HIMEM.SYS device driver. Extended memory is used by Windows, memory aware DOS programs, and DOS utilities like SMARTDRV and RAMDRIVE. SMARTDRV uses extended memory to cache information from the drives for fast access, a similar scheme to using external cache on the motherboard to improve the performance of main memory. RAMDRIVE uses extended memory to create a simulated, superfast drive, that is assigned the next available drive letter (D:, E:, F:) and is accessed just like a physical drive. Some high-end DOS applications, like AutoCAD or 3-D games, use their own extended memory managers that load with the program.

Expanded Memory

Also known as LIM (Lotus, Intel, Microsoft) specification memory, expanded memory uses a page-swapping scheme to give DOS programs mapped access to additional memory. Originally, all expanded memory was added in the form of expanded memory adapters installed on the I/O bus. Those expanded memory adapters required their own memory management software, which had to be added to the CONFIG.SYS file. Expanded memory adapters are no longer used in PCs, being both expensive and slow, but EMM386 can use extended memory to simulate expanded memory for use with old programs.

Managing Memory

Starting with DOS 5.0, Microsoft included the LOADHIGH (LH) and DEVICEHIGH commands with the operating system. DEVICEHIGH is used in CONFIG.SYS to place device drivers in the upper and high memory areas described above. LOADHIGH, abbreviated as LH, is placed before lines in the AUTOEXEC.BAT file to load them into the upper or high memory areas. For either of these commands to be used, you must first ensure the HIMEM.SYS and EMM386.EXE are being loaded in the CONFIG.SYS file. Commands in both CONFIG.SYS and AUTOEXEC.BAT are executed sequentially, and the order they appear in determines the allocation of memory and other resources.

Unless you are planning to use expanded memory, you must use the NOEMS switch. Otherwise, EMM386 will set aside a page of high memory for the swapping pages with the expanded memory, reducing the amount of space available for loading software drivers. You must also specify DOS=UMB along with DOS=HIGH in the CONFIG.SYS file, or DOS won't allow use of the upper memory area for loading device drivers "high." Once the computer has booted, you can check how efficiently you are using high memory by using MEM/C |MORE.

Example Report from MEM/C

Modules using memory below 1 MB:

Name	Total	=	Conventional	+	Upper Memory	
MSDOS	44,685	(44K)	44,685	(44K)	0	(0K)
HIMEM	1,120	(1K)	1,120	(1K)	0	(0K)
EMM386	3,120	(3K)	3,120	(3K)	0	(0K)
COMMAND	2,928	(3K)	2,928	(3K)	0	(0K)
IO	80	(0K)	80	(0K)	0	(0K)
ASPI2DOS	9,904	(10K)	0	(0K)	9,904	(10K)
EMMDSWP	3,824	(4K)	0	(0K)	3,824	(4K)
ASPICD	11,984	(12K)	0	(0K)	11,984	(12K)
ONTRACK	4,064	(4K)	0	(0K)	4,064	(4K)
EMMDSW	2,064	(2K)	0	(0K)	2,064	(2K)
SMARTDRV	29,024	(28K)	0	(0K)	29,024	(28K)
MSCDEX	57,104	(56K)	0	(0K)	57,104	(56K)
MOUSE	16,848	(16K)	0	(0K)	16,848	(16K)
Free	626,016	(611K)	602,224	(588K)	23,792	(23K)

Memory Summary:

Type of Memory	Total	=	Used	+	Free
Conventional	654,336		52,112		602,224
Upper	158,608		134,816		23,792
Reserved	0		0		0
Extended (XMS)	7,181,424		2,323,568		4,857,656
Total memory	7,994,368		2,510,496		5,483,872
Total under 1 MB	812,944		186,928		626,016

Largest executable program size   602,128   (588K)

Largest free upper memory block   23,696   (23K)

MS-DOS is resident in the high memory area.

The double reporting of memory amount, in bytes and in kilobytes (K), is just the traditional way of counting memory. One kilobyte = 1024 bytes, and the amounts (in "K") shown above were reached by arbitrarily rounding up or down. The large amount of extended memory used in the example above is being employed as cache by the SMARTDRV utility, and is released on entering Windows.

When you get a "Not enough memory to load program" type error in DOS, you want to configure memory to maximize the amount of free conventional memory. You do this by maximizing the total amount of upper memory available, then loading as many device drivers into upper memory as possible. However, simply replacing every "DEVICE=" with a "DEVICEHIGH=" in your CONFIG.SYS file, and sticking a "LH" at the beginning of every AUTOEXEC.BAT command, will rarely make the best use of your resources. The DOS memory manager sequentially loads all of the software you specify into upper memory, until the remaining free memory block won't fit another program. No errors will be generated, but the remaining drivers and TSRs (Terminate and Stay Resident programs) will be loaded in conventional memory.

For example, in the configuration above, it may become necessary to add a digitizer to the system, with a 34,000 byte driver. If you simply added a line to the end of the AUTOEXEC.BAT file, as in LH

C:\DIGITIZE\DIGIDRV.EXE, the driver would load in conventional memory since there are only 23,696 bytes of free upper memory. That would reduce the total conventional memory available to 572,128 bytes. However, if you put the new line before the command loading the mouse driver, which is 16,848 bytes, there would then be enough upper memory for the digitizer to load. The mouse driver would then load into conventional memory, but the total amount of conventional memory free would be 585,376 bytes, a 13,000-byte gain. You can see that by juggling the programs that get loaded high you can maximize the usage.

Depending on how your upper memory is organized, the total amount of upper memory free may be appreciably greater then the largest free upper memory block. In the example above, the largest free memory block is only 96 bytes less than the total amount of upper memory, but this is rarely the case. By changing the order of the lines in your AUTOEXEC.BAT and CONFIG.SYS files, you can exercise some control over this. Just remember that the order of some drivers, like placing HIMEM before EMM386, is fixed, and your system may lock up while you experiment. Just hit the "F5" key as soon as you see the "Loading MS-DOS" message during boot to bypass both startup files, or hit "F8" to step through the startup files line by line, and see exactly where the problem is coming from. In either case, when you go to re-edit the problem file, you may get a "File not found" error, because the path to the MS-DOS editor, EDIT, is missing. Just type PATH = C:\DOS then continue as usual. The system startup files, for both DOS and Windows, can be edited in Windows by selecting "Run" (under "File" in Windows 3.X, and on the Taskbar in Windows 95) and typing "sysedit" for the run file name.

Starting with MS-DOS 6.0, Microsoft added the MEMMAKER utility, which does all of the juggling for you. Another enhancement is the ability to place the drivers and TSRs in specific locations in upper memory, which really allows the programs to be shoe-horned in. Running MEMMAKER can take a bit of time and patience, since it goes through much the same process that you would be doing manually. If the system locks up during boot, MEMMAKER automatically restores the last known good boot configuration when you reboot. MEMMAKER also offers both "aggressive" and "conservative" approaches to configuring your memory, where the aggressive setting is more likely to cause lockups. If you are a "hands-on" sort of person, you can still use the manual approach that was required with DOS 5.0 when configuring DOS 6.X.

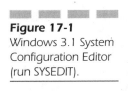

Figure 17-1
Windows 3.1 System
Configuration Editor
(run SYSEDIT).

System Configuration Editor

File   Edit   Search   Window

C:\WINDOWS\SYSTEM.INI

C:\WINDOWS\WIN.INI

C:\CONFIG.SYS

C:\AUTOEXEC.BAT

```
IF EXIST C:\WDMACS\LOCAL\FIX.BAT CALL C:\WDMACS\LOCAL\FIX
LH C:\DOS\EMMDSW.COM /D=EMMDDRV /F=C:\DOS\EMMDSW.CF
LH C:\DOS\SMARTDRV.EXE
LH c:\DOS\MSCDEX.EXE /M:20 /D:aspicd01
@ECHO OFF
PROMPT $p$g
SET path=C:\WDMACS;C:\ORAWIN\BIN;C:\WINWORD;C:\WINDOW
SET TEMP=d:\
```

PART **5**

Joining the Twenty-first Century

CHAPTER **18**

The Hand-Me-Down PC on the Web

On the information superhighway, nobody can see what CPU you're driving. A 15-year-old PC XT with a 14.4-K modem can participate in chat sessions or newsgroups just as handily as a brand new Pentium PRO with a 56-K next-generation modem. When the application is text based, the processor just doesn't make much difference. The primary difficulty in using older PCs on the Web lies in the availability of application software. Many national ISPs (Internet Service Providers) supply connection software that will only run on Windows platforms, often requiring a 486 processor and 8 MB of RAM as a minimum configuration. However, there are still local and regional ISPs who support older hardware, they just don't bombard your mailbox with floppy disks or CDs advertising their presence.

Once you move beyond text-based applications, the minimum acceptable system jumps about ten years beyond the XT. To simply handle Web browsers for Windows, a 486 is required. Standard Web features, like streaming sound (speech or music playing while you're online), require at least a very fast 486 to work tolerably well. More CPU-intensive applications, like videoconferencing, require at least a 90-MHz Pentium, often higher. Even more important than the raw speed of the PC is the speed of your connection to the Internet. In the end, this has as much to do with the quality of your ISP as the speed of your modem.

The Backbone of the Internet

Most discussions about the infrastructure of the World Wide Web begin with a history of the network, from its inception as a failsafe command and control structure for the military in the event of nuclear war. The part we need to worry about begins fewer than three years ago, when the nation's information infrastructure was essentially privatized. The term "backbone," when used for communications infrastructure, refers to the main transport mechanism for moving masses of information over long distances. The commonly used analogy of the interstate highway system, "the information superhighway," is accurate only in the geographical sense. The fiber-optic highways of the Internet backbone do crisscross the continent like the interstate system, but if an old secondary road is analogous to a POTs (Plain Old Telephone) connection, we would need a multithousand-lane highway to compare to the fiber-optic backbones.

There are seven principal companies involved in the backbone business in the United States. They range from Bolt, Beranek & Newman (BBN)—one of the original architects of the old military network—to Apex Global Information Services (AGIS), founded in 1994 solely to provide Internet related services. Advanced Network Services (ANS) operate over 12,000 miles of fiber-optic pathways, and is owned by America On Line (AOL), the world's biggest private network provider. For MCI Communications and Sprint Corporation, entering the Internet backbone business was a natural evolution from their point-to-point long-distance phone business. UUNet Technologies, now owned by MFS Communications, boasts of the most national and international connections, while PSINet employs the unique system of leasing lines from a number of regional telephone companies, but purchasing all the routing and switching gear.

All of these companies are in the interesting position of being forced to compete with each other in the marketplace while simultaneously cooperating at an operational level. There are currently no tariffs charged for network traffic, no tollbooths, tolls, or collectors. The backbone operators carry each other's traffic for free so that the favor will be returned. Bottlenecks and multicar (packet) pileups are common, and the best equipped providers staff round-the-clock command centers for traffic control and disaster response. Visit the Internet weather channel (www.mids.org/weather/us) for a look at the traffic today. The biggest challenge currently facing the backbone providers is not stringing more fiber-optic lines, but doing a better job utilizing the available bandwidth. The components that actually move the traffic on and off the fiber links are routers. These routers have to disassemble each packet of information arriving at a switch point, and determine where it is addressed to and how to move it along to the next switch point.

Most of the backbone providers also offer business and retail services. Business customers and government customers pay a premium for high-speed links to the backbones, which are incorporated into intranets, restricted access networks carrying confidential traffic. Excess capacity during off-business hours is often discounted to Internet Service Providers (ISPs), who resell the time to home users who call into local access points using PCs and modems. The big customers paying thousands of dollars a month for access often get clean paths through routers in addition to fast connections.

The Internet infrastructure business is definitely in the investment stage, where profits are measured as the relative reduction in loss as

Figure 18-1
Serving time on the
World Wide Web.

compared to the previous quarter. For companies like MCI and Sprint, money spent on communications infrastructure and know-how dovetails well with their core business. AOL bought ANS for the same reason that the movie/cable/TV/print conglomerates have been put together. It makes sense, at least on some level, for content and distribution to be controlled by a single entity. BBN is probably the strongest technical company in the Internet business, and is involved in many other advanced engineering disciplines as well. Besides having more than 30 years of experience in working with large, distributed networks, they were in desperate need of a new peg to hang their hat on at the end of the cold war, whatever the cover charge.

As companies more or less based on providing Internet backbone access and services as their core business, UUNet, PSINet, and AGIS are in a different boat. The question is not whether or not providing access to the information superhighway will one day be profitable, it's how far away that day will be. Can these three companies hang on to become to the information business what MCI and Sprint are now to the long-distance phone business. Maybe one or two, but not all three. One big wild card. AT&T may get tired of leasing access from companies that it could have once bought en masse. In the case of the BOCs (Bell Operating Companies), they may be renting Internet access on lines that actually belong to them, but are leased to the backbone companies.

Internet Service Providers (ISPs) and Business Usage

The common enemy on the Internet is time. When an employee using an intranet, or a casual surfer on the Web tries to access a server, the information will ideally appear on their screen at the maximum speed of their connection. Otherwise, the new technology will engender unhappy employees and cause surfers to hit their "Cancel" button before an impression can be made. The most critical factor impacting the speed at which that page will be served up is neither the speed of the server hardware nor the type of the connection to the ISP, although either of these also has a big impact. It's the bandwidth and proximity of the ISP's connection to a backbone.

ISPs come in a wide spectrum of cost/quality colors, ranging from backbone providers who sell directly to businesses, to mom-and-pop providers with a PC in the basement. The minimum acceptable configuration for an ISP providing server access for businesses is a T1 line (a 1.5-Mbps leased line) with a direct connection to a backbone provider's local Point Of Presence (POP). Many small ISPs are buying their access from a slightly larger ISP, who has a backbone connection. These secondary ISPs may connect to the primary ISP via a fractional T1 line (a crippled T1 implementation) or a switched 56-Kbps line. The situation degrades more and more as middlemen between the POP and the actual server location pile up, because the bandwidth of the connection from the POP to the top ISP is being shared by more and more users. Any business that really plans on doing a lot of Web traffic (tens or hundreds of thousands of accesses per day) should either get a connection directly with a backbone provider or consider using their hosting services.

A business can maintain the server (anything from a PC to a minicomputer) on premises and pay for a leased line to an ISP or can choose to have that server "hosted." There are two basic models for hosting—physical hosting and virtual hosting. Physical hosting can be further divided into two types. In the first instance, the ISP locates a server belonging to the business at the ISP's location for a fee. In the second case, the ISP leases the business a server located at the ISP's site, also saving the complications and expenses of a leased line. Virtual hosting means that the business obtains a domain name from Internic, which creates a www.yourcompany.com presence, but the home page and other HTML documents are actually located on a host server maintained by the ISP.

Virtual hosting is usually the best option for small companies, because the low initial investment ($100 to register a domain with Internic), and a cost starting around $50/month for reasonable service from a local ISP. National services like AOL offer virtual hosting anywhere in the country starting at $99/month. However, if a business wants to run proprietary server software or integrate their server tightly with a company database, a stand-alone server, usually located on the company premises, will be required. This brings into play the other two limitations on server performance—connection speed and hardware performance.

The type of leased line connection to the ISP should be decided on before the server hardware is chosen. If the leased line is slow and the server is fast, the result is analogous to a garden hose connected to a fire hydrant, while if the server is slow and the connection is fast, the situation resembles a fire hose connected to a kitchen faucet. In either case, about the same performance (water flow) results, but it is being obtained with a very inefficient and expensive approach. Leased lines vary from switched 56-Kbps lines, starting around $100/month, through fractional T1 lines, from a few hundred to a thousand a month depending on the number of 64-Kbps channels used, to full T1 at a couple thousand per month. ISDN lines can also be used, providing 56 Kbps to 128 Kbps, depending on the local phone company and whether a one or two pair implementation is used. These are the phone company charges and vary greatly from region to region. They do not include the ISP connection charge, which is often similar to the leased line cost, and varies with the ISP.

A 486 PC may make a fine server for ISDN, a switched 56-Kbps line, while a Pentium with a fast hard drive and a lot of RAM might handle a $\frac{1}{8}$ fractional T1 (four 64-Kbps channels) or a $\frac{1}{4}$ fractional T1 (eight 64-Kbps channels). At $\frac{1}{2}$ fractional T1 or full T1, a heavy-duty server such as a SunSparc or a multiprocessor Pentium makes sense, particularly since the connection cost, between the phone company and the ISP charge, is probably several thousand dollars per month. If the server will have a high processing load, i.e., database searches, forms processing, or multiuse within the company, then the above guidelines go out the window, and a $10,000 server becomes the entry-level choice.

Just about every computer company in existence offers a "Web server" product. Most of them are simply warmed-over PCs with Unix installed. Some offerings, like the Apple Internet Server Solution, are so weighed down by their "user-friendly GUI" that they perform little better than an out-of-the-box Pentium. Digital Equipment, with their Alpha Server line, offer the fastest raw processor with tremendous scalability. Sun Microsystems has a big chunk of the market with their servers based on the SuperSPARC CPUs and has done a good job leveraging their Java development to maintain high visibility. IBM can configure a great range of systems as Web servers, and offers the RS/6000 based on the PowerPC chip as a price/performance competitor. Silicon Graphics, Hewlett Packard, Compaq, and Intergraph Computer Systems all offer competitive products, though bundling practices vary.

Companies that choose virtual hosting get virtually no say in the server software used. Depending on how they are counted, the total number of servers on the Web is somewhere between 150,000 and 200,000. With millions of sites on the Web, there's obviously a lot of virtual hosting going on. If all a site will do is serve up pages and carry out some CGI (Common Gateway Interface) forms processing, the software used isn't that important. However, if security for financial transactions or integration with a certain database back-end like Microsoft SQL server are important, the choice of the right server can be crucial. According to Webcrawler, about 83% of all Web servers are running on UNIX systems. The majority of these servers are free from NCSA, Apache, or CERN. Unlike most entities giving out free software on the Web, there is no hook attached with these free servers; they simply want to see the Web grow.

There is no shortage of players in the "for-profit" server market. Some of them give away the server for free to get their foot in the door of the lucrative intranet market, estimated to be 10 billion dollars by the turn of the century. The most prominent players include Microsoft, Netscape, IBM (both as IBM and Lotus), to name just a few.

Intranets and Groupware

The subject of intranets and groupware speaks to the hand-me-down PC in corporate America. Several years ago, Lotus began marketing a new concept in software known as "groupware." Lotus Notes, a highly proprietary product that ran on top of existing LANs, may seem like a strange place to start a discussion of intranets. However, if you replace "highly proprietary" with "open standards based" and "existing LANs" with "Internet infrastructure," you get a fair picture of intranets. The first and foremost use for intranets is e-mail. Not just Paul sending Shelly a marketing idea e-mail, but threaded discussion group e-mail, automatically generated and routed workflow e-mail, and even database queries returned as e-mail. Not just text e-mails either. Sound, video, still images, spreadsheet files and documents that launch their "parent" application with a click of the mouse are all standard fare.

Intranets have often been described as a corporation's baby Internet cowering behind a fire wall. While this may ring true for the crudest installations, the real competition is occurring in the "full intranet implementation" arena, netspeak for "groupware." That Lotus Notes should be a strong competitor, with over 6 million purchased "seats," should therefore come as no surprise. Netscape, as the commercial browser pioneer, has moved systematically and aggressively into intranets, and the company recently stated that 80 percent of current revenue is coming from business customers. Last comes Microsoft, with their domination of the Windows desktop and a stable of business applications and server products. Are there other software companies pitching intranet products? Just about all of them, but barring a new "killer app," the battle is shaping up as Netscape, Lotus (IBM), and Microsoft. And never have three combatants so zealously embraced each other's standards, or announced their intention to do so in the very next revision. This bodes well for those who suffer from winter colds. Just rub some intranet promotional material on your chest and inhale the vapor (ware).

While Lotus was inventing groupware for LANs, Netscape was inventing a new kind of group. Following the basic Internet and World Wide Web model, a Netscape group consisted of people with a common interface (the Navigator browser) accessing common information (Web pages or threaded discussion groups). The difference is critical. The entire reason for Lotus's success in penetrating corporations with their Notes product is that LANs have always been held together by chewing gum and baling wire. The standard estimate for the cost of supporting each seat on a corporate LAN is $8,000 per annum, a far cry from the $0 per annum many executives were led to expect. The intranet concept (Netscape group) is really a return to the mainframe computing model. Expertise is required to program and maintain Web servers, but the browser side (terminal) is largely maintenance free. Lotus, with a remarkable show of nimbleness for a division of Big Blue, has figured this out and is working to make their Notes desktop into a full-featured browser. In the meantime, any Notes-connected user has an easy upgrade path to Internet access without requiring an IP application running on every desktop.

E-mail and collaborative discussion groups, both real-time and threaded, are the two killer apps of the intranets. Many users will also take advantage of HTML publishing, audio and video communications, and search engines indexing both the entire Internet and protected company databases. Protecting confidential information on intranets gave birth to the firewall industry. Firewalls are supposedly bulletproof solutions that can restrict access to a Web server or Internet address to authorized users. Authorization can take the form of identity, a username and password, or an IP address, the physical location. Firewalls offer no protection against the most common threat to security, which is authorized users becoming involved in unauthorized activities. This type of security is generally implemented at the operating system or database level, and the leads here belong to Microsoft and Lotus, respectively. Microsoft and Netscape browsers integrate standards-based security schemes, while the last Notes scheme was still proprietary and somewhat constricting. Netscape and Microsoft offer security solutions for commerce, validating credit card usage or banking information, but these are standard security activities that need to occur whether a transaction takes place on an intranet, the Web, or over the telephone.

The Netscape Intranet product called "Netscape One" uses the Netscape Navigator browser as the user interface and "SuiteSpot" as the server. SuiteSpot includes the Netscape Enterprise Server, Mail Server, Live Wire Pro, News Server, Catalog Server, Directory Server, Certificate Server and Proxy Server. The software runs on a number of operating systems. The solution offered by Microsoft consists of a number of add-ons to Windows NT, with MS Internet Explorer as the preferred browser and MS Front Page as a publishing tool. The server end-products include MS Internet Information Server, Windows NT Domain Name Server, MS Index Server, and MS Proxy Server, a bridge between the Internet and intranet which includes firewall level security. Microsoft achieves tight integration with their back office and database products, along with their desktop products, led by the Microsoft Office suite.

The Netscape and Microsoft solutions gather individual users and/or LANs together to create an intranet. The Lotus solution takes an existing Notes user group and turns it into an intranet via the addition of an Internet connection at the Notes Server. The new model for this connection is the Domino product which originally ran as a task on the Notes server. Because of this tight integration with the Notes server, the overall performance of a Lotus "Web Server" is relatively low and setup is complicated. Domino is probably the best choice for creating an intranet from Notes users, and the worst choice for anyone else. The new version of Domino will run as a stand-alone Web server. The biggest challenge for Lotus will be adopting the open standards of the Web without giving up the proprietary design features that make Notes the unique product that it is.

The Intranet Gospel in Verse

More for less, more bits, more megs
A higher nomenclature yet
Although performance, you may bet
Will wither in the face of code
That takes a CD-ROM to load

Groupware fashioned from the dregs
Of products fallen by the way
But dragged forth to the light of day
By starved wolves howling at the Gates
"Compete with tools and replicates"

Oh noble hardware, cruelly drowned
By layer upon layer piled
Of promises to the beguiled
Who wait amidst the growing pain
For signs of productivity gain

Then let the trumpets blare their sound
And brave consultants to the breach
Who to the flock do teach and preach
The gospel of the current year
(Behind their backs they hide the shears)

And when at last the clients beg
To know why browsers they have bought
And where's the imaging they'd sought
The experts disappear like rabbits
And leave them with their filing cabinets.

Web Browsers

Millions of Americans who have never surfed the net, much less purchased a computer, have been inundated with stories about the Netscape versus Microsoft battle, in the popular media. For the majority of us, using the Internet as a research aide or a business tool, it just doesn't matter which browser we pick. Market demands are forcing both companies to support the same standards and security implementations. The Microsoft browser, Internet Explorer, is currently outnumbered by Netscape Navigator, but the long-term advantage belongs to Microsoft, since they continue to give their browser away free and can ship it as an integrated part of the operating system. Netscape hopes to hold Microsoft off through the combination of intranet installations and court battles, along with frequent upgrades and enhancements.

In either case, Java and Active X both represent ways to add functionality to browsers. The crudest demonstrations of this are spectacles like dancing bears in tutus playing the drums. More advanced (and less silly) applications are no different from any other computer program you might run. Basically, Java is nothing more than a subset of C++ designed to be easily portable in applet form and run decently in an interpretive mode. Active X is a sort of object-oriented programming (OOP) nirvana, serving as a "container" for applets written in languages like Visual Basic, Visual C++, or the new Visual J++. At some point in the future, a new model of client/server computing may take advantage of either technology to do more actual data processing at the client end. In the meantime, neither technology stands to inherit the Web, which continues to be ruled by good, old, HTML (HyperText Markup Language).

Finding Information on the Web

There are tens of millions, soon to be hundreds of millions of different places you can visit on the Web. Surfing the Web, following hyperlinks from one site to the next by clicking on words or pictures, is a great entertainment for many people, but it's not a very efficient way to find specific information. The card catalogs to the Web are called search engines, and they vary in scope from attempts to index every page on the Web to catalogs for specific professions or hobbies. Learning to use the big search engines, like AltaVista, Webcrawler, and Excite, is well worth the twenty minutes or half hour it will take to master the "Advanced Search" capabilities. Some major search engines employ a layer of "reviewing," which means your search is limited by the prescreening of people who probably don't understand your subject of interest as well as you. Most reviewers are also biased in favor of sites with heavy multimedia content, fine for entertainment, useless for serious research.

As of this writing, AltaVista is the search engine that has the quickest reaction time to newly listed sites, so we will use it for our example. In the first example screen shown, a search is done on Morris Rosenthal. The result of the search is that over 20,000 matches are found, in this case 263,235 instances of Morris and 26,297 instances of Rosenthal.

In the second example, we put the entire name in quotes before submitting the request, which tells the search engine to find an exact match for "Morris Rosenthal". In this case, the search engine returns only 40 instances, which makes sifting through the resulting links that are listed below the result statistics much more efficient.

AltaVista, and indeed most search engines, offers an "Advanced" option, which lets us add conditional statements to our search, like AND, OR, NOT, and NEAR, rank our results according to the words found, and specify a range of dates to search. In the third example screen, we search for "Morris Rosenthal" AND "PC," looking only at pages created between January 1 and April 10 of 1997.

The result of our search consists of two hits, down from the 20,000+ returns from our first crude search. The amount of time and frustration you can save by using advanced search options when you know precisely what you are looking for is tremendous. The best technique is usually to ask for the most specific information you could possibly want, than slowly broaden your search if no matching pages are found.

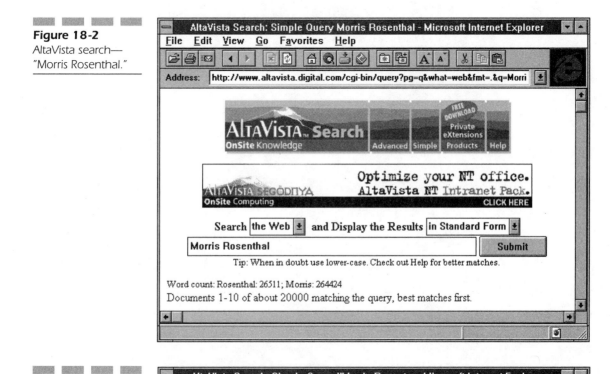

Figure 18-2
AltaVista search—
"Morris Rosenthal."

Figure 18-3
AltaVista search—
"Morris Rosenthal."

Figure 18-4
AltaVista search—
"Morris Rosenthal"
and "PC."

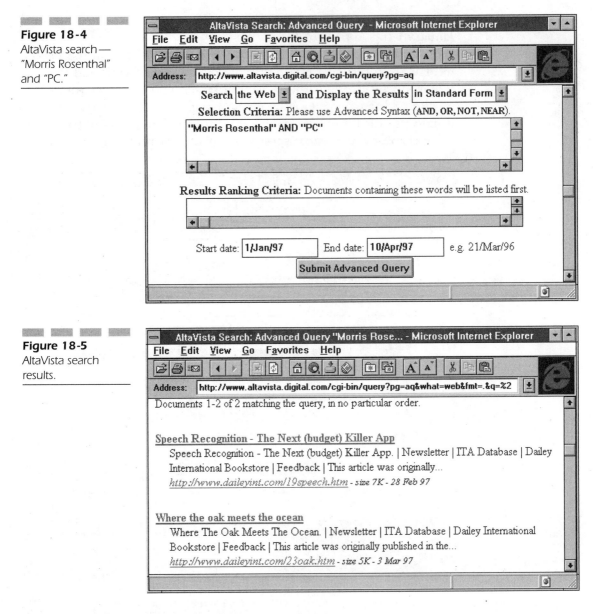

Figure 18-4
AltaVista search—
"Morris Rosenthal"
and "PC."

Figure 18-5
AltaVista search
results.

Publishing Your Own Web Pages

There are two classes of users on the Web, surfers and contributors. The most revolutionary thing about the Web is it enables anybody to create a potential audience of millions for their words, art, or ideas, and there are even places in cyberspace which will host your Web pages for free. Most monthly Web services that you sign up for come with an allowance of server space for hosting personal Web pages, usually allowing you 1 or 2 megabytes of space. Two megabytes translates into about 500 double-spaced pages of text with a dozen pictures thrown in for good measure.

If you are thinking about creating your own Web content and have already been up and surfing on the Web, you may be intimidated by the professional look of most commercial and some personal Web sites. Don't give it another thought. If you have something to say about restoring clipper ships, pruning fruit trees, or using a microwave oven to create your own broadcast TV station, there are people out there who are waiting to hear from you. The important thing is that your text or pictures are actually informative, otherwise you're just wasting your readers' time. Although pictures are the main draw for many Web surfers, it's your text content that will draw people to your site via search engines. On the Web, a picture is not worth a thousand words, but the opposite is sometimes true.

When planning your Web page, keep in mind that the typical photograph, heavily compressed to save space, takes as much time to load as about 5,000 words of text, ten single-spaced pages. The best approach to a site that includes multiple photographs is to give visitors an index to them on your home page but to store the photographs in small groups on individual pages of their own. The index you create might include "thumbnails" of the images, shrunk down to about ten percent the size of the original artwork, so your visitors can decide whether or not it's worth a minute or more of their time to call up the full-sized image.

The number one feature of HyperText Markup Language (HTML), the basic formatting language of the Web, is clickable links. A word or an image that is tagged as a hypertext link will change the contents of the screen when selected (clicked on by the mouse). The hypertext links can be local or remote. Remote links refer to another page, on the same Web server or on the other side of the world, which are described by their HyperText Transfer Protocol (HTTP) address, as in the familiar "http://www.somesite.com". The other type of link is known as an "anchor," and serves as an entry point to the currently loaded page, somewhere other than at the very top. Local links utilizing anchors are the ideal way to navigate lengthy text documents, and if your page is more than three or for screenfulls long, you should use anchor links to prepare a hyperlinked table of contents at the top of your page. Links can also be used to launch applications on your machine, like your e-mail program.

Secondary in importance to hypertext links is the ability to format text in a variety of ways. Hypertext now supports most of the formatting options present in word processors, such as font size, bold, italic, bullets, etc. HTML also lets you control the color of the text, the color of the background page, and the color of links both before and after they've been selected. Along with the basic page formatting options, you can include an image to serve as wallpaper, that will be repeated over and over again to fill the screen. The problem with wallpaper is it takes additional time to load, and usually detracts from the readability of the page. One compromise is to use a very wide image that is all one color after the first inch or so on the left. This translates into a colorful left margin, with an nice solid background on the rest of the page for your text. All the same, unless you have artistic aspirations, you're better off skipping background images altogether. Another basic feature of HTML is the use of tables to organize information. More advanced features like forms and frames are equally dependent of server and browser capabilities, and are often unsupported in personal Web spaces.

There are three or four different ways you can prepare information, or "pages," for Web publishing. The oldest and most time-consuming way is to use a standard text editor to insert HTML tags into your document. There is really no reason to use this approach today, so steer clear of books or classes that will teach it to you for a price. Even if you are a hardcore programmer, you're much better off producing the basic Web page using one of the approaches described below, and then using the "Show HTML" option to go in and fine-tune the output.

The easiest way for most people to publish Web pages is to use the tool that comes free from their ISP, such as America On Line. This approach ensures that you won't end up using features your server doesn't even support and also gives you an easy way to upload the finished pages to your Web space without having to use a separate FTP (File Transfer Protocol) utility. Personal Web publishing tools include all of the functionality of HTML and are easier to use than most word processors. You can prepare the basic text for your Web pages in a word processor and import or convert them, but it's often simpler to type them from scratch in the publishing tool. Make sure to periodically use your Web browser to open the page you are creating on your hard drive to see if it really looks the way you expect it to. If you believe you are particularly concerned about the appearance of your pages, check them using both Netscape Navigator and Internet Explorer, and don't be surprised if the more advanced formatting options produce unexpected results.

Another simple way to produce Web pages is using your word processor, providing it is new enough to support the option to generate HTML documents. A good implementation of this option will create all of your local links for you from your existing table of contents, embed or link any artwork, convert tables, and do a decent job with formatting. However, unlike printed documents, the actual fonts displayed (Times New Roman, Helvetica, Arial) will be a function of the browser settings of your visitor as opposed to the fonts you have chosen, so don't go overboard with fine-tuning such details. Using your word processor means you'll also have access to the integrated spelling and grammar checkers. The drawback with word processors is that they are released much less often than new versions of Web tools, so you aren't likely to have the latest, greatest bells and whistles.

Any of the above methods of preparing Web pages are more than enough for producing award-winning content and worldwide attention. However, if appearance and special effects are your game, you can invest in the latest full-blown publishing tools from Netscape or Microsoft, or in one of the popular Web design-only packages like Hotdog. These tools emphasize using advance features like frames, forms, and animation. They can also help with support for Common Gateway Interface (CGI) programming, the ability to process data entered in forms to take orders, perform database searches, and generally provide a higher level of interaction with your visitors. However, in order to use CGI programming, you must have a higher level of access to your Web server, something few ISPs allow for noncommercial accounts.

CHAPTER 19

The Future of the Hand-Me-Down PC

The basic model of a PC, as a box with a power supply that has a motherboard with a couple of peripheral adapters and drives stuffed into it, has changed very little since the introduction of the IBM PC more than 15 years ago. As more and more functions have been integrated onto the motherboard, new adapter cards like modems and sound cards have gained popularity to take their place on the bus, so the basic part count hasn't really changed at all. We've come to expect leaps in speed and capacity every year, and the standard PC in the year 2000 may well be a 750-MHz, 128-bit CPU with 64 megabytes of RAM, a 25-gigabyte hard drive, a DVD (Digital Video Disk) drive, and a cable or ADSL modem. The one thing you can be sure about is that software producers will eat up all that capacity and tell you that you'd get much better performance out of their product if you would just upgrade to the next generation of PC.

At some point in the future, whether that time is five years or fifteen years from now, the basic model of the box with the power supply and all these generic parts stuffed into it is likely to change. This change, which will replace the PC, TV, and telephone with an integrated HCC (Home Communications Center), is less dependent on advances in computer technology than on investment in basic communications infrastructure, but barring famine and pestilence, the time is coming. The real obstacle to the infrastructure upgrade is determining who gets to charge whom to pay for it, and how much. The services that will make the HCC a compelling purchase will be your standard computer, entertainment and telephone functions, combined with video phone, video disk, speech recognition capacity and a vastly improved World Wide Web. The term "couch potato" will have to be updated to something less dynamic, since the sprouts grown by potatoes will demonstrate ten times the physical activity shown by a hard-core HCC addict.

Video Phone and Conferencing

One of the most basic futuristic functions for the hand-me-down PC is the video phone, which is already here in many different forms. Each end of a video phone or videoconferencing hookup requires a PC equipped with a video camera, a video capture card, a microphone, a sound card, and a modem or other networked link—either direct or using the Internet as a transport mechanism. Implicit in this setup is the requirement for a fast PC, a 90-MHz Pentium being the very bottom end. The horsepower requirement is based on the tremendous computer processing overhead needed to compress and decompress the voice and video information flowing between the computers. In the case of a PC connected on a hard-wired corporate network, the processing load is less because the compression required to squeeze the information out of a modem and phone line in real time is bypassed. However, any type of hookup using the Internet as the transport layer is subject to stutters and hiccups that can't be cured with faster PCs.

There are two basic approaches to compressing and decompressing the audio/video stream — hardware and software. Hardware implementations require a special adapter, though it will also integrate the functions of a standard video capture card and sometimes also a sound card. The positive points for hardware include guaranteed performance, relative ease of setup, and one stop support. While there are standards for hardware compression, such as MPEG, that can be engineered from off-the-shelf chip sets, many solutions are completely proprietary, requiring identical hardware at all of the sites involved. Another downside of hardware solutions is that they are often non-upgradable and thereby short lived.

Software CODECs (COmpression DECompression) can also be standard or proprietary, depending on the supplier. One of the biggest advocates of software codecs is Intel Corporation, which gives away internally developed software at their Web site. The reason for Intel's active support of software codecs is that they help sell the faster Pentium processors that are required to use them effectively. The two biggest advantages of software codecs are cost and upgradeability. The downside is you won't have a clear idea of how well it's going to work until you try it.

At the moment, setting up a video phone using a PC is a time-consuming job for techies or hobbyists, whatever approach is chosen. When the dust settles and the new standards emerge in a few years, video phone technology will be integrated into home entertainment centers, and later into home communications centers. Expect early offerings to take advantage of what are becoming fairly common household items, like camcorders, to help hold down the cost and justify the expense for the average technophile. As previously mentioned, somebody is going to have to pay for the upgrades to our national and international communications infrastructure for these new technologies to be widely used, and those somebodies will probably be us.

Speech Recognition (Talking to Your PC)

The next killer app for PCs is speech recognition. Speech recognition will run exclusively on PCs, with no connection to LANs, servers, or Internet providers required. What speech recognition will demand is more PC. More memory, more storage, more horsepower. That's fine with the computer industry, since PC power has been growing at a geometric rate over the past decade. The problem for end users can be summed as follows: a geometric progression makes for a slippery slope. As the power of PCs grows, the rate of obsolescence moves in lock step. Never mind anecdotes about XTs and ATs running as fax servers, or how a 386 is really all a sane person could ever need. Running today's software without serious corner cutting requires a Pentium PC with 16 MB of RAM, not to mention the gigabyte plus of hard-drive space and the 8X CD-ROM. A decade ago, a corporate buyer might squeeze four years out of a PC purchase. The current figure is probably closer to three.

The final goal for speech recognition is to render obsolete or secondary all other input devices, including the keyboard and the mouse. This will probably also bring about a change in the current window graphically oriented operating environments, which are idealized more for mouse usage than anything else. The first application for speech recognition is simply to replace typing with dictation, something that the current products on the market are targeting. The control function, navigating around the operating system environment with spoken commends, will remain awkward for some time, until good shortcuts are devised. In other words, if you want to reprint the letter you wrote to your Uncle Sam last month, you want to be able to say, "print the letter I wrote to Uncle Sam last month," not "goto word processor," wait, "open file," wait, "samlett.doc", wait, "print", wait, "OK".

Speech recognition is in its infancy, with the first products capable of understanding continuous natural speech recently being introduced. Minimum requirements are generally a fast Pentium with MMX technology and plenty of RAM. In other words, this application requires the latest, greatest hardware and operating system, just to get out of the box! The current "big three" of speech recognition are IBM, Kurzweil, and Dragon. By the year 2000, the "big three" will be Microsoft, IBM, and TBD (to be determined). With Microsoft migrating the world to NT, you can be sure that their speech recognition product will favor

NT over Windows 95. The problem for Intel is that NT runs well on a variety of processors, including Digital's Alpha series. DEC, which currently ships a 500-MHz version of the Alpha, is a potential player in the speech recognition game, along with Compaq, which is trying to move beyond being just the number one clone vendor. Other contenders for the number three slot in speech recognition may include Sun, Oracle, and Netscape.

Today's standard clone can't run today's best speech recognition package, much less tomorrow's. Along with speech recognition, we can expect the long awaited arrival of AI (Artificial Intelligence), though initially it will be rather stupid, since functionality will be achieved through the brute force approach. The traditional emphasis in interactive artificial intelligence has been on neural network learning, sentence parsing and logic, but speech recognition combined with PC power will allow for a whole new range of "intelligent" products. For example, a CD might contain 1,000 answers to common medical questions. Never mind parsing and analysis, just include 1,000 different versions of each question pointing at the same answer. The one million questions required by this approach fit easily on a CD, with plenty of room left over for some gruesome medical pictures.

Digital Video Disc (DVD)

Digital video discs are finally here, after nearly two years of delays fostered by competing standards and resistance from Hollywood studios worried about pirating. DVDs were originally envisioned as primarily a replacement for VHS tapes and laser video discs, but it's become apparent that their initial sales will be strongest in the computer market. DVDs will eventually supplant CDs, but expect a long period of cohabitation, particularly with the installed base of CD drives and their plummeting cost. DVD drives read manufactured CDs, but have problems with older recordable discs, another reason for many of us not to throw away our CD drive.

The first wave of DVD drives play 4.7 GB (Gigabyte) discs, single-sided, single-layer media. The next iteration of DVD will be single-sided, double-layered discs, storing 8.5 GB, and the final goal is double-sided, double-layered discs storing 17 GB. At the 17 GB level, a single DVD disc will hold as much information as about 26 CDs. For about $300, that's a lot of storage capacity, but don't expect to be able to play movies on your hand-me-down PC screen for that price. Movies will be encoded in MPEG 2, probably using the new Dolby Digital for audio tracks, so you'll need an additional expensive decoder board in a fast Pentium to turn your monitor into a big screen.

The first impact of DVDs in PCs will be in the game and reference tile market. Many leading games, particularly those with large amounts of video, are currently shipping on multiple CDs. Although the manufacturing costs for CDs are fairly trivial (well under one dollar each in quantity), the attraction of not having to open the drive to change CDs in the middle of a game will be enough reason for many gamers to upgrade. The quality and quantity of video included with games will increase dramatically, but the old tradeoffs between picture size, compression quality, and video length will eventually reassert themselves at higher limits.

One of the most obvious marketing tactics for DVD will be to sell compilations of old CDs, just like early CDs sold compilations of floppy software and games. Other early adopters should include software vendors like Lotus, Microsoft, IBM, and Corel, who already ship multi-CD versions of many of their products. As with CDs, some developers will be unable to resist the urge to create "shovelware," shoveling everything that they can get the rights to onto a DVD just to be able to market it as "One million photographs from NASA" or "Every book published before 1890." The positive side about shovelware is that it is cheap, and if you're willing to pan for gold, there are plenty of grains mixed in with all the sand.

CD Recording

Inexpensive DVDRs (Digital Video Disc Recorders) are still over the horizon somewhere, so DVDRs will probably cost twenty times as much as CDRs (CD recorders) for the near future. CD recording isn't yet quite so straightforward as copying files to a floppy disk, and at $5 to $10 per blank disc, you don't want to waste too many. Recordable CDs store up to 650 MB of whatever you what to put on them, and unlike tapes and portable cartridge disks, almost anybody you could want to share the information with will have a CD drive that can read it. In its simplest form, CD recording consists of copying files from your hard drive to the CD. If you want to produce CDs as an interactive multimedia product, you should look into authoring packages like Director from Macromedia or Icon Author from AimTech. Recordable CDs are perhaps the most ideal way to archive information, with an unattended shelf life outstripping magnetic tapes and disks.

The standard software included with a CDR will give you the ability to write not only CD-ROM, the current format used for multimedia computer CDs, but also CD-DA, the digital audio format used by your stereo equipment, and CD-XA, extended architecture. Remember to disable Smart Drive and any antivirus programs before you start to record. Eliminating TSRs (Terminate and Stay Resident programs) and disabling the write caching of Smart Drive to the CDR are recommended to prevent untimely interruptions of the data stream flowing to the CD. An example of the sort of disastrous interruption that can be caused by a TSR would be an incoming fax or modem call being answered, and the safest way to prevent this is to unplug the phone line from your modem.

Don't buy a CDR without a 1-MB buffer to insulate it from extremely short-lived interruptions, but even recording at single speed the buffer provides a maximum breathing space of less then eight seconds. At double speed the maximum tolerance is less than four seconds, and at either speed many other factors in transferring data from the source to the CDR buffer will prevent this maximum from being reached. In any case, recording at double or quad speed is riskier than recording at single speed, so cut your first disc at single speed to ensure that any problems encountered aren't due to buffer underrun. Most software does include an option to nondestructively test the ability of the system to successfully output a given amount of data at either speed, but since the test takes as long as actually writing the data, it's only for the very patient.

A CDR recorder doesn't require a superfast system to operate successfully. In fact, I've cut many CDs of different formats on an old 486DX40. For those with the foresight and budget to plan a CD recording system, the following suggestions could be helpful. Start with a Pentium based system with 16-MB RAM. Get a PCI SCSI card, and hang on it the following: a 2-GB hard drive, a quad-speed CD player, and your CDR. Having all the devices on the same SCSI bus will allow for the maximum transfer speed, and you will be able to easily copy prerecorded CDs from your player to the recorder. Most experts will advise you to invest in an AVI (Audio Visual) hard drive, a high performance drive that will not force interruptions to do thermal calibration in the middle of your recording session. I haven't found AVI drives to be necessary, and have gotten by fine with older IDE drives, but I always record on single speed. A sound card and video capture card or a color scanner will provide you with lots of big files to fill your CDs with. Invest in a high-end sound card with good dubbing software if you want to record professional music CDs from demo tapes or other media.

CDs produced in CDRs are not 100 percent compatible with all older players, particularly multisession CDs. The failure of a CD player to read a multisession CD won't result in an error message, it's just that the player will only be able to access the first session you wrote to the CD. Since gold recordable CDs are not erasable, information is added or deleted by writing a new version of the table of contents each time a new session is recorded. Some CD players lack the circuitry to find these newer versions of the table of contents; they just use the one at the start of the disc. Another incompatibility is likely to be with DVD players, although the newest CDRs coming on the market are said to be capable of writing DVD readable CDs.

Multisession recording is about as simple as single session recording with one additional step up front; either loading a saved virtual image for the particular CD you are working on or reloading the contents of the last track you recorded so your software can include it in the new version of the table of contents for the disc. In general, multisession recording only makes sense for experimental discs or backups. You'll rarely be delivering CDs to somebody with the expectation of ever getting them back, and the economic motivation to reuse gold CDs is lessened now that they've fallen under $5 in quantity.

The PC Life Cycle

In the course of this book, we've often discussed the cost/benefit trade-offs between upgrading a hand-me-down PC and buying a newer model. The decision to buy new is often driven by the desire to load new software that would work poorly or not at all on the older system. Windows 95 is often the straw that breaks the camel's back, but since most new software packages are written exclusively for Windows 95, it's often a load of straw that you really need to bring home. The other likely reason for buying new is the need for speed. If you use your PC a lot and find yourself waiting a minute here and twenty seconds there, you may easily see where your time savings on a machine four times as fast could more than pay for itself.

The benchmark PC often referred to in this book is the $1000 discount store clone, a 150-MHz Pentium with a 1.2-GB hard drive loaded with Windows 95, an 8X CD-ROM, 16-bit sound, a 33.6 modem, and a 14" monitor. A couple of these numbers may pick up a notch or two before you bring this book home, but the importance of this benchmark PC is in the price, not in the exact components. For many years, $1,000 in the hands of a good shopper has bought new a PC that is much better than the average PC in general use.

You can always pay up to $3,000 for a top brand name loaded with software and the biggest, fastest components available, but you're only buying yourself an extra nine months to a year before your $3,000 PC has become the $1,000 generic model. In the meantime, you can be sure that very little software will be sold that actually needs the $3,000 PC to work, because software developers want to create products with the largest market possible. Don't buy a real brand-name PC for $1,000 or under; the low price in this case will just mean that it is a close-out, approaching obsolescence.

There are some advantages to buying brand-name PCs at any performance level, a choice that will increase the overall price tag from $200 to $500. These include longer warranties, better technical support, software bundles that will include an office suite, and sometimes better hardware. However, an Intel CPU is an Intel CPU whatever box it's in, and most of the other components are also commodities produced by a limited number of dominant international manufacturers. The only components most brand-name manufacturers actually produce themselves are the system box or case and a highly integrated motherboard.

The life cycle of a PC is much shorter than that of a refrigerator or a washing machine. Unlike these appliances that continue to serve their function if you change your diet or your wardrobe every few years, your PC will almost certainly need at least some sort of upgrade if you change your software. The problem with buying into the high end of the PC food chain is that unlike a Lamborghini or a Cadillac, you couldn't get your old PC stolen if you leave the keys in it. Never buy twice as much PC as you need on the theory that you may need it someday. Wait for that day, then buy a PC four times as good with the money you saved on your original purchase. Give your old PC to the kids, and be glad you aren't still paying credit card installments on something that was old a year ago.

APPENDIX A

Important Web Addresses

3Com   www.3com.com

Acer   www.acer.com

Adaptec   www.adaptec.com

American Megatrends (AMI)   www.megatrends.com

American Micro Devices (AMD)   www.amd.com

ATI   www.atitech.com

Award   www.award.com

Aztech Labs   www.aztechca.com

BOCA   www.bocaresearch.com

Calcomp   www.calcomp.com

Cardinal   www.cardtech.com

Chips & Technologies   www.chips.com

Cirrus Logic   www.cirrus.com

Colorado   www.hp.com/go/colorado

Compaq   www.compaq.com

Conner Peripherals   www.conner.com

Creative Labs   www.creativelabs.com/zonemenu.html

Cyrix   www.cyrix.com

Dallas Semiconductor   www.dalsemi.com

Dell   www.dell.com

Diamond Flower International (DFI)   www.dfiusa.com

Diamond Multimedia   www.diamondmm.com

Data Technology Corporation (DTC)   www.datatechnology.com

ESS   www.esstech.com

Evergreen Technologies   www.evertech.com

Future Domain   www.adaptec.com

Gateway 2000   www.gw2k.com

Hayes   www.hayes.com

Hewlett Packard   www.hp.com

IBM   www.ibm.com

Iomega   www.iomega.com

Intel   www.intel.com

Magitronic   www.magitronic.com

Maxtor   www.maxtor.com

Micropolis   www.microp.com

Microsoft   www.msn.com

MicroTek   www.mteklab.com

Mitsumi   www.mitsumi.com

MR Bios   www.mrbios.com

Novell   www.novell.com

Oak Technologies   www.oaktech.com

Olivetti   www.olivetti.it

Packard Bell   www.packardbell.com

Phoenix   www.phoenix.com

Quantum   www.quantum.com

Realtek   www.realtek.com

Seagate   www.seagate.com.tw

Summagraphics   www.calcomp.com/summagraphics

SyQuest   www.syquest.com

Tandem   www.tandem.com

Teac   www.teac.com.jp

Trident Microsystems   www.trid.com

Tseng Labs   www.tseng.com

Turtle Beach   www.tbeach.com

UMAX   www.umax.com

US Robotics   www.usr.com

Western Digital   www.wdc.com

Winbond   www.winbond.com.tw

Zoom   www.zoomtel.com

APPENDIX B

Upgrade CPUs

There are three basic upgrade paths for Intel Pentium OverDrive Processors. Systems based on Intel 486DX or 486SX processors may be upgradable to Pentium OverDrive Processors at a clock speed of either 63 MHz or 83 MHz. PCs based on the older Pentium processors, the 60-MHz and 66-MHz models, can be upgradable to the 120-MHz or 133-MHz Pentium OverDrive Processors. Computers based on the 75-MHz, 90-MHz, or 100-MHz Pentium CPUs are often upgradable to the 125-MHz, 150-MHz, or 166-MHz Pentium OverDrive processors with MMX technology. The performance gain you will see with these upgrade processors varies with the system and the software you are running.

Intel publishes the *Intel Pentium OverDrive Processor Upgrade Guide*, a frequently updated book which lists thousands of brand-name systems, along with the upgrade part, if available. The Web version of this guide is available at:

```
http://www.intel.com/overdrive/upgrade/index.htm
```

Information about upgrading unbranded systems is available at:

```
http://www.intel.com/overdrive/unbranded.htm
```

The following list is a short reference to what brand name systems had one or more models listed in the *Upgrade Guide* as of the 15th revision.

Warning! You must consult the published Intel *Upgrade Guide* or the Intel Web Site for information about your exact model. Appearance of your system manufacturer on this list in no way guarantees that your system is upgradeable.

Acer Incorporated
Advanced Integrated Research, Inc
Amax Engineering Corporation
Ambra Computer
American Megatrends, Inc
Amstrad PLC
Apricot Computers, Ltd
AST Research, Inc

AT&T Global Information
 Solutions
Bold Data Technology, Inc
Caliber Computer Corporation
Compaq
CompUSA
CompuTrend Systems, Inc
Cumulus

Daewoo Telecom Ltd
Dan Technology, PLC
Data Storage Marketing, Inc
Datavarehuset AS
Dell Computer Corporation
Digital Equipment Corporation
DTK
Elonex
Epson
Escom
First International Computer
Fountain Technologies, Inc
Fujitsu
Gateway 2000
Goldstar Co. Ltd
Hewlett Packard
Hyundai Electronics Industries
IBM Corporation
ICL Personal Computers A.B.
Intergraph
IPC Corporation Ltd
IPC Technology, Inc
J&W Computers
KBS (K T Tech)
Leading Edge Products, Inc
Lion America Corporation
Memorex Telex
Metrovision Microsystems

Micro Professionals
Micron Computer, Inc
Micronics
Mitac International Corp
NCR
NEC Technologies, Inc
Olivetti
Opus
Packard Bell
Peacock
Quantex Microsystems
Research Machines
Samsung Electronics Co, Ltd
Seiko Epson Corporation
Siemens Nixdorf Information
  Systems
Supercom, Inc
Swan Technologies
Tandy
Toshiba Corporation
Trigem Computer, Inc
Tulip Computers International, BV
Unisys Corporation
Viglen Computers Ltd
Vobis
VTech Computers Ltd
Zenith Data Systems
Zeos International, Ltd

APPENDIX C

Error Codes

There are three BIOS manufacturers who dominate the clone market: AMI, Award, and Phoenix. The current Award BIOS only generates beeps for video failure or memory problems. Video failure consists of one long beep followed by two short beeps; any other beeps are probably a RAM problem.

The Phoenix BIOS always produces a single beep when everything is okay. Beyond that, they advise that beep codes are not necessarily similar across systems, and you should find your original documentation. If the BIOS produces three series of beeps before repeating or stopping, and the first series consists of two beeps, you should try swapping RAM. Series starting with three beeps can be the video adapter or CMOS, so try replacing the video adapter.

The AMI BIOS produces the following beep codes.

#Beeps	Error Message
1	Refresh Failure. The motherboard refresh circuitry has failed
2	Parity Error. A parity error was detected in the first 64 KB of the base memory (System RAM SIMMs). For all practical purposes, this is the same as 3 beeps
3	Base 64-KB memory failure. A memory failure in the first 64 KB of RAM
4	Timer Not Operational. Timer #1 on the motherboard has failed
5	Processor Error. The CPU has generated an error—replace CPU
6	8042 Gate A20 Failure. The Gate A20 switch, integrated in the keyboard BIOS chip has failed. The system cannot swith the CPU into protected mode
7	CPU Exception Interrupt Error. The CPU has generated an exception interrupt
8	Display Memory Error. The video adapter has failed
9	ROM Checksum Error. The ROM BIOS has failed its self-check
10	CMOS Shutdown Register Read/Write Error. CMOS register error

GLOSSARY

10Base-T A type of LAN that uses twisted-pair cable (telephone wire) to connect the PCs.

286 PC based on the 16-bit Intel 80286 or compatible CPU, a clone of the IBM PC-AT.

386 PC based on the 32-bit Intel 80386 or similar CPU.

486 PC based on the 32-bit Intel 80486 or similar CPU.

586 PC based on a post-486 generation CPU, not of Intel manufacture.

access time The amount of time it takes for a memory subsystem (RAM, cache) or a drive, to find the requested information and make it available to the bus. Measured in nanoseconds for memory, and in milliseconds for drives.

active hub See Hub.

adapter A card or board that is installed in the motherboard to add functionality. Almost all systems will have a video adapter (on a few brand-name systems it is integrated on the motherboard). Other common adapters include SCSI cards, IDE adapters, internal modems, and network adapters.

application program Any software, besides the operating system, with which the computer user interacts. Games, databases, and word processors are application programs. MS-DOS, Windows, and networking software are not.

AUTOEXEC.BAT A batch file (collection of commands) that DOS executes automatically on startup. You can add commands to AUTOEXEC.BAT to do things like start Windows automatically whenever you start the computer by making the last line on this file read "win". Games and other programs often modify this file and can cause the system to freeze.

back up Making a copy of computer data to guard against hard-drive failure.

baud The data communications rate in bits per second. Com ports in the PC have a maximum baud rate associated with them (19.6-K baud on most SIDE cards), over which they cannot operate, so hooking up faster devices, like a 28.8-K baud external modem, does not result in the rated modem performance.

bare bones   A minimal configuration in which the PC has enough parts to power up and light the monitor but lacks a hard drive and other necessary parts.

BIOS   Basic input-output system. The permanent program stored in a ROM chip on the motherboard that allows the CPU to communicate with the other hardware present when powered on.

bit   The basic information unit that computers work with, either a 1 or 0. Eight bits make a byte.

board   Another word for adapter or card, meaning a computer circuit board. See adapter.

boot disk   A disk is bootable when it can be used to load an operating system when the computer is started. Only the A: drive (and the floppy disk in it) or C: drive can be bootable on PCs.

boot sector   The first area of real estate on a disk where the BIOS looks for boot information.

burn-in   The amount of time a PC is tested, or left powered up, before being sold. Often an exaggerated number.

bus   A general-purpose data pathway shared by two or more devices.

byte   Eight bits. All memory and storage used by PCs is measured in bytes. A kilobyte is 1024 bytes. A megabyte 1024 kilobytes, a little more than one million bytes, A gigabyte is 1024 megabytes, a little more than one billion bytes.

cache memory   Hardware cache consists of superfast SRAM (static RAM) used to hold a small amount of working information for the CPU. Hardware cache speed is usually about four times faster than regular RAM. Software cache is information held in RAM to complement the performance of the drives.

CAD   Computer aided drafting (or design). CAD software has completely replaced pencil-and-paper drafting at most companies.

CAM   Computer aided manufacturing. CAM software controls milling machines and other industrial processes.

cards   See adapters.

carrier   The tone or transmitted frequency onto which a modem encodes information.

cartridge drive   A removable media drive, usually from SyQuest or Iomega, that performs on par with hard drives.

CD drive A drive that reads compact discs containing computer software, music, or other information.

CD recorder A drive that can write to gold recordable CDs that can be read in other CD drives or played in stereo systems.

centronics The standard connector on printers, giving name to the centronics printer cable.

chip Any ceramic- or plastic-encapsulated electronic circuit used in electronics.

clone Originally a PC capable of running all of the software that ran on the IBM PC AT. Now refers to any PC that follows the herd and remains compatible with all PC software and add-in adapters.

CMOS memory A tiny amount of RAM that is kept alive by a battery while the computer is turned off. The CMOS memory stores settings needed by the computer to operate, such as the hard drive type.

CMOS setup CMOS setup is a permanent program stored in the system's BIOS that allows you to change the settings permanently stored in CMOS memory.

Com port A communications port for attaching external devices to a PC.

CONFIG.SYS The first file read by the operating system after boot-up. DOS requires CONFIG.SYS to be present to install any device drivers or advanced utilities, such as HIMEM or EMM386.

coprocessor See math coprocessor.

CPU Central processing unit. The brain, either an "86" series chip (386, 486, etc.) or a Pentium variation, which is mounted on the motherboard and serves as the brain for the whole computer.

crash Either a "head crash," a disastrous hard-drive failure, or a "computer crash," any lockup or radical failure resulting in the need to reboot.

device driver A special piece of software that controls optional hardware attached to or installed in your PC. Device drivers are installed by the CONFIG.SYS or AUTOEXEC.BAT files on DOS systems.

DIMM Dual inline memory module. An extra-long SIMM which is accessible 72 bits at a time.

directory A logical structure, like folders in a filing cabinet, in which files are stored.

display adapter   See video adapter.

DMA   Direct memory access. The DMA controller allows the CPU and any other DMA-capable devices to independently access memory and give instructions for data transfers.

DOS   Disk operating system. Will be Microsoft DOS on most hand-me-down PCs.

download   Copying a computer file from a remote location, like an Internet server, onto your PC, via a modem or a network connection.

DRAM   Dynamic RAM. The main memory of the computer, which needs to be constantly refreshed by the motherboard (electronically read and rewritten) so that it doesn't lose its stored bits.

EISA   Extended ISA. An enhanced bus for the adapters on the motherboard that provides a high-speed, 32-bit interface.

EMM386   A program used by DOS to simulate expanded memory, which must also be present for some other DOS memory management options to be used.

ethernet   A type of network protocol commonly used for local area networks.

executable   A program, stored on disk with an ".EXE" file extension, i.e., PROGRAM.EXE.

expanded memory   A method used in old computers to allow for larger programs than would have otherwise been possible in the DOS environment.

extended memory   Any memory installed beyond the first megabyte is extended memory. If you have 16 MB of RAM, you have 15 MB of extended memory.

external cache   A small amount of SRAM used to enhance the speed of main memory. Most systems have between 64 KB to 512 KB of external cache installed.

external modem   A modem that comes with its own power supply and is connected to the PC by way of a serial port. External modem performance is limited to the Com port limitations.

fragmentation   The tendency of files on a computer disk to get spread out into pieces over time, slowing down performance. Utilities like DOS DEFRAG easily remedy the problem.

file   Any collection of information in permanent storage with an associated file name.

floppy   A floppy drive or disk, so named because the original plastic disks were very flexible.

format   The process by which a disk is prepared for use by the operating system. All of the current data on a disk is lost when it is formatted.

game port   A port for attaching a joystick to the PC.

gigabyte   1024 megabytes. See byte.

GUI   Graphical user interface. A software interface based on icons, pull-down menus, and graphics that is operated with a pointer.

gold recordable CD   A type of CD coated with gold dye that is used in CD recorders.

hard drive   A permanent storage device that holds computer files. Hard-drive capacity is measured in megabytes or gigabytes.

hardware   Any electronic device that can be included in or added to a PC.

HIMEM   The DOS utility invoked in the CONFIG.SYS file that allows the system to conserve program memory by using otherwise inaccessible areas to store device drivers.

hub   A type of junction box necessary for 10Base-T networks.

HTTP   HyperText Transfer Protocol. The Internet protocol used by the World Wide Web.

hyperlink   Underlined text or a clickable image on the WWW that loads a new Web page or launches another application.

IDE   Intelligent drive electronics. A type of interface used primarily for hard drives and CD drives which allows for a very simple and inexpensive interface to the motherboard.

IDE adapter   A simple card which allows up to four IDE devices to talk to the I/O bus.

internal cache   Superfast cache that is actually integrated with the CPU and stores 8 KB or more of the most used information at any given time.

interlace   A mode in which a monitor lights every other line of pixels each time it redraws the screen, in order to decrease flickering.

Internet   The international computer network that grew out of the old military failsafe network. The fastest growing segment of the Internet is the World Wide Web.

interrupts The electronic triggers that are used by devices in the system to get the attention of the CPU to process a request. A limited number of interrupts are available, and they can only be shared in special situations.

internal modem An adapter that sits in a motherboard slot and acts as an additional Com port. See modem.

I/O adapter Adds the Com ports, printer port, and game port on older PCs. The I/O adapter is integrated with the SIDE adapter on many systems and is integrated onto the motherboard on the newest PCs.

ISA Industry Standard Architecture. The basic PC design used by IBM with their PC-XT and PC AT that allowed PC parts to be largely interchangeable. All PC buses, until the advent of PCI, were backward compatible to the ISA bus.

joystick A control device used for games that is often similar to the control stick in an airplane.

jumper A small, plastic-encased short, like a tiny automobile fuse, which is used to make circuit pathways and select options on drives, adapters, and the motherboard.

kilobyte 1024 bytes. See byte.

LAN Local area network. A means by which computers are physically linked together to share information and resources.

low-level formatting A software process that prepares a disk for use by the operating system. All hard drives currently sold are low-level formatted in the factory and should only be re-low-level formatted if unrepairable by any other means.

master The primary or boot drive on an IDE controller. The setting is jumper selectable on the drive.

math coprocessor A chip which does floating-point (as opposed to integer) math very quickly. Starting with the 486DX CPU, math coprocessors have been built into CPUs and are no longer present as separate chips.

megabyte 1024 kilobytes. See byte.

microcomputer Fancy word for a PC, not necessarily a clone.

microprocessor Any "intelligent" chip, but normally reserved to describe the CPU.

MMX Multimedia extension technology integrated with the newest CPUs.

modem A device which allows computers to transmit information to each other over the phone lines. Most PC modems work with audible tones, requiring the information to be encoded on one end and decoded on the other. The newest modems can receive digital information, doubling the potential speed.

monitor The TV screen on which a computer displays information.

motherboard The main circuit card in your PC, on which the CPU, main memory, and adapter cards are mounted.

mouse A pointing device that is moved around on the desk to move a cursor on the screen.

multimedia Enhancement to the PC which generally includes the minimum of a sound card, speakers, and a CD drive, along with an SVGA video adapter that is capable of displaying a minimum of 256 colors.

network Any type of communications infrastructure for computers or intelligent devices.

network adapter The adapter that lets your PC communicate on a network.

operating system The basic software required by every computer to run. DOS, OS/2, Windows 95, and Unix are examples of operating systems.

parallel port See printer port.

partition A method of dividing the hard-drive capacity into artificial segments which are each treated as a separate drive by the operating system and are assigned their own drive letter (C:, D:, E:, etc.).

path A DOS variable which defines the directories the computer will search for executable programs. The path is set in the AUTOEXEC.BAT file and can be checked at any time by typing "path" at the DOS prompt.

PCI Peripheral connect interface. The newest and highest-speed bus in use for connecting adapters to the motherboard. PCI is not backwards-compatible with older cards.

Pentium The next generation of Intel CPU after the 486.

Pentium PRO An enhanced version of the Pentium.

peripheral   Any computer component that resides outside of the system box.

PnP   Plug and play. An adapter whose physical settings are made through software rather than jumpers. On Windows 95 and NT systems, the operating system controls the settings.

port   An attachment point for devices connected to a PC.

printer port   A port for attaching printers or other devices to the PC.

power supply   The PC component that takes the AC voltage from your wall socket and turns it into the small, regulated DC voltages that the internal computer components use.

RAM   Random access memory. Usually refers to the main memory in the PC, measured in megabytes.

ROM   Read-only memory. A permanent storage device such as a ROM chip or a CD.

screen   See monitor.

SCSI   Small computer system interface. A high-speed computer bus used for connecting drives, scanners, CDs, and other peripherals to the PC.

serial port   See Com port.

setup   See CMOS setup.

SIDE adapter   Super IDE adapter. Integrates the IDE adapter with the I/O Adapter.

SIMM   Single inline memory module. A small circuit board that carries multiple RAM chips.

slave   A second drive attached to an IDE controller. A master drive must be present. The setting is jumper-selectable on the drive.

software   The program instructions your computer works with, anything from the operating system to the BIOS, from games to databases.

sound card   The adapter which gives your PC the ability to play or record voice and music.

SVGA   All modern video adapter displays can function in SVGA mode, displaying 800 horizontal pixels by 600 vertical pixels on the monitor.

system box   The desktop or minitower case which holds the motherboard, power supply, drives, and other PC parts.

tape drive   A drive which uses tape cartridges, similar to cassette or VHS tapes, that is used to back up information from a computer hard drive.

terminator   A dummy load (a resistor) used on SCSI buses and Thin Ethernet LANs to absorb the leftover RF energy when it reaches the end of the bus.

Thin Ethernet   A type of LAN that uses a bus topology built from 50-ohm coaxial cable and BNC connectors.

trackball   A pointing device that sits in one place while you roll the ball with your hand to move the cursor on the screen.

turbo   An option on older PCs that switches the computer between high speed (regular) and a lower speed useful for some very old games or troubleshooting.

VGA   Video graphics adapter. VGA has come to mean a screen resolution of 640 horizontal pixels by 400 vertical pixels.

VESA   Video Electronics Standards Association. An industry group that creates hardware and software standards for enhanced video operation.

VESA local bus   A bus design that takes advantage of the CPU's ability to talk directly with a small number of adapters at high speed.

Video adapter   The computer component that generates the control signals for the monitor.

virus   A self-replicating program that is generally designed to infect your computer in a way that causes harm. Viruses can be deterred with virus-shield programs or removed by virus-doctor software.

Web page   A file stored in hypertext format on an HTTP Internet server.

Web surfing   Following hyperlinks on the WWW from one web page to the next.

Windows   Microsoft Windows 3.1, Windows for Workgroups, Windows 95, and Windows NT are all examples of Windows-based operating environments, which take the GUI approach to displaying information.

WWW   World Wide Web, the graphically oriented segment of the Internet.

ZIFF   Zero insertion force. A type of socket for the CPU which uses a lever to release or lock in the CPU.

INDEX

About the Author

Morris Rosenthal is a writer and independent computer consultant. He holds degrees in electrical and computer engineering, has built or repaired thousands of PCs, designed and installed networks for schools and businesses, and trained many PC technicians. He has been featured on the *Dateline NBC* Web site as an expert on computer repair, and his own popular Web site at http://www.daileyint.com includes "The Midnight Question," an interactive page where a new PC question is answered each day.